Towards a Malawian Theology

of Laity

Published by

Luviri Press

P/Bag 201 Luwinga

Mzuzu 2

ISBN   978-99960-66-60-3

eISBN   978-99960-66-61-0

Cover: Luis Miguel Paulo

The Luviri Press is represented outside Africa by:

African Books Collective Oxford
(order@africanbookscollective.com)

www.luviripress.blogspot.com

www.africanbookscollective.com

Towards a Malawian Theology of Laity

Edited by

Volker Glissmann

Luviri Press
Mzuzu
2020

Contents

Notes on Contributors

Hany Longwe received training in Mechanical Engineering in Blantyre (Malawi) and in London, and in teaching at Bolton (UK). He taught at the Malawi Polytechnic and later worked for Dwangwa Sugar Corporation. He holds a Diploma in Theology from the Baptist Theological Seminary of Zimbabwe, and is a graduate of the Baptist Theological Seminary of Zambia (BTh) and of the University of Malawi (MA and PhD). For about thirteen years, he served as the Principal of the Baptist Theological Seminary of Malawi, and later taught at the University of Livingstonia. He has also served as a visiting lecturer at Mzuzu University. Hany Longwe is a member of South Lunzu Baptist Church in Blantyre.

Joseph Andrew Thipa was born on 4th May, 1953 in Chiradzulu District, Malawi. He holds an MA in Theological Studies obtained in 1998 from Austin Presbyterian Theological Seminary in Texas, USA, a PhD in Systematic Theology in 2009 from Stellenbosch University, South Africa. He is currently a Lecturer in Systematic Theology, African Christian Theology and Christian Ethics at the University of Malawi, Chancellor College. Before coming to Chancellor College, he taught at Zomba Theological College in Zomba, Malawi. In 2019, he published a book titled, "The Doctrine of Atonement for Building Human Rights in Malawi."

Rt Rev James Tengatenga, PhD, is Distinguished Professor of Global Anglicanism at The School of Theology, University of the South, Tennessee, USA. He is the former bishop of the Anglican Diocese of Southern Malawi. Before becoming bishop he taught at Zomba Theological College and then in the Department of Theology and Religious Studies at the University of Malawi.

The Rt Rev Dr Fanuel Magangani, bishop of the Anglican Diocese of Northern Malawi since 2010. Before his ordination he obtained a Licentiate at Zomba Theological College. He went on to complete his Diploma in Theology through Theological Education by Extension (TEEM). He further obtained his Bachelor's Degree

6

(First Class) at Mzuzu University. While preparing for his studies in Masters at Nashotah House, Wisconsin, USA, he was elected Bishop of Northern Malawi. Meanwhile completed his Doctor in Ministry at Nashotah House and he is currently completing his PhD with Mzuzu University. He has passion for lay ministry.

Manuel Kamnkhwani is a seasoned theologian working with Logos Institute, a ministry that he founded in 2005, in Lilongwe, Malawi. Born and raised in a pastor's home, the author had an early exposure to Theology and Philosophy. Kamnkhwani studied at African Bible College in Lilongwe where he obtained a Bachelor of Arts degree in Biblical Studies. Upon graduation he taught at Evangelical Bible College of Malawi for a year before proceeding to Westminster Theological Seminary in California, where he obtained a Master of Arts degree in Theological Studies. Back home in Africa, Kamnkhwani taught Systematic Theology and Church History at Harare Theological College and African Bible College in Lilongwe. He is also a visiting Lecturer at Mukhanyo Theological College in South Africa. Kamnkhwani currently lives in Lilongwe with his wife Karen, their two daughters, Tamanda and Stacy and their son Herman II.

Chatha Msangaambe holds a Doctorate Degree in Practical Theology from Stellenbosch University in South Africa. He has more than 20 years of practical experience in transformational leadership and congregational pastoral work combined with lecturing in a few theological seminaries. He has been Moderator of CCAP Nkhoma Synod for more than 10 years. He was recently decorated with a Chancellor's Meritorious Award by the Nkhoma University for his academic and leadership contribution to the church in Malawi. Rev. Dr. Msangaambe is currently the National Chairperson of the Evangelical Association Of Malawi.

Rev Dr Blair D. Bertrand is a Lecturer and the Director of Research and Educational Quality Assurance (DREQA) at Zomba Theological College (ZTC) as well as serving as Educational Consultant for Theological Education by Extension Malawi (TEEM). In addition, Bertrand serves the Blantyre Synod (Church of Central Africa

Presbyterian) in the youth department developing training for youth leaders. Bertrand is an ordained minister of Word and Sacrament in the Presbyterian Church in Canada and holds a PhD in Practical Theology from Princeton Theological Seminary.

Rev Dr Gertrude Aopesyaga Sulumbu-Kapuma PhD (University of Pretoria). Senior Lecturer at Zomba Theological College since 2010. Lecturer in Practical Theology and Gender and Theology at the University of Fort Hare 2000-2005. Lay Leader for 23 years before Ordination in 2003. Published a number of articles with The Circle of Concerned African Women Theologians and NetAct. Co-Edited a book on Gender Equality with NetAct. Serving as TEEM's first female board chair. Proud grandmother. Continues to work with a small congregation.

Watson Rajaratnam currently serves as New Initiatives Consultant with SIM Malawi, focusing on mobilizing churches for world missions and sending missionaries to reach the unreached people groups. He is a College Lecturer turned Journalist turned Mission Consultant & Mobilizer, sent by his church and partners in Singapore to serve in Malawi. During the last 9 years he has been mobilizing African churches and missionaries for world missions. Prior to his ministry in Malawi, he served as SIM Singapore National Director and later as New Initiative Consultant with SIM Zambia. He also serves as an International Faculty of Haggai Institute where he facilitates the topic "Biblical and Contemporary Models of Evangelism." Watson believes that Africa are still untapped gold mines for world missions.

Paul Mathews Louis Mawaya is an ordained Presbyterian Minister of Word and Sacrament who has served CCAP Blantyre Synod for 16 years. He is married to Geertrui den Ouden with three children; Joel Dalitso (12 years), Joshah Mangalisoh (9 years) and Josephine Tadala (6 years). He is currently the National Mission Mobilizer for Society for International Ministries (SIM) Malawi. He holds a BA in Biblical Studies from African Bible College, a BD from the

Theological Board of Malawi and has successfully defended his MA in Theology and Religious Studies with University of Malawi.

Isabel Apawo Phiri is Deputy General Secretary of the World Council of Churches responsible for Public Witness and Diakonia since 2012. A Presbyterian lay person from Malawi. She has been engaged with the churches and the ecumenical movement from 1984-1991 as a commissioner for Programme on Theological Education of WCC and from 2002-2007 as general coordinator of the Circle of Concerned African Women Theologians. She edited the Journal of Gender and Religion in Africa, published numerous articles and co-edited books in the area of gender, mission and African theology. Among various international degrees, she earned a PhD in Religious Studies from the University of Cape Town. She was a professor of African Theology, Dean and Head of the School of Religion, Philosophy and Classics, and Director of the Centre for Constructive Theology at the University of KwaZulu Natal, Pietermaritzburg, South Africa. She also taught in the Department of Religious Studies and Theology at the University of Malawi 1983-1996.

Volker Glissmann, PhD, was the Executive Director of TEEM (Theological Education by Extension in Malawi) from 2010-2018. He has a PhD in Old Testament from Queen's University Belfast and an MA in Theological Education from the London School of Theology/Middlesex University. He is a global mission worker of the Presbyterian Church in Ireland and works as a Programme Developer for the TEE College in Johannesburg, South Africa. He is involved in theological educational consultancy and facilitates a course on Designing and Delivering Effective Theological Education at London School of Theology's Master in Theological Education programme. He has published a number of articles on theological education as well as on diaspora theology.

"Only when every member of the Church realizes that the responsibility in this matter devolves upon him too can there be an intelligent critical appreciation of what is or is not done in this regard. If a part—and probably much the greater part—of the Church declines its responsibility for this task, it signifies nothing more nor less than that this section of the Church is renouncing the freedom which it is offered under the Word, and wishes to live only by authority in the Church. In this case, how soon it will be manifest that for this party there is no ecclesiastical authority either. Those who are silent in deference to scriptural learning, the congregation which is passive in matters of biblical exegesis, is committed already to secret rebellion. It is emancipated from the Canon and confession, and therefore from the Word of God and from faith. Therefore it is no longer a true congregation of Jesus Christ. Whoever will have nothing to do with this secret and one day open rebellion, whoever wants ecclesiastical authority for the sake of the authority of God's Word, must affirm freedom under the Word as the freedom of all Christian men, and must wish the congregation to participate in scriptural exegesis with real responsibility."[1] –

Karl Barth

Introduction

Nearly forty years ago, the great African theologian John S. Pobee made the following assessment about the importance of lay participation: "we believe the future of the church in Africa lies with knowledgeable and committed laymen."[2] Lay empowerment and lay participation have indeed huge potentials to change the witness of the church in Africa and beyond. But it is also something of an unfulfilled promise. Why is that? Agustin Garcia-Gasco y Vicente highlighted the essential importance of the steps that need to be taken in order to fulfil the potential of the laity in the church. He insisted that, "theological formation is considered to be a right, and a fundamental Christian obligation rather than a privilege limited to a

---

[1] Karl Barth, *Church Dogmatics: The Doctrine of the Word of God, Part 2* (vol. 1), trans. G.W. Bromiley and T.F. Torrance, London: T&T Clark, 2004, pp. 714-715.

[2] John S. Pobee, "News of Developments in Ministerial Formation in Ghana," *Ministerial Formation*, 7 (1979), p. 20.

few."[3] To which we can add Jey J. Kanagaraj's affirmation that, "the church is a corporate community in which all, not just the clergy, have a ministry. This of course includes women, youths, and children."[4] On paper (or at least in the writings of these few selected theologians) the empowerment of the laity seems to be both a theological necessity as well as a foundational theological requirement for the church if it wants to be a faithful witness to the incarnate Word of God. But something, somewhere tempered the hope attributed to the empowerment of the laity. Peter Stone, citing the selected works of Mark Gibbs, points to a fundamental implementation problem -- which is not unique to Malawi and in the case of Gibbs is based on his observations about the church in Britain -- namely, "the reluctance and inability of the clergy to promote the laity in ministry within the churches and in the world." For Gibbs and Stone this is one of the reasons for the "the low strength of the evangelical churches."[5] This is especially surprising as typically evangelical churches are strong on *biblicism* (a high regard for the Bible), *conversionism* (the belief that lives need to be changed), *activism* (the expression of the gospel in effort) and *crucicentrism* (the stress on the sacrifice of Christ on the cross) -- all which are prioritized in the movement and would be vital to the right empowerment of the laity. Yet somehow, the movement's clergy was reluctant to empower the laity to participate.[6] Historically, all of this seems again a little bit surprising when we consider a key moment of the history of church renewal, namely the Reformation, which gave birth to the Protestant churches. A central emphasis of

3   Agustin Garcia-Gasco y Vicente, "International Institute of Theology at a Distance (Spain): Continuing Theological Formation for Priests, Religious, and Laity," *Ministerial Formation* 17 (Jan 1982), pp. 3-6 [3].

4   Jey J. Kanagaraj, "The Involvement of the Laity in the Ministry of the Church," *Evangelical Review of Theology*, 21:4 (October 1997), pp. 326-331 [329].

5   Mark Gibbs cited in Peter Stone, "Theological Education for the Laity: Part 1: Policies and Practices at the London Institute for Contemporary Christianity," *Journal of Christian Education* (1989), Papers 94, p. 7.

6   See David W. Bebbington, *Evangelicalism in Modern Britain, 1730s-1980s*, London: Routledge, 1989.

the Reformation was the doctrine of the priesthood of all believers. "Everyone can understand the Bible and therefore needs to learn how to read it; all human vocation comes from God and requires training."[7] Sidney Rooy continues to stress that both great Reformers: Martin Luther and John Calvin founded schools to educate the church not only the clergy. The same sentiment is picked up again and theologically aligned with our contemporary theological understanding,

> The late Orlando Costas suggested that theological education is to equip the people of God for the service of his kingdom; for the whole people of God to serve in all walks of life. The whole people of God should be equipped in the whole counsel of God within and from his total context: laity, those in specialized ministry (pastors and teachers); theologians; men, women, young people and children; marginalized people such as Latin American Indians, women, Afro-Americans.[8]

The essential pillars of lay empowerment which are fundamentally twofold: (a) a right to theological formation for laity based on membership of the Christian community, combined with (b) the call on the laity to fully participate in ministry – often a call to a general but also to a specific ministry on behalf of either the church or - wider than that - the kingdom of God. These are the essential pillars of lay empowerment and lay participation.

Reflection by African church leaders and theologians in general on the issues of lay participation and training is quite rare. Though this is not just true for the continent but is an unfortunate global phenomenon. All of this is slightly surprising as 99% of the church is made up of lay Christians and their contribution is usually locally valued because they are indeed the central pillar of the church.

---

[7]   Sidney Rooy, "Historical Models of Theological Education," in C. René Padilla (ed), *New Alternatives in Theological Education*, Oxford: Regnum, 1988, p. 64.

[8]   Tito Paredes cited in [author unknown], "Institutional Development for Theological Education in the Two-thirds World: Summary of findings of the 1995 consultation at the Oxford Centre for Mission Studies," *Transformation: An International Journal of Holistic Mission Studies* 12:4 (Oct 1995), pp. 18–32 [18].

Malawian churches utilize heavily the skills and talents of their lay members, yet do not provide a systematic reflection about the role of lay people in the life and ministry of the church. The majority of Malawian churches are hierarchical in governance and leadership structure and one possible result of this is the lack of ownership by lay people of the affairs of the church. At the same time institutions of theological education predominantly focus on (at least in intent) ministerial theological education or on academic theological education. Which raises the question, how does theological education empower the grassroots church – the laity? The Western and also the Far Eastern Protestant Churches are heavily clergy driven yet maintain *in principle* (not always in practice) the priesthood of all believers. Which path is the right one for the Malawian church?

The aim of the book is to bring together different contributors to address biblically and theologically the role of the laity within the context of the Malawian church. The experience of the contributors was deliberately chosen to include active church leaders within the Malawian church, theological educators reflecting within institutions here in country as well as Malawian theologians who serve outside of Malawi. At the same time, the contributions from practitioners who are actively involved in grassroots and church ministry are highly valued, since their voices might not always make it into publications of this kind. Then finally, the voices of Malawian lay Christians were also collected through interviews so that their voice is heard and can contribute towards the development of a Malawian theology of laity.

Finally, a word of appreciation to all contributors who contributed their ideas and time to make this book become a reality. It is highly appreciated. A special appreciation to the 15 lay Christians who were interviewed for the research published in the chapter "Voices from the Grassroots: Meaningful Partnership" -- your sharing from the heart and your openness are highly appreciated. A special appreciation goes to Prof Klaus Fiedler from Luviri Press who has been such a strong supporter of this project from the moment the project was first suggested to him. My appreciation to my daughter, Lina Glissmann for her invaluable help with editing and also to Prof

Kenneth Ross for his help in assisting to get the publication to a better standard.

Bibliography

[author unknown], "Institutional Development for Theological Education in the Two-thirds World: Summary of Findings of the 1995 Consultation at the Oxford Centre for Mission Studies," *Transformation: An International Journal of Holistic Mission Studies*, 12:4 (Oct 1995), pp. 18-32.

Barth, Karl, *Church Dogmatics: The Doctrine of the Word of God, Part 2* (vol. 1), trans. G.W. Bromiley and T.F. Torrance, London: T&T Clark, 2004.

Bebbington, David W., *Evangelicalism in Modern Britain, 1730s-1980s*, London: Routledge, 1989.

Garcia-Gasco y Vicente, Agustin, "International Institute of Theology at a Distance (Spain): Continuing Theological Formation for Priests, Religious, and Laity," *Ministerial Formation* 17 (Jan 1982), pp. 3-6.

Kanagaraj, Jey J., "The Involvement of the Laity in the Ministry of the Church," *Evangelical Review of Theology*, 21:4 (October 1997), pp. 326-331.

Pobee, John S., "News of Developments in Ministerial Formation in Ghana," *Ministerial Formation*, 7 (1979), p. 20.

Rooy, Sidney, "Historical Models of Theological Education," in C. René Padilla (ed) *New Alternatives in Theological Education*, Oxford: Regnum, 1988, pp. 51-72.

Stone, Peter, "Theological Education for the Laity: Part 1: Policies and Practices at the London Institute for Contemporary Christianity," *Journal of Christian Education* (1989), Papers 94.

Chapter 1

The Church, the Laity, and the Priesthood

Hany Longwe

Introduction

The distinction of "royal priesthood, holy nation" mentioned in Revelation 5:9-10 and in 1 Peter points out a particular problem for Christian churches that have an ordained priesthood in their structures, as much of Protestantism ceased to designate Christian ministry as priesthood.[1] Formerly, it was the unquestioned premise that the ministry of the church belonged to the ordained clergy who were conceived as the ministers, and the rest of the Christian community as the laity. That meant that in the life of the church the clergy were the ones doing something on the laity. This view of ministry came under sharp attack in both theory and practice.[2]

Sometimes the ministry of the laity has been interpreted to mean that there is no privileged class, and that all services by both clergy and non-clergy are of equal importance before God and in the life of the church. From time to time, it has been conceived as the complete mobility of functions within the church, with each person being empowered to perform any function. Further still, the ministry of the laity has been understood to mean that the real ministry of the church is in the world, and thus the laity constituted the fundamental ministry of the church, with the clergy serving as resources to and enablers of, the laity in their *secular* mission. At times it is seen to be the only ministry, with baptism as the act of ordination, and the necessity of a clergy, in any sense of the word, is put radically in

---

[1] Raymond E. Brown, *The Churches the Apostles Left Behind*, Ramsey: Paulist Press, 1984, p. 80.

[2] Gabriel Fackre, *The Christian Story: A Narrative Interpretation of Basic Christian Doctrine*, Grand Rapids: Eerdmans, 1984, p. 175.

15

question. As a result, it is the lay people who assume the functions normally associated with the clergy in the inner life of the church as well as the ministry to the world.[3]

Such views of ministry have contributed to the loss of a sense of identity among the clergy who have attempted to honour the enlarged perception of ministry. In response, some have recognized the need for an official, ordained clergy who fulfill authoritarian ministerial functions within the community of faith. Nonetheless, balancing the authority of laity and clergy has proven to be a delicate exercise. That has seen a rising generation of women not only seeking ordination and equal participation in the church as pastors or clergy, but also their rightful place in theology.[4] This challenge assumes there is a unique and important meaning to worship and the proclamation of the Word.[5]

Historical Developments

The word lay derives from the Anglo-French *lai*. This is from late Latin *laicus*, and Greek *laikos,* meaning of the people, and from *laos* meaning the people at large. At first there was a sense of unified ministry for the whole people of God, but later, in the patristic era, there was a growing distinction between the clergy and the laity. In the Middle Ages there was a rise of clerical authority and status, which was followed by a monastic and sectarian reassertion of lay ministry in the church. It was the Church Reformation that emphasized vocation and the priesthood of the believers. The Free Church Tradition produced democratic polity, and voluntary church membership. Although there has been a growing trend toward ministerial professionalism, there also has been a reassertion of the

---

3   Gabriel Fackre, *The Christian Story*, p. 175.

4   Erhard S. Gerstenberger, *Yahweh the Patriarch: Ancient Images of God and Feminist Theology*, Minneapolis: Fortress Press, 1996, pp. 111-128.

5   Gabriel Fackre, *The Christian Story*, p. 176.

role of the laity through lay renewal, and the growth of clerical authoritarianism among evangelical Protestants.[6]

The Entire Church as the People of God - *Laos*

A history of the laity or a theology of the laity is a history and theology of the whole church. The entire church was, and is *laos*, people of God, sharing a priestly function as members to respond to each other and to the world (1 Pet 2:9).[7] 1 Peter 1:13 – 2:10 applies to Gentile converts, sharing the whole Exodus experience of Israel. They have left their former servitude, and have been redeemed by the blood of a lamb, while going through a period of wandering toward a promised inheritance. The Levitical priesthood has been replaced by Christ, and now Christians constitute a royal priesthood.[8] Yet the distinction between clergy and laity is a real one in Christian history and must not be underestimated. Its earliest roots were evident in the struggle over questions of authority, order, and leadership in the New Testament churches. It would be a mistake to interpret the priesthood of all believers to mean "an unstructured, democratic fellowship."[9] The priesthood of all believers, like other metaphors of the church, speaks of order and design. The church can be described as "structural," "spiritual," or a "gathered" community. Although some churches have embarked on a lifelong relationship with the doctrine of the priesthood of all believers, they have had a difficult time agreeing on the precise language for describing this most important belief to which they hold fast.[10]

---

[6] Bill J. Leonard, "Southern Baptists and the Laity," in *Review and Expositor*, vol. 84, no. 4, (1987), p. 633.

[7] Bill J. Leonard, "Southern Baptists and the Laity," p. 634.

[8] Raymond E. Brown, *The Churches the Apostles Left Behind*, p. 26.

[9] Bill J. Leonard, "Southern Baptists and the Laity," p. 634.

[10] Hany Longwe, *Christians by Grace, Baptists by Choice*, Zomba: Kachere; Mzuzu: Mzuni Press, 2011, p. 19.

The Vision of Equality

The picture of the first Christian church made plain a revolutionary vision of equality. When Habakkuk complained to God about the violence and injustice God's people had experienced, God told him to write down the vision and spell it out on tablets (2:2-5). Joel made it plain the vision of the Spirit's empowerment, of all that would result in the demolition of barriers erected on the basis of gender, age, race and class (Joel 2:28-29). On the day of Pentecost, Peter declared the vision (Acts 2:17-18). Not everything mentioned by Joel happened that morning, but the Spirit empowered believers to live out the discipleship of equals initiated by Jesus.

The Development of Divisions between the Ordained Clergy and the Laity

Around A.D. 96 the term *layman* (*ha laikos anthropos*) first appeared, in the earliest presumed sub-apostolic writings, the Epistle of Clement of Rome to the church at Corinth,[11] in which he stated that "the layman is bound by the lay ordinances." It appears that the Corinthian church had deposed some presbyters, and Clement urges the church to reinstate these presbyters to the office and comments at length on the evils of jealousy and faction.[12] The letter is an indication that already certain divisions had developed between the ordained clergy (presbyters and deacons) and the rest of the congregation, yet, Clement acknowledged that all Christians had a priestly function in the church's worship. Every believer received this "ordination" to a royal priesthood by virtue of baptism, symbolized by the laying of hands as a sign of the coming of the Holy Spirit.[13]

---

[11] A.M. Renwick, *The Story of the Church*, Guilford: Billing & Sons, 1958, p. 25.

[12] Robert A. Baker, *A Summary of Christian History*, Nashville: Broadman, 1959, p. 26. See also, Cyril C. Richardson (ed), *Early Christian Fathers*, New York: Touchstone, 1996, p. 64.

[13] Wayne Grudem, *Systematic Theology: an Introduction to Biblical Doctrine*, Leicester: InterVarsity, 1994, p. 961.

As early as the beginning of the second century, the Christian leaders began to make a distinction between the clergy the laity. The very names they adopted showed the official attitude of superiority; for the clergy means, "those who have been called of God', while laity means, "the people."[14] By the fifth and sixth centuries, the distinction was becoming more pronounced, partly due to controversies over heresy, authority and order in the rapidly growing congregations. Efforts to develop order, fight heresy and maintain orthodoxy, influenced the rise of an elaborate clerical hierarchy.[15] The church regarded the clergy as having special grace, being indispensable in the Christian's approach to God.[16] The priesthood of all believers was practically forgotten.[17]

Reassertion of the Role of the Laity

The Church Reformation of the sixteenth century produced a reassertion of the role of the laity. Martin Luther rediscovered the claims of Scripture, with its gift of justification by grace through faith restoring the idea of the church as a spiritual communion of believers, all of whom were priests to God.

Primacy of the Word and the Priesthood of All Believers

Luther held that ordination was an invention of the church, nonetheless, he admitted that as a rite that had been practised for many ages it was not to be condemned, but all Christians were priests. That resulted in a distinction between calling and office. All followers

---

[14] Robert A. Baker, *A Summary of Christian History*, p. 37. See also, Kenneth Scott Latourette, *A History of Christianity* vol. II, New York: Harper & Row, 1975, pp. 133, 183.

[15] Bill J. Leonard, "Southern Baptists and the Laity," p. 634.

[16] A.M. Renwick, *The Story of the Church*, p. 72. See also Cyril C. Richardson (ed), *Early Christian Fathers*, p. 47.

[17] A.M. Renwick, *The Story of the Church*, pp. 72, 73.

of Christ were called to the gospel, and no vocation was less Christian than any other. All Christians had equal access to God, but not equal ability to interpret the Word correctly. Those that were called priests were ministers, selected from among the Christians to act on their behalf, and their priesthood was the community's ministry.[18] Luther and other Protestants stressed the primacy of the Word of God as contained in the Scriptures and, holding to the priesthood of all believers, insisted not only that all Christians read the Bible, but also on their competence, guided by the Holy Spirit, to understand it appropriately.[19]

Unity, Equality and Spirituality

Among the Radical Reformers were the Anabaptists, who went beyond Luther and reemphasized the equality of all believers. They sought to restore the New Testament church as a community of adult believers bound by covenant in faith, witness and discipline, and called to minister to the people of God. To them the distinction between the clergy and the laity undermined the nature of the church itself for it created a church organized around religious professionals. They suggested the laity should become again what they were in the early church: the carriers of the faith. Immediate individual experience of the grace of God became central.[20] That encouraged the unity and equality of all believers; the clergy and the laity were co-labourers in ministry.

Some of the descendants of the Radical Reformers looked to the New Testament church equality, which originated in the common experience of baptism. They emphasized the evangelical identity and spiritual unity of all believers as witnesses to and as followers of Christ. The various groups promoted the equality of believers and

---

18 Bill J. Leonard, "Southern Baptists and the Laity," p. 635.

19 Kenneth Scott Latourette, *A History of Christianity* vol. II, p. 719.

20 Bruce Milne, *Know the Truth: A Handbook of Christian Belief*, Nottingham: InterVarsity, 2006, p. 302.

denounced the ecclesiastical elitism, inherent in the knowledge and work of the priest. They also insisted upon a spiritual, often political, egalitarianism in the face of clerical and aristocratic hierarchy. To be a Christian was to be a minister.[21] These egalitarian notions led to results quite different than those intended by the Reformers themselves. Nevertheless, the priesthood of all believers and the obligation of private judgment conserve the root of individuality.[22] The individual was and could be moved and guided only by their own personal experience of such grace, and herein lay their autonomy – their independence in Christ.[23]

Congregational Form of Church Government

Various groups continued to insist that all believers were called to minister to the church and the world. They believed all persons could preach and teach without regard to ministerial training. They made it possible for laity to perform all ecclesiastical functions when authorized by the congregation. The laity had final authority under Christ in the endeavours of the church.

Voluntarism

This congregational spirit became even more powerful when united with the ideals of democracy and religious freedom which was based on the non-coerced consent of the individual. The church became a voluntary association. The voluntary principle in religion had a powerful influence on the role of the laity. Voluntarism meant church leaders were dependent as never before on the laity for spiritual and temporal support. It was more evident in the basic ecclesiastical organization, the denomination. Voluntarism shaped the

[21] Bill J. Leonard, "Southern Baptists and the Laity," p. 636.

[22] George F. Thomas (ed), *The Vitality of the Christian Tradition*, New York: Harper & Brothers, 1945, p. 140.

[23] Bill J. Leonard, "Southern Baptists and the Laity," p. 637.

understanding of the nature of the church as "operating through democratic process under the Lordship of Jesus Christ."[24]

Evangelical Conversion

Perhaps evangelical conversion – warm, personal, and individual – was the greatest equalizer. Conversion transcended race, education, or class. In turn, the converted were called to convert others; that was the universal Christian ministry. In common spiritual experience, congregational polity, and communal responsibility of the nineteenth-century cultivated a "people's church," which accentuated the call to ministry as given to all Christians. Final authority for church government came from Christ through the congregation. The clergy derived their authority to preach and administer the ordinances from Christ through his churches. That does not suggest, though, that churches refused to distinguish between clergy and laity. Free Church traditions recognized that some individuals were called to particular ministerial functions within the churches. The congregational form of church government has maintained a tension between the universal calling of all believers and the "strange" calling of ordained ministers.[25]

In the congregational form of government everything must come to the congregational meeting, and as the church grows, decision-making reaches a point of near paralysis. While this structure does attempt to do justice to the scriptures, regarding the need for final governing authority to rest within the congregation as a whole, it is unfaithful to the New Testament pattern of recognized and designated elders who have actual authority to rule the church.[26]

---

24 Bill J. Leonard, "Southern Baptists and the Laity," p. 637.

25 Bill J. Leonard, "Southern Baptists and the Laity," p. 639.

26 Wayne Grudem, *Systematic Theology*, pp. 935-936.

Training Programmes for the Laity

On one hand, Congregationalists have developed one of the most far reaching programmes for equipping and motivating lay ministry. The Sunday school represents the most important source of lay education and activity in the life of a local church. Church programmes for lay witnesses place emphasis on the need for every Christian to be a soulwinner, properly trained in witnessing, that was to be an integral part of every Christian's life. Nonetheless, history reveals an increasing theological and practical segregation between clergy and laity in the churches.[27]

The Laity – A Prominent Feature of Protestantism

Laymen and laywomen gradually came to the fore, partly through their financial gifts to the churches and various religious organizations and institutions. Layman's organizations sprang up, first in connection with local churches, and then as denominational fellowships. Some of the outstanding evangelists were not ordained. This made for a kind of lay Christianity that for the most part, had little patience with what it regarded as theological details. Lay Christianity respected, studied and taught the Bible, sought to win individuals to a personal Christian commitment. They were activists, generous in giving their time and money.[28]

The lay component and the emphasis upon evangelism and revivalism with the consequent mass conversion were phases of a kind of popular Christianity. Among other expressions were hymns which had the quality of folk songs about them. Here was a singing faith which voiced and helped to shape the aspirations, prayers and actions of multitudes. Undoubtedly nothing of this kind of similar

---

[27] Bill J. Leonard, "Southern Baptists and the Laity," p. 639.

[28] Kenneth Scott Latourette, *A History of Christianity*, vol. II, p. 1265.

dimensions had previously appeared in the history of Christianity or of any religion.[29]

Women as Laity

In his time on earth, Jesus was very attentive to women as human beings on a par with men which was radical in the Jewish culture. Jesus did not proclaim a part of the gospel to women and most of it to men. At the beginning of his movement, Christianity seemed to follow Jesus' lead in his treatment of women, many of whom were among the organizers and leaders of the early church. The early history of the church reflects an active participation of women in the spread of Christianity, not only as listeners and followers, but also as leaders.[30] "Biblically and in Christian teaching, women have a right to nothing less,"[31] because in the high dignity and respect Jesus accorded to them, there is a remarkable affirmation of equal access to all the blessings of salvation for both women and men.[32]

Jesus had more than twelve disciples; once he sent out 70 among whom were women (Lk 8:1-2) as *apostles*. He also chose to meet his female disciples first after his resurrection (Mt 28:10). Jesus perceived both men and women as his disciples. They all joined together constantly in prayers (Acts 1:14). Women were also there when the promised Holy Spirit came upon the disciples. God gave the gift of Pentecost to both women and men (Acts 2:17-18).[33]

The apostle Paul has been accused and viewed as being anti-women, and yet the New Testament evidence is against this assessment as is evident in Romans 16. Paul introduces Phoebe and greets 25

[29] Kenneth Scott Latourette, *A History of Christianity*, vol. II, p. 1265.

[30] Patricia Wilson-Kastener, *Faith, Feminism, and the Christ*, Philadelphia: Forttress Press, 1983, pp. 72-73.

[31] Erhard S. Gerstenberger, *Yahweh the Patriarch*, p. 115.

[32] Wayne Grudem, *Systematic Theology*, p. 937.

[33] Klaus Fiedler, *Baptists and the Ordination of Women*, Zomba: Lydia Print, 2010, pp. 8-9.

individuals, nine of whom were women,[34] prominent in the advancement of Paul's mission to the Gentiles particularly on Macedonian and Roman soil. While this reflects the greater freedom enjoyed by women in such areas, it also testifies to Paul's flexibility of practice where that would not lead to offence. His approach resulted in the elevation of women to a place of religious work of which there is little contemporary parallel.[35] From the first days of the church and grand proclamation of Paul in Galatians a change can be traced, that in Christ there is neither male nor female, but all are one in Christ, compared to the much more restrictive legislation of the Pastoral Epistles in the third quarter of the first century. As the church became more organized and hierarchical, the place of women was being moved toward the periphery.[36]

Women in Ministry

In the Free Church movement there was openness to women in ministry. Women were encouraged to evangelistic work especially in the foreign countries, but men had serious reservations about it.[37] The continued influence and energy of women's missionary organizations served as the centre pieces for the "women's sphere" of activities in the churches and the denominations. On the British Isles, Congregationalists admitted women to their ministry. One of these, Agnes Maude Royden, who became an assistant pastor in 1917, was the first woman to hold that post. From the 1920s to the 1940s, she made several worldwide preaching tours.[38] In 1931 Agnes Maud

---

[34] Klaus Fiedler, *Baptists and the Ordination of Women*, p. 11.

[35] Robert Banks, *Paul's Idea of Community: The Early House Churches in their Historical Setting*, Exeter: Paternoster, 1980, p. 160. See also: Janet Kholowa and Klaus Fiedler, *Mtumwi Paulo ndi Udindo wa Amayi mu Mpingo*, Zomba: Kachere, 2000.

[36] Patricia Wilson-Kastener, *Faith, Feminism, and the Christ*, p. 73.

[37] Ruth A. Tucker and Walter Liefeld, *Daughters of the Church: Women and Ministry from New Testament Times to the Present*, Grand Rapids: Academie Books, 1987, pp. 379-380.

[38] Ruth A. Tucker and Walter Liefeld, *Daughters of the Church*, p. 379.

Royden was the first woman to become Doctor of Divinity and was well known on both sides of the Atlantic.[39] Although there were at the time a few gifted speakers, these lay preachers were crucial in the early development of the Free Church movement.[40]

Women and Ordination

Questions regarding the role of lay women increasingly involve ordination for both clergy and laity.[41] As a vocation, ordination was reserved for men.[42] The argument is the ordained priest represents Christ, who is the husband of his bride, the church. Limiting ordination to men was also based on patriarchal culture.[43]

In some churches, ordination is given to two types of ministers, clergy and deacons, the latter being a lay officer of a local church. Through the office of a deacon, the churches created a class of ordained lay leaders. Recent developments have stressed the servant role of the deacon, with less distinction between temporal and spiritual functions. This trend suggests that the deacon – male and female in a growing number of churches – represents the ministry of the laity. Deacon family ministry and leadership in worship and teaching activities of the church have tended to foster a ministry centered approach to the diaconate.[44] Throughout the history of modern missions, women have been more strongly attracted than men to the

---

[39]   Kenneth Scott Latourette, *A History of Christianity* vol. II, p. 1387.

[40]   Ruth A. Tucker and Walter Liefeld, *Daughters of the Church*, p. 390.

[41]   See Klaus Fiedler, *Baptists and the Ordination of Women*, p. 11.

[42]   Klaus Fiedler, *The Story of Faith Missions*, Oxford: Regnum; Sutherland: Albatross, 1994, p. 308.

[43]   See Isabel Apawo Phiri, *Women, Presbyterianism and Patriarchy: Religious Experience of Chewa Women in Central Malawi*, Blantyre: CLAIM-Kachere, 1997. See also Rachel NyaGondwe Banda, *Women of the Bible and Culture: Baptist Convention Women in Southern Malawi*, Zomba: Kachere, 2005.

[44]   Bill J. Leonard, "Southern Baptists and the Laity," p. 643.

challenge of sharing the gospel worldwide, especially with other women.[45]

The Laity and Missions

God expected or demanded Abraham and his successors to be missionaries. God brought Abraham's descendants to himself, which means they were to encounter the living God and enter into a new covenant relationship with him. Abraham's descendants' entry into the covenant had to be of their own free choice. But, if they chose to enter the covenant, it had to be in accord with conditions laid down by God. They had to be willing to obey his voice and keep his covenant. If they were obedient and kept the covenant, they would enter into a unique relationship with God. The uniqueness indicates three ministries for Abraham's descendants:

They were to be God's own possession or special treasure emphasizing the portability of the message and the fact that God has placed such high value in people.

They were to be a kingdom of priests. Here Israel's mission became explicit; the whole nation was to function on behalf of the kingdom of God as an intermediary role in relation to the nations. This became the basis for the New Testament doctrine of the priesthood of all believers. Unfortunately for Abraham's descendants, they rejected this priesthood of all believers and urged Moses to go up to the mountain of Sinai on their behalf and as their representative. Even though God's original plan was for a moment frustrated and delayed until New Testament times, it was not defeated, substituted or scrapped; it remained God's plan for believers. In addition, Abraham's descendants were to be a holy nation, "wholly" the Lord's. They were to be set apart not only in their lives, but also in their service.[46]

---

[45] Ruth A. Tucker, "Women in Missions," p. 279. See also, Klaus Fiedler, *The Story of Faith Missions*, pp. 292-309.

[46] Walter C. Kaiser, Jr., "Israel's Missionary Call," pp. 29-30.

Israel and the Church – "People of God"

One would argue that Israel is not the same with the church. The fact is what separated the two and demanded death for any Gentile that transgressed and passed its boundaries in the temple complex, has now been knocked down by Christ's death. Maleness, femaleness, Jewishness, Gentile-ness, slave status or whatever no longer matter. All who believe are one "people of God." Peter calls the Gentile believers of his day "a chosen race, a royal priesthood, a holy nation, God's own people" (1 Pet 2:9). The use of Exodus 19 is very obvious and transparent. The point is to recognize the continuity in the purpose and plan of God. The reason why Israel and now Gentile believers have been named a royal priesthood, a holy nation, the people of God, a chosen race, his special, moveable possession, is that we might announce, declaring the wonderful deeds of the One who called them out of darkness into his marvelous light and be his missionaries and witnesses. Peter is trying to show that the people of God in all ages have been one. The unity of all believers and the continuity of that plan between the Old and New Testaments is a certainty.[47] The primary emphasis of this passage is missionary outreach as a response to this privileged status.

The Laity as Effective Communicators

Multiplication of congregations must become a part of the joyful obedience of every Christian, clergy and denomination. If trained in evangelism, the laity are the most effective communicators for they reach their fellow workers, faculty members, fellow employers and employees.[48] Effective evangelism is carried on by a joint effort of the clergy and the laity. In it the clergy perform a small and very important percentage while the laity does a larger percentage of the total work. If any denomination or congregation wishes to become

---

[47] Walter C. Kaiser, Jr., "Israel's Missionary Call," pp. 30-31.

[48] Donald A. McGavran, *Effective Evangelism: A Theological Mandate*, Phillipsburg: Presbyterian and Reformed Publishing company, 1988, p. 6.

effective in its proclamation of the gospel, it must inspire and organize a substantial number of its laity to become ardent and well trained lay evangelists.[49] The training of committed Christians to find and nurture unsaved relatives, friends and neighbours is the key to growth needed by every ordained clergy.

> If the entire life of the church is missionary, then there is need for a theology of the laity. It does not mean that the laity should be trained to become little pastors. Instead, their ministry or service is everywhere. The contingent form this ministry must be recognized as the contingent shape of the clergy ministry, and it will not be the same for every age, context and culture. Where the church's efforts may be more than those of the government, and where the church is left as almost the only voice of the voiceless, in most cases, it will be a combined ministry of the clergy and the laity so that it becomes impossible to distinguish who is doing what.[50]

Ecclesiology of the Laity

Some form of ordained ministry is indeed essential and constitutive as guardian, to help keep the community faithful to the teaching and practice of apostolic Christianity. The clergy do not do this alone, but together with the laity. The priesthood of the ordained ministry is to enable and not to remove the priesthood of all believers. The clergy are not prior to or independent of or against the church; rather, with the rest of the laity, they are the church sent into the world. As a result, there is need for a more organic, less sacral ecclesiology of the laity.[51]

Creeping Clericalism

"Clericalism," that is, the increasing dominance of ordained professionals in the churches was developing which would influence the

[49] Donald A. McGavran, *Effective Evangelism*, p. 131.

[50] David J. Bosch, *Transforming Mission: Paradigm Shifts in Theology of Mission*, Maryknoll: Orbis, 1996, pp. 472-473.

[51] David J. Bosch, *Transforming Mission*, p. 474.

understanding of the role of the laity. This trend may be attributed to several developments.

Tension between Clergy and Laity

The historic distinction between congregational polity and ministerial leadership continues to create tension. In some Protestant churches the congregation is the final authority. Pastors have long known frustration of congregational divisions and lay inflexibility. Power struggles between clergy and laity have often characterized these churches. These conflicts have sometimes led ministers to claim greater authority for the ministerial office, less by virtue of congregational approval than by divine mandate. These churches increasingly view the ministerial call as a divine imperative which is confirmed, though not necessarily verified, by the congregation through ordination. The call is seen as unique in and of itself apart from confirmation of the community.

Professionalization and Multiple Ministers

The increasing professionalization of multiple ministers has had a significant effect on the theology of the laity. Once the pastor was the only ordained cleric in the congregation, but now, in increasing numbers, churches are hiring and ordaining ministers to serve specialized functions. These ministers provide valuable services for the church and the denomination. Their presence, however, implies that ministry or at least ministerial leadership may best be done by specially trained, preferably seminary educated professionals who are paid to direct various facets of church life. While this may be a reality of modern ecclesiastical life, it has significant implications for attitudes toward the priesthood of all believers. This approach may foster a view of the laity as clients who hire a professional to perform certain special services for a particular community. There is no real need to motivate the believers to be involved in ministry.[52]

---

52 Bill J. Leonard, "Southern Baptists and the Laity," pp. 644-45.

Denominationalism added another dimension to the issue of ministerial professionalism by creating the office of a "denominational worker," lay or clergy, an employee of the denomination who produces and administers programmes but is not related directly to the traditional ministerial functions evident in local congregations. In contrast, denominational workers serve as religious professionals, not "pure" laity, but neither are they preachers or ministers in the traditional sense. Denominational professionals have had limited authority in shaping and even addressing controversies and policies.[53]

Autocratic Model of Ministry

Most significantly, some Protestant denominations have been confronted with one particular model for ministry which emphasizes the ultimate authority of the pastoral office. This view suggests that there is only one biblical model for ministry and congregational authority, the pastor. As "under-shepherd" he (women are not considered) represents Christ in the congregation and is responsible only to God. Spiritual, financial, and practical ministries are directed by the pastor who articulates the Word of God to the people. Church growth studies frequently confirm that this autocratic model for ministry produces significant numerical advancements for many congregations. Practically speaking, this style of ministry reflects the business model of the chief executive or chairman of the board whose powerful direction leads the corporation to ever expanding statistical and financial success. Therefore, the laity are considered constituents to be guided by a caring chief executive who, by virtue of divine enlightenment and spiritual responsibility is called to lead and direct the church authoritatively.[54]

---

[53] Bill J. Leonard, "Southern Baptists and the Laity," p. 645. See also Klaus Fiedler, "The 'Smaller' Churches and Big Government," in Matembo S. Nzunda & Kenneth R. Ross (eds), *Church, Law and Political Transition in Malawi 1992-94*, Gweru: Mambo-Kachere, 1997 (1995), pp. 164-65.

[54] Bill J. Leonard, "Southern Baptists and the Laity," p. 645. This is a development that shows in many of the Charismatic churches.

"Creeping clericalism" among the clergy, plus spiritual inferiority complex among the laity, have continued to minimize believers' perception and fulfillment of their priestly call. However, that call remains God's call and commission for all God's people to accomplish.[55]

Conclusion

The presence of an ordained priesthood can have unfortunate side-effects on minimizing an appreciation of the priesthood of all believers. There is a need to recover for the Church membership, 1 Peter's sense of priestly dignity and spiritual sacrifices is a way of understanding the status conferred on all Christians – the priesthood of all believers. The ultimate aim of the priesthood of all believers is the joint service of all believers, men and women, who are theologically competent in a unified mission to the world. Incidentally, this is an encouragement to theological training institutions to develop programmes for training the laity in specialized ministry rather than requiring all who provide such ministries to acquire a professional, clerical identity.

The priesthood of all believers gives each Christian, male or female, the responsibility to be a witness for their faith as an individual and as a part of the local church or denomination. Although churches are growing so quickly that coping with the ever-increasing numbers is a major problem, they lack missionary vision. There is much energy for missions available on the level below that of the clergy, and that is the laity. All Christians are priests, and all priests are Christians. The greatest of power is not in the pulpit, but in the lives of those in the pews.

---

[55] *What Presbyterians Believe*, www.pcusa.org/believe/past/mar04/priesthood.htm, [10.12.2017].

Bibliography

Baker, Robert A., *A Summary of Christian History*, Nashville: Broadman, 1959.

Banda, Rachel NyaGondwe [Fiedler], *Women of the Bible and Culture: Baptist Convention Women in Southern Malawi*, Zomba: Kachere, 2005.

Banks, Robert, *Paul's Idea of Community: The Early House Churches in their Historical Setting*, Exeter: Paternoster Press, 1980.

Bosch, David J., *Transforming Mission: Paradigm Shifts in Theology of Mission*, Maryknoll: Orbis, 1996.

Brown, Raymond E., *The Churches the Apostles Left Behind*, Ramsey: Paulist Press, 1984.

Fackre, Gabriel, *The Christian Story: A Narrative Interpretation of Basic Christian Doctrine*, Grand Rapids: Eerdmans, 1984.

Fiedler, Klaus, "The 'Smaller' Churches and Big Government," in Matembo S. Nzunda & Kenneth R. Ross (eds), *Church, Law and Political Transition in Malawi 1992-94*, Gweru: Mambo-Kachere, 1997 (1995); Mzuzu: Luviri Press, 2020.

Fiedler, Klaus, *Baptists and the Ordination of Women*, Zomba: Lydia Print, 2010.

Fiedler, Klaus, *The Story of Faith Missions*, Oxford: Regnum; Sutherland: Albatross, 1994.

Gerstenberger, Erhard S., *Yahweh the Patriarch: Ancient Images of God and Feminist Theology*, Minneapolis: Fortress Press, 1996.

Grudem, Wayne, *Systematic Theology: an Introduction to Biblical Doctrine*, Leicester: InterVarsity, 1994.

Kaiser, Jr., Walter C. "Israel's Missionary Call" in Ralph D. Winter & Steven C. Hawthorne (eds), *Perspectives on the World Christian Movement: A Reader*, Pasadena: William Carey Library, 1981.

Ketcherside, Karl, *The Priesthood of All Believers*, http://house church.org/basics/ketcherside.html, [10.12.2017].

Kholowa, Janet and Klaus Fiedler, *Mtumwi Paulo ndi Udindo wa Amayi mu Mpingo*, Zomba: Kachere, 2000.

Latourette, Kenneth Scott, *A History of Christianity: Reformation to the Present* vol. 2, New York: Harper & Row, 1975.

Leonard, Bill J., "Southern Baptists and the Laity," in *Review and Expositor* vol. 84, no. 4, (1987), pp. 633-647.

Longwe, Hany, *Christians by Grace, Baptist by Choice*, Zomba: Kachere; Mzuzu: Mzuni Press, 2011.

McGavran, Donald A., *Effective Evangelism: A Theological Mandate*, Phillipsburg: Presbyterian and Reformed Publishing, 1988.

Milne, Bruce, *Know the Truth: A Handbook of Christian Belief*, Nottingham: InterVarsity Press, 2006.

Phiri, Isabel Apawo, *Women, Presbyterianism and Patriarchy: Religious Experience of Chewa Women in Central Malawi*, Blantyre: CLAIM-Kachere, 1997.

Renwick, A.M., *The Story of the Church*, Guilford: Billing & Sons, 1958.

Richardson, Cyril (ed), *Early Christian Fathers*, New York: Touchstone, 1996.

Thomas, George F. (ed), *The Vitality of the Christian Tradition*, New York: Harper & Brothers, 1945.

van Koevering, Helen E.P., *Dancing their Dreams: The Lakeshore Nyanja Women of the Anglican Diocese of Niassa*, Zomba: Kachere, 2005.

What Presbyterians Believe, www.pcusa.org/believe/past/mar04/priesthood.htm, {10.12.2017}.

Wilson-Kastener, Patricia, *Faith, Feminism, and the Christ*, Philadelphia: Fortress Press, 1983.

Chapter 2

The Place of the Laity in the Church under the Priesthood of All Believers

Joseph Thipa

Introduction and Background

Many leaders of Christian churches in Malawi and world-wide are acting in a way that seeks superiority and honour from followers, as was the case of some priests and prophets in Old Testament times. Many Christian leaders would like to be called by such names as prophet, major prophet, apostle, *et cetera,* which make them look outstanding and superior to the people to whom they minister. In the Old Testament of the Bible, priests and prophets were designed by God to be mediators between him and the people. Also, the idea that priests and prophets are mediators between God and his people has created inequality between many Church leaders and the rest of Church members, whom we call laity. As a result, such Christian leaders tend to occupy superior and holier positions in the Church and society. They even go as far as acting as Old Testament prophets; they act as mediators between God and his people. Yet the Bible is very clear, especially in the Letter to the Hebrews, that Jesus Christ is the ultimate mediator between God and the People after the Old Testament prophets and priests (Hebrews 1:2). This chapter there-fore aims at investigating about the position of laity in the Christian Church with regard to the principle of "priesthood of all believers."

"Laity" is a term that has grown out of general agreement (con-ventional), and it refers to church members who are not clergy or those church members that are not ordained into priesthood or ministry of Word and sacraments.[1] In connection with the word "laity" there is the Greek *laos*, "people," that is used in the New Testament of Israel (inclusive of the priests and other leaders). The term *laos*, *"people"* is used in the New Testament for the church (inclusive of pastors and other leaders). In Titus 2:14 we read, "Jesus Christ, who gave himself for us to redeem us from all wickedness and to purify for himself a people that are his own." Here, *a people that are his own* means the church inclusive of everyone in it. 1 Peter 2:9-10 reads, "But you a *chosen people*, a *royal priesthood*, a *holy nation*, a *laos* (people) belonging to God ...now you are the *laos* (people) of God," shows that both "laity" and "priesthood," even though they are different positions, are equally valued by God.

With reference to the "priesthood of all believers," the phrase does not mean that there is no difference between ordained and lay people, but that both share together in the common ministry of the whole people of God.[2] That is the reason why in the New Testament we find that there was no distinction between clergy and laity in terms of service to the people of God. That is why 1 Corinthians 12 shows the church in an organic unity. Believers in the New Testament times believed that in the organism of the living body of Christ, no member is purely passive. Also, in Ephesians 4:16, each and every member shares in the life of the body Jesus of Christ, which is the Church, as much as each member also shares in its activity. Therefore, it means that in the church there must be diversity of ministry by all members of the body (laity included) but having unity of Christian ministries.

History of the Priesthood of All Believers

"Priesthood of all believers" is a doctrine which was classically formulated by Martin Luther, affirming the common dignity, calling

---

1   David F. Wright, "Laity" in S.B. Ferguson, D.F. Wright and J.I. Packer (eds), *New Dictionary of Theology*, Leicester: InterVarsity, 1988, p. 375.

2   J. Stacey, *Groundwork of Theology*, London: Epworth Press, 1977, p. 249.

and privilege of all Christian believers before God.[3] "Priesthood of all believers" means that the Christian Church no longer needs priests similar to those of the Old Testament to offer up animal sacrifices because Jesus Christ has made once for all and perfect atoning sacrifice of himself for humanity's redemption.[4] Every Christian believer has access to the throne of God by the merits of Jesus.[5] "There is no New Testament warrant for ascribing any special qualifications of priesthood to ordained persons within the priesthood of the Christian Church."[6]

With reference to the "priesthood of all believers," the early Christian Church Fathers spoke of all Christians as representing pure sacrifices to God.[7] Wright says that the designation of bishops, presbyters as sacrificing mediatorial priests of Old Testament terms obscured the general priesthood of Christian believers.[8] That is the reason why in the Middle Ages Christians, who were not clergy or monks, were in effect relegated to second class status.[9] It is, therefore, against such distortions that Martin Luther protested to say that Christian baptism consecrates all Christian believers without exception and makes them all priests.

The Reformation emphasized the priesthood of all believers and recovered the doctrine of Christian vocation in which every Christian is called upon to serve God in his or her own particular occupation. That is why the great Evangelical movement, which spread through Protestantism in the 17th and 18th centuries, gave a far larger place to the laity. The laity were used as instruments in worldwide

---

[3]   David F. Wright, "Priesthood of All Believers," in S.B. Ferguson, D.F. Wright and J.I. Packer (eds), *New Dictionary of Theology*, Leicester: InterVarsity, 1988, p. 531.

[4]   G.P. Duffield, and N.M. van Cleave, *Foundations of Pentecostal Theology*, Los Angeles: L.I.F.E. Bible College, 1983, p. 452.

[5]   Hebrews 4:14-16.

[6]   David F. Wright, "Priesthood of All Believers," p. 532.

[7]   Malachi 1:10.

[8]   David F. Wright, "Priesthood of All Believers," p. 532.

[9]   David F. Wright, "Priesthood of All Believers," p. 532.

evangelism that was prevalent in that age. They were to become active participants in gatherings for Christian nurture, in winning souls, and in transmitting the faith.

The Methodist Church itself was in its beginning largely a lay movement. In Europe Anglican lay preachers were encouraged to go into worldwide Christian mission and they operated under the supervision of an Anglican clergyman, John Wesley. In England and in America a number of voluntary societies grew up apart from any ecclesiastical control but supported by clergy and laity in fruitful co-operation. In contemporary Malawi, too, we see a lot of lay participation in the Christian churches. For example, in the Church of Central Africa Presbyterian there are more lay preachers every Sunday than ordained preachers.

The Need for Priesthood of All Believers in the Contemporary World

Renewal of Temporal Orders[10]

In our contemporary world, priesthood of all believers means that men and women should work in harmony; they should renew the temporal order and make it increasingly more perfect. Such is God's design for the world. Temporal order refers to personal and family values, culture, economic interests, trade, professions and political institutions, international relations, and so on, as well as their gradual development. All these possess a value of their own, placed in them by God, both in themselves or as parts of the integral temporal structure. "And God saw all that he had made and found it very good" (Genesis 1:31). This natural goodness of theirs receives an added dignity from their relation with the human person, for whose use they have been created.

This was what was in the mind of the World Missionary Movement that was born at Edinburgh in 1910. In its Life and Work programme,

---

[10]   Austin Flannery, *Vatican Council II*, New York: Costello, 1996, pp. 412-413.

it sought to find out how Christians could assist one another in bringing their faith to bear on the general life of society – in politics, industry, education, international relations, et cetera. The Life and Work prong held that the task of the Church, besides saving souls out of the present evil world and preparing them for an eternal destiny, includes the transformation of this world. Certainly, the mission of the church is not only to bring the message and grace of Christ to the world but also to permeate and improve the whole range of temporal things.

A good example about transformation of this world would be of a humble cobbler, who as he hammered in the nails, or pegs, or drew the thread through the tough leather, making shoes that were strong and comfortable, felt that he was serving God. As he was fair and kind, he knew that through his everyday work, which otherwise might have been drudgery, something to rebel against, he was co-operating with God in the advancement of His Kingdom. Another example is of a boy who accepts the doctrine of Christian vocation and is able to work in a filling station, or as a clerk, or as a day labourer, with the same joy in service that a church minister knows, or a missionary.

Ordained Members will Find it Difficult without Lay Participation

Our contemporary world is very complex and very difficult for the ordained members to do it alone without lay participation. Ordained members should know that the Laity is already involved in dealing with societal issues outside the Church. They work for government institutions, non-governmental institutions, *et cetera,* out there, and are in a better position to advise the Church on how it can best handle issues concerning people and the environment in which they live. The success of the church in this contemporary world is seen to depend upon its laity, not because of their particular ability, but because of their involvement in the life of the world out there.

Again, most of the great benevolent work of the church had its birth from lay participation in the work of the church – for example, organized home missions, foreign missions, Sunday schools, educational societies, and the like. Only gradually were these organizations taken over by the denominations as a part of their normal operations. The role of the Pastor changes, here, becoming not less, but more important as the Pastor seeks to aid the laity to function as the People of God in the totality of their lives. Therefore the difference between Pastors and Laity is theological rather than functional. The difference is theological, rather than functional in the sense of the different roles that God has placed upon the ordained and Laity. Here, no one role is inferior or superior to the other.

Conclusion

First and foremost, whatever every Christian believer will do, lay or ordained, they should aim to do charity work, social aid and proclamation of the gospel, rather than competing for status. Moreover, Christ himself has as signs of his messianic mission works of charity as given in Matthew 11:4-5. In the text, "Jesus replied, 'Go back and report to John what you hear and see: The blind receive sight, the lame walk, those who have leprosy are cured, the deaf hear, the dead are raised, and the good news is preached to the poor.'" Here Christ avoided telling people sent by John his status. Instead, he portrayed himself as having come into this world to serve the people and proclaim the gospel.

Again, in Matthew 22:37-40 Jesus states the greatest commandment of the law as that of loving God with one's whole heart and one's neighbour as oneself. Also in John 13:35 Jesus has made charity the distinguishing mark of his disciples, in the words, "By this will everyone know you for my disciples, by your love for one another." The Laity as belonging to priesthood of all believers should therefore support as far as they can, in private or public works of charity and social assistance movements, including international schemes.

Bibliography

Duffield, G.P. and N.M. van Cleave, *Foundations of Pentecostal Theology*, Los Angeles: L.I.F.E. Bible College, 1983.

Flannery, Austin, *Vatican Council II*, New York: Costello, 1966.

Stacey, J., *Groundwork of Theology*, London: Epworth Press, 1977.

Wright, David F., "Laity," in S.B. Ferguson, D.F. Wright and J.I. Packer (eds), *New Dictionary of Theology*, Leicester: InterVarsity, 1988, p. 375.

Wright, David F., "Priesthood of All Believers," in S.B. Ferguson, D.F. Wright and J.I. Packer (eds), *New Dictionary of Theology*, Leicester: InterVarsity, 1988, pp. 531-532.

Chapter 3

Not Just Loyal Sheep: Informed Ministry of the Laity

James Tengatenga

Introduction

In one of our catechisms the interrogation goes:

Q. Who are the ministers of the Church?

A. The ministers of the church are lay persons, bishops, priests and deacons.[1]

For me this is a telling Q and A. It is on this basis that one begins to look at what qualifies one to be a minister. It also begs the question as to what ministry is. We have, by and large, tended to think of ministers as only those who are ordained. In fact, in some of our churches that is how we refer to the clergy: as ministers. This has led us to not recognize the work of laity as ministry. They are the sheep who are to be led and fed by the *abusa*. What we see in this is that there is a clericalization of ministry. In turn, our people have also believed that they are nothing more than "sheep" [sic]. If they have any contribution to make to church life; theirs is merely to complement the pastors. It is not ministry in its own right but contingent on that of the pastor. What I am leading to, here, is that this is a false understanding of ministry and ministers. Secondly if the ministry of the laity is indeed ministry in the same way as that of the clergy, it requires formation as well. This is where the training and equipping for ministry comes into play. Hence, as one Church of England report in 1985 says, "Adult Christian commitment means an

---

1   "The Catechism" in *Episcopal Church Book of Common Prayer*, New York: Church Publishing House, 1979.

informed commitment. It is not a matter of being loyal sheep."[2] In order for us to appreciate this I will give a sketch of the context in Malawi with special reference to my own denomination and propose a way in which the ministry of the laity can be made not only effective, but also restored to its rightful place in the *missio Dei* and in doing so, demonstrate its value.

Our Context

When one is repeatedly told something, one tends, in the end, to believe that it is true. In spite of the quotation from the Catechism I referred to above, most lay people do not recognize that they too are ministers and hence can be specially commissioned for particular ministry in the church. One is also cognizant of the fact that for some, it is willful ignorance and for even others blatant denial. Fredrica Harris Thompsett, in *The Study of Anglicanism*, says:

> What is at stake is not the task of convincing people that they are 'ministers'; rather the basic goal is encouraging persons to live authentically as 'Christians' in their daily life. In the global village of the twenty-first century, the exact ordering of ministry will surely not be as critical as the ethical witness of laity in a post-Christian world.[3]

Thus, being a Christian is being a minister.

Most of our people believe that they are consumers of the wares the clergy have to offer. It is expected of the clergy (*abusa*) that they will lead their sheep to good pastures like their exemplar the Good Shepherd (Jesus). The clergy are expected to make sure that the church runs, and in extreme cases (in the Anglo-Catholic tradition) it even goes further to say that "Father knows best and Father does it all." Should the laity find themselves doing something it tends to be understood as helping Father out! This is not to ignore the fact that there are *Wardens* and *Elders* in the parish whose duty is to carry out

---

[2] *All are Called*, Church of England Report, 1985, p. 23.

[3] Fredrica Harris Thompsett, "The Laity," in Stephen Sykes, John Booty and Jonathan Knight (eds), *The Study of Anglicanism*, London: SPCK, 1988, p. 288.

various duties in the pastoral and administrative work of ministry. According to the laws of our denomination they can be licensed to perform other functions in the church, such as leading prayers and ministering to the various pastoral needs of the people in their wards. Some are even selected and trained to be *Lay Readers* (in Malawi now known as *Lay Leaders*) who do the readings and lead non-sacramental services. These are the volunteers.

A similar breed of people are *Catechists*. These are the full-time employees in our denomination and have full-time teaching (*catechesis*: hence the name) and full-time pastoral responsibilities as assigned by the priests. These are few and far between and are the exception and not the norm. Their ministry is still very much contingent on that of the priest. However, it has to be recognized that they are considered ministers, albeit of a lower order. And as ministers, they are trained for that particular ministry. This training or formation suggests that the church takes their ministry seriously enough to warrant the effort. It is for the likes of these, that programmes like TEEM tend to be set up.[4] However, even TEE is not taken seriously enough. There is a tendency to train only for liturgical practice, a little homiletics and a little pastoral theology. By and large it is not the full breath of theology that they get. The TEE course is only partially used. Lay Training Centres are generally used for this partial formation. Even where it is used in full, the course of choice is the most basic introductory one. It is as if "real" theology is only reserved for the priests. Does this suggest that the clergy would like to hold the keys to the "theology franchise" as a domain for the clergy alone?

---

4 [Note from the Editor: Theological Education by Extension in Malawi (TEEM) was founded in January 1978. According to *Ecclesia* of February 1978 (which was an Anglican newsletter published monthly in Chichewa and English from 1962-1980, "six churches in Malawi have agreed to set up Theological Education by Extension in Malawi ... the six Churches are the Church of Central Africa Presbyterian's two Synods of Blantyre and Nkhoma, the Anglican Church's two Dioceses of Lake Malawi and Southern Malawi, the Churches of Christ and the African Baptist Assembly."]

If this were not an anomaly enough for the "teaching elders" (as our Presbyterian compadres call clergy), more often than not priests are not too keen to be animators for the learners. It is seen as an extra responsibility to be such. The assumption behind it being that there are regional coordinators who are paid to do this job. The teaching elders delegate their role to those who would be their support. It, thus, is an attitude problem on their part. To be blunt, it is an abdication of their role in training and equipping their lay leaders for ministry. The need for a well-trained laity is, therefore, not appreciated. We will return to this point anon.

A further point in describing our scenario is: The growth of the church in our denominations in Malawi is not matched with priestly vocations and/or with the resources to train the requisite number of clergy. This has meant that most of our congregations are run by voluntary lay leaders and occasionally by the paid ones as described above. These volunteers' qualifications are (more often than not) that they know how to read and write. Theological training is not expected. It seems to me that this is an acceptable position in the church in Malawi. The hope being that at some point in the future there will be enough clergy to fill the vacancies and thus there will be no more need for lay ministers. What happens in the meantime is anybody's guess! No wonder there is an ignorance of the faith among our people.

As a matter of contrast, our clergy are formed in seminaries for not less than three years and the clever ones even get more training to graduate and postgraduate levels. The church is ready and willing to spend a lot of money training its clergy for ministry. The assumption here is that the clergy are trained for ministry and those who do not receive the training are not into ministry! Of course, it is not intended to say that but that is the perception this scenario creates. The other assumption is that the church trains the clergy so that they, in turn train their laity. As we have hinted above, this does not happen to the degree of the investment.

Congregations fight over well-trained clergy in the belief that they are better priests. In many ways that is a correct expectation. It is expected that the clergy will be "properly" trained for ministry. It is considered a disgrace when the church ordains to the priesthood "half-baked" people but we think nothing of the "unbaked" lay leaders who lead our many congregations. It is as if these lay leaders are not ministers to the same degree as clergy but just "glorified laity." They are nothing but sheep dependent on the ministry of the pastors. I am not suggesting here that the ministry of clergy is the same as that of the laity. They are different charismata but both are "ministry." Barring the sacramental and other sacerdotal aspects of ministry, the formation required is the same, just as the expected fruit is the same. It may be argued that laity have not had the time for the training to that level but it is my belief that this is just a cop-out. Special programmes have been devised when exigencies of time and other constraints have dictated that clergy be trained in non-traditional ways. "Where there is a will there is a way," goes a saying. Given the scenario painted earlier, the church in Malawi would be expected to have prized lay training and formation for ministry more than in other parts of the world. The only explanation I can come up with, in this respect is that the laity are not considered ministers in the way that clergy are. In fact, their work is not considered ministry. After all laity are but sheep.

What's the Fuss About?

This begs the question of what the fuss is about. To begin with the attitude and stance described above goes counter to the concept of "the priesthood of all believers" as understood by the church. It has a tendency to an over clericalization of the church that borders on the medieval abuse. It does not take into consideration the place and role of all believers which the Reformation (among other things) ushered in. The various Reformed traditions, including the Anglican traditions, were concerned about the literacy of the laity hence the use of vernacular languages in worship and Bible translations which sought to bring the faith to the people. For it not to be just the property of the clergy.

Not only is this situation retrogressive towards the medieval, it also goes some way towards negating the spirit of our predecessors of the church in Malawi. They identified the need and formed two institutions dedicated to the training of the laity, namely Lay Training Centres and TEEM. This was in addition to the seminaries. It may be argued that seminaries were not for the laity but that is not entirely true (at least in the Universities' Mission to Central Africa).[5] If one wanted to be a *Lay Reader* (those laity who worked alongside clergy and were the catechists, readers and preachers) in the church one had to be trained, first as a school teacher (which training had a religious studies component), work for at least one year being monitored and mentored by the local clergy while working alongside them in the school and local church, and then one would be sent to theological college for a further year of training. After that training they would then be qualified to be a *Lay Reader*. At the theological college, they would have been training alongside those who would be training for the ordained ministry. This suggests that catechesis *(and the catechumenate)* was considered serious business, to the extent that such rigorous training was needed. In the 1960s leading to the 1970s the *oecumene* realized what had been lost through the demise of this type of training and resolved to do something about it. This resulted in TEEM (Theological Education by Extension in Malawi). This new institution was to cater for the barely literate and for the educated – hence the two programmes that it ran. In the one hundred plus years that the church had been in the country (at that time) it was not lost on those leaders that the ministry of the laity was integral to the *missio Dei* in Malawi. This was recognizing that ministers are not born but they are formed.

Let me digress briefly in order to return to a point mentioned earlier. Many clergy have felt lonely and in danger of stunted or stymied

---

5   See James Tengatenga, *The UMCA in Malawi: A History of the Anglican Church*, Blantyre: Kachere, 2010.

theological development. There is not a ready community of theologians with whom to engage in discourse. Even their sermons are not professionally critiqued and neither are the clergy quizzed on the theological content of their sermons and teaching. During church synods or conventions, the discussion hinges more on tradition as experienced without theological depth or *raison d'être*. This has left many clergy persons wondering where and when they are to engage in theological discourse. In the end, this theological atrophy has led to a less effective theological engagement with the issues of the day making the church irrelevant or simply one that regurgitates thoughts from somewhere else without itself making any offerings by way of language or theological method to the theological and ethical discourse in the international arena. In extreme cases, it has led to theologians who are unable to offer appropriate theological (or otherwise) responses to challenges from both within and without. This suggests that the church has ceased to be a community of learners and a community of discourse. Given the dearth of theologians there is no one to engage with. Had it been that the laity are formed well for ministry, the clergy would have a community of discourse. As the prophet Isaiah says (about the Servant of the Lord) he is like one who "listens like one who is taught." Listening and teaching go together! It is, as the Bible says, "Deep calling to deep and iron sharpening iron" (Proverbs 27:17). This will only happen if laity are not considered simply as sheep.

Discourse is not the only missing thing in the life of most clergy but also support in their teaching ministry. I am here referring to more than "mere" *catechesis*. Regular in-depth Religious Education fails to take place in our parishes to a large extent because the clergy do not have enough time to do all the teaching in the many congregations (and even in the one congregation) under their cure. It would be a great help if they had other theologians beside themselves to do the teaching. A well-formed laity both those in recognized ministry like *Lay Readers, Catechists* or *Evangelists* and those who have theological training without any particular official capacity in the church can be an asset to the church. The task of making disciples is not just for the clergy alone.

Not Loyal Sheep but Ministers

The blame cannot be on the church as institution and the clergy alone but also on the laity themselves who have imagined themselves as not being called to ministry. As we saw above, being an authentic Christian is being in ministry by virtue of our baptism. The church as a community of discourse requires both: an informed and well-formed clergy and informed and well-formed laity.

If the work that laity perform in the church is ministry, it should follow that we make the same requirement on them (in terms of formation) as we have on the clergy. This is where a properly run TEE programme can be useful in the equipping of the saints for the work of ministry. The TEE method is helpful in this enterprise because it is flexible, time commitment-wise. However, for it to be effective the "teaching elders" have to rise to their God given charism and be the local animators and facilitators in the study groups. It is not only clergy who can be teachers. Laity can be teachers as well. An added advantage to the clergy tutoring their own flock is that they get used to doing and speaking theology with their own people and conversely the laity become comfortable with clergy in the same way, to the extent that theological discourse will become a normal way of being for them. Certainly not all are teachers and neither are all mere learners. Teaching is a charism and like all charismata it is given by the Holy Spirit according to his wish. It is for this reason that we have to look at laity as not just sheep but laity committed and equipped for ministry.

Bibliography

All are Called, Church of England Report, 1985.

The Catechism in *Episcopal Church Book of Common Prayer*, New York: Church Publish House, 1979.

Tengatenga, James, *The UMCA in Malawi: A History of the Anglican Church*, Zomba: Kachere, 2010.

Thompsett, Fredrica Harris, "The Laity," in Stephen Sykes, John Booty and Jonathan Knight (eds), *The Study of Anglicanism*, London: SPCK, 1988, pp. 277-293.

Chapter 4

The Laity as Church in the World: The Need to Equip them in their Apostolate

Fanuel Magangani

The ideal of grace is not lived in isolation but in community. This presentation is a call to be living members of the Church Community into which we have been incorporated through our Baptism without the mark of separation of being clergy or laity but the Church of God in sharing the privileges of training.

The Church is a visible sign of Christ who lives on in history. In Scripture the Church is described in images rather than in rational terms only, more as a living reality than as rational. The Church is Mystical Body (1 Corinthians 12:27) and as "People of God" (1 Peter 2:9-10). We are the hand, eye, feet, ears of Christ, to make him present in the world.

The Old Testament uses two words to denote the Church namely *qahal* and *edhah*. The words are sometimes used interchangeably but were not synonymous at the beginning. *Edhah* (appoint) is a gathering by appointment and it applied to Israel or its representatives whether assembled or not. *Qahal* (call) on the other hand properly means the actual meeting together of the people. Sometimes we find the *qahal edhah* which means the assembly of the "congregation," (Exodus 12:6; Numbers 14:5; Jeremiah 26:17). It seems that the actual meeting was sometimes a meeting of the representatives of the people (Deuteronomy 4:10; 18:16; 2 Chronicles 5:2-6 and 1 Kings 8:1-3, 5). "As in the OT (Exodus 12:6; Numbers 8:20; Ps. 74:2) the *edhah* of

God is Israel or the Jews in an organic unity, and the *qahal* (of God) is simply the assembled *edhah.*"[1]

Edhah is commonly more used in the book of the Exodus, Leviticus, Numbers and Joshua but is absent from the book of Deuteronomy and is rarely found in the later books. *Qahal* is often found in Chronicles, Ezra and Nehemiah. "The Septuagint translates the word for gathering or assembly, Hebrew *qahal* with the Greek term εκκλησιαζώ; to summon an assembly and the verb that is cognate to the New Testament noun εκκλησια."[2]

Synagogue is the usual translation of *edhah* in the Septuagint[3] and also in the Pentateuch.[4] In the later books of the Bible, *qahal* is generally translated *ecclesia*. Ecclesia is the primary Greek translation of *qahal* for the Greek speaking Jews.

The New Testament has two words for the Church; Ecclesia and Synagogue. The word synagogue is derived from the meaning of the two Greek words συν-αγω meaning to "come together" it ordinarily means either the religious gathering of the Jews or the building in which they assembled for public worship. It was mostly being used after the fall of the Temple when the Jews were taken into captivity in Babylon. When they came back the word synagogue in the Septuagint meant the gathering of the Jews in local areas apart from the gathering in the Temple as described in the New Testament (Matthews 4:23; Acts 13:43; Revelation 2:9; 3:9).

The *qahal* translated *ecclesia* and *edhah* rendered synagogue in the Septuagint are used in the New Testament to show that the Church

---

[1] George Johnston, "The Doctrine of the Church in the New Testament" in Matthew Black, H.H. Rowley (eds), *Peake's Commentary on the Bible*, 1962, London: Nelson, pp. 719-723.

[2] Wayne Grudem, *Systematic Theology*, Leicester: InterVarsity, 1994, p. 853.

[3] Septuagint is the Greek Translation of the Hebrew Text commonly known as LXX.

[4] Pentateuch means the first 5 books of the Old Testament, commonly known as the Books of the Law.

has its basis in the Old Testament. The term ecclesia generally designates the Church of the New Testament though in a few places it denotes common civil assemblies (Acts 19:32, 39, 41), the Jewish group Acts 7:38 (assembly in the wilderness at Mount Sinai). But in many cases, it was assumed that this was a term being used to mean the Church in the New Covenant of God.

Since the idea of the Church is a many-sided concept, it is quite natural that the word ecclesia as applied to it does not always have exactly the same meaning. Jesus was the first one to use the word in the New Testament and he applied it to the company that gathered about him, "*on this I will build my Church*" (Matthew 16:18), recognizing him publicly as the Lord, and accepted the principles of the Kingdom of God. It is also found in Matthew 18:17 where he speaks of how the fellowship of believers were to conduct themselves towards each other if one goes astray: "*And if he refuses to hear them, tell it to the church. But if he refuses even to hear the church, let him be to you like a heathen and a tax collector.*"

The basic meaning of *ecclesia* from the verb *ek-kaleo* is "to call out." So it's a called out group selected from a larger group by a call. In this call it does not only refer to the clergy but to the Church as a whole.

The Book of Acts gives us a fundamental outline of the Church. The apostles began their work of reaching out to the world from the day of Pentecost when about three thousand believers were added to them (Acts 2:41). In verse 47 Luke tells us what he meant in verse 41 by "to them" when he explains "*And the Lord added to the church daily those who were being saved*" (Acts 2:47, New King James Version).

Later on, as a result of the extension of the Church the word acquired various significations and definitions. Local Churches were established everywhere and were also called ecclesia since they were manifestations of the one universal Church of Christ. In this context the understanding of the Church means all the believers in Christ were part of the membership of the Church.

All baptized -- Priests/Ministers/Pastors, religious, and laity -- are the Church; there is a unity of mission though there is a diversity of functions. All have responsibilities springing from their Baptism. The main point to be made in this presentation is that Christ did not intend merely to save individuals but to save the world, and for this He founded the Church to continue His mission to the world. As members of the Church, the laity have a specific mission to the world and in the world to be fully Christians just like the clergy. They are the Church in the world for they live the life in the world doing everything they can do but living the life of the Church. As the Church in the world through the transformation of their lives, they are to penetrate and transform society through the power of the Gospel hence the need to equip them in their apostolate.

Lay Person

In religious organizations, the laity comprises all people who are not in the clergy. A person who is a member of a Religious order who is not ordained legitimate clergy is considered as a member of the laity, even though they are members of a religious order (for example a nun or lay brother).

In the past in Christian cultures, the term *lay priest* was sometimes used to refer to a secular priest, a diocesan priest who is not a member of a religious order.

There is diversity in how Christian communities have considered the roles of the lay faithful in the life of the Church. Some denominations have specific roles for the laity and others do not have unique terms for this distinction.

Anglicanism

In the Anglican tradition the term "laity" refers to anyone who is not a bishop, priest, or deacon, that is, the fourth order of ministers in the Church. In this tradition all baptized persons are expected to minister in Christ's name, such that during a time of emergency a lay faithful may baptize and that action is duly considered as a Sacrament.[5] The orders of ministry are thus lay people, deacons, priests, and bishops.

The ministry of the laity is "to represent Christ and his Church; to bear witness to him wherever they may be; and, according to the gifts given them, to carry on Christ's work of reconciliation in the world; and to take their place in the life, worship, and governance of the Church."[6] Much of the ministry of the laity thus takes place outside official church structures in homes, workplaces, schools, and so forth. Laymen also play important roles in the structures of the church as they are the Church in the world. There are elected lay representatives on the various governing bodies of churches in the Anglican Communion.

Roman Catholicism

The Second Vatican Council (1962–65) spent a great deal of time exploring the purpose and mission of the Laity in the Catholic Church. One of the main documents specifically relating to the Laity was *Apostolicam Actuositatem* which includes the following statement:

> The term laity is here understood to mean all the faithful except those in holy orders and those in the state of religious life specially approved by the Church. These faithful are by baptism made one body with Christ and are constituted among the People of God; they are in their own way made sharers in the priestly, prophetical, and kingly functions of Christ; and they carry out for their own part the mission of the whole Christian people in the Church and in the world.[7]

The Second Vatican Council taught that the laity's specific character is *secularity*, i.e. as Christians who *live the life of Christ in the world*, their role is to sanctify the created world by directing it to become more Christian in its structures and systems. Due to their baptism, they are

---

5   *Mapemphero ndi Nyimbo za Mulungu.*

6   *Book of Common Prayer*, p. 855.

7   Pope Paul VI, *Apostolicam Actuositatem.*

members of God's family, the Church, and they grow in intimate union with God, "in" and "by means" of the world. It is not a matter of departing from the world as monks and nuns do in order to sanctify themselves; it is precisely through the material world sanctified by the coming of the God made flesh, i.e. made material that they reach God. Doctors, mothers of a family, farmers, bank tellers, drivers, by doing their jobs in the world with a Christian spirit are already extending the Kingdom of God. According to the repeated statements of Popes and lay Catholic leaders, the laity should say "we are the Church" in the same way that the saints said that "Christ lives in me."

Presbyterians

They understand lay ministry in a more equal way in the running of the Church where they are considered to be ruling elders if elected to that position. In this case they work side by side with the teaching elder although the teaching elder takes a first place in practical life. In every Church tradition lay apostolate has a profound place and cannot be avoided.

The Mission of the Church

If we are the Church, then together as the Church we have a mission. That mission is to continue the *missio Dei* in the world which is to evangelize the world. There is only one mission of the Church and of all its members - it is the evangelization of the world. Pope John Paul II states that the Lord has entrusted a great part of the responsibility of the Church's mission to the lay faithful, in communion with all other members of the people of God[8] it is clearly the mission of the laity to engage in evangelism in the same way as it is the mission of the clergy. The Anglican Church for instance has advanced into many parts of Malawi through the work of the lay faithful. When the Church leaders were hindered from going into other spheres of

---

[8]   Pope John Paul II, *Christifideles Laici*, p. 32.

operation due to comity arrangements the laity resisted and remained Anglican, Presbyterian or Roman Catholic in the areas where they settled. In time the Priest or the Minister followed them. This is the trend that is prevailing even today. The lay faithful are the ones who are doing Church spawning in most mainline Churches.[9]

In addition, Pope Paul VI, in his apostolic exhortation, "On Evangelization in the Modern World," provides us with a definition of evangelization when he says:

> The Church evangelizes when she seeks to convert, solely through the divine power of the message she proclaims both the personal and collective conscience of people, the activities in which they engage, and the lives and concrete milieus which are theirs.[10]

Plainly stated, evangelization is a process whereby others are, through divine power, converted in mind and heart and then live out the Christian ideal in their families, workplaces and other environments seeking to bring others to the same consciousness. For this to happen we need to make a deliberate effort to equip them so that they will bring this fire of evangelism into the world in which they live.

The laity comprises the vast majority of the membership of the Church. The laity witness to the Church and to the world by bringing Christ to all of the structures of life of the world, each one of them acting in accordance with their unique talents given to them by God.

They are all, each at their own level, co-responsible with the clergy for the unique mission of the Church. In 1 Corinthians 12:4-6 Paul writes, "There are different kinds of spiritual gifts, but the same spirit gives them. There are different ways of serving, but the same Lord is served. There are different abilities to perform services, but the same

---

[9] In many places we have Anglican prayer houses not because of evangelism by the Priest with a fully supported programme of the Church but because the laity in that place did not want to join another Church but to remain Anglican and thereafter their story is not told. You would only hear the first Parish Priest was Father So-and-So while, in fact, the station was opened by the laity without the support of a Priest.

[10] Pope Paul VI, *On Evangelization in the Modern World*, p. 18.

God gives ability." We may perform various and diverse functions, but all are directed to the same mission.

We have been called to the Christian vocation and sent with the message of Christ to evangelize the world. This role or function as an evangelizer is not an incidental aspect or luxury of the life of a Christian; rather it is the only true response to the call. The redemptive work of Jesus extends to every aspect of life. It extends to our families, friendships, work situations and social gatherings this is only possible when the Church finds ways of equipping the laity not with the sense of ordained ministry but for them to serve better in their own right as the lay faithful to Christ's call to mission. In his great commission he did not just call upon the apostles only but also those who are called according to his purpose. If that call was only meant for the apostles then none of us who are not an apostle par excellence should claim the authority of being sent into the mission field for we were not there as eye witnesses. But if we can claim this authority then the laity also is sent out for mission just as we are.

It is this universal calling into the mission field that we need to find ways of equipping the laity for their apostolate. Sadly, this is not taking place; the institutions that were meant to help the lay people to gain the much-needed knowledge are today turned into business institutions for a different purpose. If we look around and find out what is happening now in the lay training centres we shall see that they have outlived their purposes. Even in Theological Education by Extension (TEE), the ideal purpose was perverted into professional training for Teachers and Clergy to upgrade their professional papers. We need to be there for the initial training of the lay faithful for their apostolate. This can be done if we can consider every parish, or station as a lay training centre through which we can reach out to the lay people in a cost-effective way and also in a convenient place.

Conclusion

We are people who are taking the marvellous realities of Grace seriously. We are people who can live fully as God's children, as brothers and sisters of Christ, and as temples of the Holy Spirit (1 Corinthians 3:16-17). We are people disposed to project Christ in all the crossroads of life. We are people who judge all the problems of life by Christian criteria, and we live in grace. Then we will be people who realize in their lives the beautiful definition of a Christian as stated by Pope John XXIII, the Christian is joy - a joy for God and a joy for other people. We can be that joy in the world by leveling the ground for the lay people to show their skill in theological studies. We can do this by providing the means for them to study theology in the clearest available language.

Bibliography

Book of Common Prayer of the Episcopal Church in the United States of America, New York: Oxford University Press, 2007.

George, Johnston, "The Doctrine of the Church in the New Testament" in Matthew Black, H.H. Rowley (eds), *Peake's Commentary on the Bible*, London: Nelson, 1962, pp. 719-723.

Grudem, Wayne, *Systematic Theology*, Leicester: InterVarsity, 1994.

Mapemphero ndi Nyimbo za Mulungu, Lilongwe: Anglican Church in Malawi, 1996.

Pope John Paul II, *Christifideles Laici*, 1988., www.vatican.va/content /john-paul-ii/en/apost_exhortations/ documents/hf_jp-ii_exh_ 30121988_christifideles-laici.html [18.4.2019].

Pope Paul VI, *Apostolicam Actuositatem*, 1965, www.vatican.va/ archive/hist_councils/ii_vatican_council/documents/vat-ii_de cree_apostolicam-actuositatem_en.html [18.4.2019].

Pope Paul VI, "*On Evangelization in the Modern World*," 1975, www. papalencyclicals.net/paul06/p6evan.htm [18.4.2019].

Chapter 5

Servants or Masters? 21st Century Pontification of the Church in Africa

Manuel Kamnkhwani

The media nowadays is awash with scandals involving church leaders, ranging from sexual promiscuity to embezzlement of church funds. A week does not go by without hearing an embarrassing incident involving a pastor or elder of the church. Amidst the true stories that can be proven, are a myriad of fake news and scandals still targeting church leaders and their followers. The fake news and rumours that surround the pastoral ministry are an indication of the rot that has found its way into the supposed noble profession.

Indeed, modern day church leadership has fallen into a great deal of disrepute because some of the personalities who have found their way into this noble calling are in it for selfish reasons. The vetting processes of even the once conservative denominations have been seriously breached by wolves in sheep's clothing who have worked their way to the top hierarchies of a lot of denominations, infecting whole systems with worldly ideals and values at the expense of the rule of scripture. Today church policy is no longer determined by what scripture says, but by what would be of material and economic gain to the leadership of the church. The church, once a source of solace and comfort to the poor and lowly, is now a cash cow to a few greedy masters who claim only by word of mouth to be servants of the Lord.

It is common knowledge to any church goer today that the pastor is the central focus of worship in most churches. Instead of the historic wooden pulpit that drew the congregation's attention to the spoken word of God, most churches are now adorned with glass lecterns which draw the worshippers' attention to the preacher, high and lifted up on a gold studded throne draped with expensive linen and a red carpet leading up to the podium. This elevation of the office of a pastor is a replay of the historical eleventh century elevation of one man in the church, otherwise dubbed Pontification, whereby absolute power over the church was given absolutely to one leader of the church, who later became too powerful and ceased to serve the almighty God but rather himself and his cronies.

More than a decade ago, I attended a denominational strategic planning review that was intended to recap and reiterate the contents of a strategic plan that the said church was supposedly implementing at that time. On the second day of the session, in the course of reviewing the organizational organogram, I was shocked to hear the facilitator of that particular session telling the then secretary general of the church that, "...you are the CEO of this denomination." After a short pause, the Secretary General enquired rather quizzically; "I am the CEO of the denomination?" and the statement was emphatically repeated to him, "Yes, you are the CEO of the denomination." The facilitator at this time was a professional businessman working in the secular business world where the concept of a Chief Executive Officer is often understood as a boss who is above everybody else in the organization, whereas his audience largely consisted of church ministers, who supposedly are considered to be elders of a church that have been assigned a leadership role among their peers. It would be wise if we, as a church, went back to our source of knowledge and direction, which is the Bible. There is need to theologically reflect about biblical leadership models and those promoted by society. This will help us to find guiding principles that will help us formulate an appropriate theological understanding of what church leadership should look like, instead of borrowing secular terms and values.

In the secular world, the CEO has the final authority in the organization he/she is heading, whereas an elder in a church, regardless the responsibility vested in their office, is supposed to be guided by the rule of scripture. A good friend, who has specialized in Management studies, once told me that the CEO in an organization is supposed to be resourceful for the organization; meaning that the decisions he makes should either bring financial gain or social recognition to the organization. The same principle, applied to the church or para-church organization would translate the financial and social recognition into the glory of the Lord alone. Somehow, the church has lost its true identity over the years and has become a marketplace for profit instead of a medium for winning souls for Christ and ultimately growing the kingdom of God on earth.

Despite the shock and dismay, I was a mere backbencher, who did not have a voice in the session. I reserved my comment and sat through the rest of the session, confused and amazed at how the rest of the participants could sit and not enquire further as to what the introduction of the title of CEO really would really imply in a church setup. Did it not occur to any of the participants that the designation of a CEO and its implications did not belong in the church? Could it be that the once clear line of demarcation between worldly values and standards and Kingdom values and standards has been completely obliterated? As a church, are we still conscious of our duty to influence the world? Are the words of our Lord still relevant, especially such passages as Matthew 5:13 that, "You are the salt of the earth, but if the salt has lost its saltiness…it is no longer good for anything…." Given what surrounds us in church circles has the church lost its influence on the world and instead, is it the world which is influencing the church?

Today, a good percentage of church leaders are in ministry not to serve the Lord, but to serve their own interests. In most churches, the worship services and other church programmes are being altered to create opportunity for the leaders to benefit. Instead of worshipping the Lord, churches are busy with raising funds during worship time. Instead of hearing the Lord speak to the congregation through the teaching and preaching of God's word, pastors are busy manipulating congregants to dig deeper in their pockets for an offering. Both inside and outside the church, pastors are demanding earthly respect and recognition. Indeed, just as Jesus reprimanded the Pharisees and Sadducees in Matthew 23:6-8 for seeking public honour, so too does modern church leadership seek to be honoured much more than they are willing to serve. Pastors and even elders today are expecting and even demanding to be accorded the same respect and honour as the secular leaders get from their subordinates. Church leaders get offended when they are addressed as Mr. So and So, instead, they want to be addressed by the title of their supposed ministry, for example Elder So-and-So or Pastor So-and-So. Some have even gone to the extent of creating new offices that do not exist anywhere in the early church. Titles like, Apostle, Prophet are clear indications of seeking special recognition among the ordinary.

Besides titles, some pastors' personal grooming and adornments give away their pride. A flamboyant mega church pastor in the big city will have bodyguards, drive the latest top of the range cars, adorn themselves in the finest and most expensive clothes and sit on a 'throne' in the centre of the church podium. Even in the rural areas, much as we may not see such flamboyance and elegance, the pastor will still get the best seat at a funeral; he will not carry his own bible, but the elders and deacons will carry it for him.

Church discipline today is used by some church leaders as a weapon with which they can exert selfish influence and generate unhealthy fear and respect among church members for their personal gain. When Paul gave guidelines of church discipline and emphasized its importance, he intended for such steps to be used with the intention of bringing the wayward sheep back to its senses in love. However, the same is being used by some as a tool to silence dissension and criticism among the flock. Someone once said if you put a weapon in the hands of a fool, he will hurt both himself and everybody around him.

The above analysis, is probably true of the universal church today, differing only in the degree of contamination from one church to another. It is, however, obvious when we refer to scripture that such leadership does not belong in the church. The Lord Jesus Christ, himself taught by his words and actions that a true leader is a servant leader who has the interests of their followers at heart. Indeed, a pastor is a shepherd leader, who is supposed to lay down his life and comfort for the sake of his flock.

Has church leadership always been like this? Probably not. We are well aware of what kind of leaders the apostles were. They were the kind that sat under the mentorship of Christ himself, who towards the end of His earthly ministry demonstrated true leadership by literally washing the feet of His disciples. His example is what the apostles emulated, while modern day church leadership despises the same. Indeed, the disciples were able to get it right because they learned from the best servant leader ever; one who despite being the very Son of God, left His glory above and reduced himself to take up the lowliest form of human existence possible. Servant leadership is only possible with Christ. A lot of church leaders today are going into ministry without a personal knowledge of Jesus Christ, and that is a recipe for failure in ministry. Worse still, even those that go into ministry while they are born again, end up making the same mistakes as the unbelieving leaders simply because they have never been taught anything about servant leadership.

In my fifteen years of training Lay church leaders, I have discovered that Lay leadership of the church has become more ceremonial than practical in recent years, whereby it is more about filling a vacant position than equipping the church with a leadership that will move the congregation from one degree of glory to the next. In a typical Presbyterian church (popularly known by the acronym CCAP)) in Malawi, Elders and Deacons get trained for three days on average in a rural congregation, whereas in the more urban areas, where the potential leaders will be working during the week, the best they can get is a full day training on a Saturday. Previously the process of electing and ordaining Lay leaders in the church was quite lengthy, whereby those that have been identified as potential Elders and Deacons had to undergo a rigorous training, both theoretically and practically.

Jesus Christ spent three years training the twelve disciples for ministry. They heard him speak, they saw him heal, preach and teach people from all walks of life and just before his crucifixion, Jesus dedicated them to the father and pleaded for their protection and strengthening (John 17). Those twelve were indeed readied for the task ahead. Despite having their individual shortcomings, the apostolic church leaders had remained faithful shepherds of the flock that the Lord himself had handed over to them. They faithfully and wholeheartedly cared for the believers that had seen and heard Christ himself teaching. They were even dedicated to making more disciples by faithfully following the formula of the great commission, but somewhere along the way something happened. The salt had lost its saltiness, and the sinful human element crept in and it has stayed on and continues to threaten to dominate the leadership landscape to the end of time. The further the church moves away from scripture for guidance, the worse it will become in all aspects, leadership included.

A Historical Overview

A discussion of modern church leadership would be incomplete without a mention of the Papacy, the official head of the universal Roman Catholic church. Beginning in the eleventh century, we begin to see the bishops of Rome being referred to as "Pope," meaning father. It is a title that came about to depict what is understood as the role that the Lord Jesus Christ in Matthew 16:18 said the apostle Peter would play in the life of the community of believers. Much as the interpretations of the reference to the 'rock' may vary, it is obvious that the Roman church took it to mean that Peter and all the subsequent heads of the church after him would be the foundation of the church's life and teaching. It was further understood that the decisions of the bearer of the office were sacred and could not be questioned as they had the blessing of Christ himself.

Out of this understanding of the office of the Pope, came lots of abuses as the office was beginning to be a tool of political machinations in secular politics, hence the term "pontification." The zenith of the pontification came during the reign of Pope Gregory, when the prestige of the papacy was enhanced and enjoyed temporal sovereignty in Italy, and in the years following, the office became the centre of political controversy throughout Europe. In this era, the scriptural qualifications of church leadership became irrelevant in the choice of the individual to fill the position of the Pope.

It is implied in the recorded history of the church that the turning away from biblical church leadership was perpetrated by a gradual departure from the rule of scripture to a gradual adoption of worldly standards. When church leadership tasted worldly political power and influence, God's will was thrown out the window and scripture was used selectively to support the human approach to leadership. What started, in the Roman Catholic church, as an honest attempt to protect the true teaching of scripture by consolidating all interpretive authority of God's word in one office, took a turn for the worse and was abused, by the Popes, as a license to control the faithful the way kings controlled their subjects.

Worse still, the rise of the papacy coincided with a secular government arrangement called Feudalism. The Feudal system of government gave land owners absolute powers over anyone living and working on their land. Subsequently, this system made things even worse since the church also turned the land that was given to it into such fiefdoms where they controlled the affairs of the societies that existed in church owned land. The earthly rewards of Feudalism turned the church leadership into rich and powerful men who had influence in commercial and political circles. The more the church turned to commerce and enterprise, in the name of growing the kingdom of God, the more the control it got over the poor and the more powerful and corrupt the papacy became.

The events of the history of the papacy obviously had both positive and negative universal influences, and the church in Africa has not been spared. Today we can point back to the same history as the source of the multiplicity of denominations and much of the church's practices and traditions. We continue to see not only the Roman Catholic church vesting a lot of power and control in individuals that have been elected to lead the churches. With time, such individuals are becoming too big and too powerful to be controlled by their fellow elders and whenever someone points out their shortcomings, schisms are inevitable. Today, universally, there are lots of denominations and sects that are being established by power hungry men masquerading as men of God, who use the church to amass power and have control over the masses that follow them out of real spiritual hunger. These power-hungry individuals have probably seen how rich and powerful some church leaders of mainline historical churches have become.

On the side lines, we have a number of home-grown pontificating practices and traditions in the modern African church that are unique to the geographical African church. A very good example is the practice of elders and deacons carrying the pastor's Bible. I have grown up all my life in Africa, having been privileged to travel to several African countries both as a dependent of my parents and as an independent adult. In the few African countries I have been to, I have noticed that elders and deacons feel it is not honourable for the pastor to carry his own Bible all over, except when he is coming from the vestry to the pulpit. Such, to them, is a way of identifying the pastor as their superior. To most African elders, there is no such thing as a pastor being considered as one of the elders of the church. They have put a clear line of distinction and hierarchical order within the offices of the church whereby the supposed teaching elder, otherwise known as the pastor is at the top, the ruling elders are below him and the deacons are at the bottom. Practically, the pastor gives the orders, the elders chart a course of action and the deacons implement. If chairs need to be carried, or the vestry cleaned, it is the deacons' job. All menial tasks are, in fact, the deacons' duties, while tasks with authority are the elders' duties, and the pastor gets the reports and preaches on Sundays and special occasions. I have never seen an African church where a pastor is and behaves like a mere elder among other lay leaders of the church. Pastors are monarchs in churches either by design or by default.

In the New Testament's Pauline epistles of Timothy and Titus, Paul dedicates all three epistles to define and refine the true biblical understanding of the offices of church leadership, hence the designation of Pastoral Epistles to the three letters. In his discussion of the whole concept of church leadership, Paul interchangeably uses the terms elder, overseer and pastor to refer to church leadership, meaning that they are all at par. On a few occasions, for instance in 1 Timothy 5:17, he gives a special accolade to "...those who labour in preaching and teaching," as "...worthy of double honour." It is such few instances of a higher profile given to the preacher, that the world has used to set a preaching elder, otherwise known as a pastor, above the other elders of the church. However, the biblical truth is what we see depicted in the pastoral epistles, that all leaders of the church are in equal standing before the Lord. John MacArthur in his commentary on the meaning of "double honour" in 1 Timothy 5:17, says, "Elders who serve with greater commitment, excellence, and effort should have greater acknowledgement from the congregation ... implicit is the idea that some elders will work harder than others and be more prominent."

Besides seeking or accepting undue honour, a lot of modern-day pastors are also caught up in worldly definitions and strategies of leading. Followers of most religious leaders today are compelled, coerced and deceived into believing the otherwise unbelievable with the expectation of getting divine favours through their leaders. Stories of religious leaders sleeping with their female followers are commonplace today. Stories of followers remitting all their earnings to the church are not strange. The Bible gives us a job description of a pastor, in 1 Peter 5:1-4 whereby all the modern-day religious myths and scams are debunked. Peter exhorts elders to "...exercise oversight, not under compulsion, but willingly...not for shameful gain, but eagerly, not domineering over those in your charge, but being examples to the flock."

Given this understanding, we could ask should a preaching elder be given a throne in the church? Should he be given final authority in the financial matters of the church? Should he be accorded the best position at the dinner table? Absolutely not, as it is against the teaching of scripture.

All these damages to the pastoral office have happened in full view of knowledgeable people who have stood aside and watched like spectators. Some have been silent out of a desire to remain relevant and maintain good relations with the church leaders who are guilty of desecrating the pastoral office. Others have remained aloof because they feared being disciplined and left out in the cold. 'Suppose I die while on discipline, and the church does not officiate my funeral, what embarrassment to be buried like a dog,' they have thought. These and many other reasons have choked church members from pointing out the shortfalls of modern-day church leadership, yet scripture is full of examples of how some people stood up and pointed out the mistakes of even the greatest leaders of God's people. In Exodus 18, Jethro, Moses' father-in-law went all the way from Midian to advise Moses about delegation. Prophet Nathan used a story to rebuke great King David's adultery and subsequent murder, and many other instances of prophets either rebuking or advising kings and great rulers about their departure from God's will. Church leaders are mere humans just like the kings and rulers of Israel of old, hence they also need to be guided and counselled whenever they go wrong.

'What do pastors do in Theological College then, if they do not learn about biblical leadership?', some may ask. Indeed, it is expected that Theological Seminaries should produce well trained men in all areas of ministry, but some still manage to come out half baked. Maybe it is time theological seminaries got back to the drawing boards to rethink their real mission. A lot of seminaries have become more academic than ministerial, meaning that they are more interested in producing academics than making disciples for Christ. Historically, seminaries emphasized mentorship in their theological training, whereby they put ministerial students under the practical tutelage of experienced and devoted godly men, who would not only teach them the art of preaching, but would also be interested in their students' personal lives and spiritual growth. The men that graduated from such seminaries knew why the pulpit was in the position in which it was. They knew why they sang Psalms and hymns and not dance music in the Lord's house. They knew very well why they could not have a salary but an honorarium instead. Indeed, they knew why any communicant church member was at liberty to question and enquire more about what they said in the pulpit.

As for the rest of the ruling elders and deacons, where would they learn all the insights that a pastor learns in seminary? This is a very relevant question here in Africa, where theological education is mostly for the academic interest or for training to be a pastor. It is such lack of theological education opportunities that has contributed to the decay and subsequent departure from biblical ideals in church leadership in the African church. On the one hand the pastors who have undergone some training will look down upon other elders who have not had such an opportunity and this becomes a recipe for their pride, arrogance and abuse of their office. On the other hand, the elders who have not undergone any theological training begin to admire their learned colleague and eventually submit to him unquestioningly.

Unfortunately, some theological training initiatives that directly seek funding from secular sources and detaches themselves from the church's mission are bound to fail (in the long run) and soon become advocates of a secular gospel in the church's leadership matters. History shows that these theological training institutions that detach themselves from the church will compromise on their interpretation of Bible doctrines and soon become adherents of socially and politically correct interpretations of scripture.

Way Forward

It is because of such situations at stated above that Lay Leadership training institutions and programmes were created especially for the church in the developing world. Theological education, like any other tertiary level learning is too expensive in the developing world. Unlike, Western countries, where an elder has an opportunity to go study theology and learn everything that a pastor learns, the only hope for an elder in the developing world is to get some theological training is through Lay training initiatives and perhaps theological distance learning. Theological training is not an option or a choice for the Church in Africa, it is an essential need that cannot be ignored but must be offered to all elders. Churches in Africa are encouraged to adopt lay training initiatives closest to them and enrol their leaders into the programmes. Most effective is to enrol the leaders not one by one but as a team. In places where individual congregations or full denominations have adopted Lay training programmes, they normally have the elders and deacons trained in the absence of the pastor, this heightening the impression that the pastor is not a fellow elder with the rest of the leadership team. Ideally, the full leadership of the church should be trained together to solidify the equality of the offices. Another mistake that churches make whenever they have an opportunity to conduct elders' training is to make attendance optional instead of mandatory. Given the understanding that is prevalent in the African church, that ministry only requires zeal and passion, and does not need any training; a handful of elders would turn up for training. It would be preferred if any person earmarked for eldership (or leadership) in the church, would first be required to undergo a reasonable length of training and mentorship before they are given eldership (or a leadership position). Unfortunately, the biblical criteria for eldership has been replaced with worldly standards such as popularity, or one's ability to contribute reasonable amounts to the church coffers.

In recent years, there has been a gradual shift of the church away from all forms of theological education, to the degree that churches no longer feel a sense of ownership of their own theological training initiatives. Some have suggested that this trend has been fuelled by a desire of most theological training institutions and programmes to be independent of denominational control and bureaucracy. Regardless of who is to blame for the unfortunate situation of alienation between the churches and their theological institutions, one obvious fact is that theological education is owned by, and exists for, the church. If the church owns theological education it will support, endorse, promote and value all training initiatives designed and offered by theological training institutions (both the ones that the church owns and those that it co-owns with other churches). At the same time, theological institutions and all other initiatives should be tied into the local church if they are going to make an impact with their programmes.

Chapter 6

The Place of the Laity in Doing Theology at Grassroots

Chatha Msangaambe

Introduction

Theology is not only a noun, it is also a verb. Its essence and flavour is more in doing than in being. In simple terms, 'doing' theology is living and working with God in His church and world today. Since the laity section forms the major part of the church world-wide, an early presupposition can be made that if the church is to make any significant difference in the world, it has to depend on committed and informed lay people. While the church's clerical members are recognized and respected for providing leadership in the church, especially in Africa, the church's life depends mostly on the quality of the laity. An African proverb says that *it is not the one who beats the drum that makes the dance, but the one who sends the dust into the air.*[1] The point is not to undermine the trained ordained clergy who *beat the drum* and set the rhythm in the church, but it is to highlight the laity's significant role in the life of the church. The discussion that follows aims at a rediscovery of the place of the laity in the church's on-going efforts to remain missional and relevant in the contemporary world.

The Missional Church and Theology at Grassroots Level

More than ten years ago I was privileged to represent my church at the annual General Assembly of the Church of Scotland in

---

[1] *Mwini gule ndi uyo apalasa fumbi osati wang'oma.* A Chewa proverb which literally means that the most entertaining person in any dance is the one who is dancing, not the drummer, regardless of the fact that both are needed for the dance.

Edinburgh. During my free time, a friend of mine who was once a missionary to Malawi, took me for a walk downtown. He led me to a coffee shop where he offered me a cup of coffee. It was a magnificent building that looked like several of the 18th century houses along that street. As we chatted over the cup of coffee, he drew my attention to the setting of the coffee shop. In his explanation of the interior appearance of the cafe, he told me that the entire building had once been a church building that belonged to one of the established churches. It was first sold to a circus owner after World War II, who later sold it to a coffee shop family. I was slightly disturbed, as I pounced on my old missionary friend with a series of inquisitive questions. I could not fathom why such churches, that were once crowd pullers and a centre of human activities should be reduced to circuses and eventually coffee shops. In his analysis as a seasoned missionary, my friend said something that forms the base of our discussion's conclusions. The 19th century churches in Europe, excelled in sending missionaries to the rest of the world, but failed to be missional churches. They brought the gospel to the unreached remote areas of Africa and other continents but fell short in the sustenance vision of the church in their own communities. The church declined in the home backyard while it thrived in the missionary field. While church buildings were mushrooming in the missionary-invaded Africa, churches were closing and church buildings sold in missionary-sending Europe. As we drew these conclusions, our coffee cups were dry and it was time for the assembly once again. It remained my task to find out more about what a missional church is all about.

Examining a Missional Church

A faithful healthy church in our world today is the one that is missional. By missional I mean a church that is having an energizing faith; outward-looking focus; and frequently participating lay people. A missional church does not exist for itself but makes itself relevant to the context in its pursuit of the Great Commission. Kimball says,

"To be a missional church is more than just to evangelize."[2] In an effort to come up with a summarized explanation of a missional church, he ended up with the following compilation:

- Being missional means that the church sees itself as being missionaries, rather than having a missions department, and that we see ourselves as missionaries, right where we live.
- Being missional means that we see ourselves as representatives of Jesus "sent" into our communities, and that the church aligns everything it does with the *missio Dei* (mission of God).
- Being missional means we see the church not as the place we go only on Sunday, but as something we are throughout the week.
- Being missional means that we understand we don't "bring Jesus" to people but that we realize Jesus is active in culture and we join him in what he is doing.
- Being missional means we are very much in the world and engaged in culture but are not conformed to the world.
- Being missional means we serve our communities, and that we build relationships with the people in them, rather than seeing them as evangelistic targets.
- Being missional means being all the more dependent on Jesus and the Spirit through prayer, the Scriptures, and each other in community.

For the missional church to effect transformation and self-sustenance, it has to start by doing theology at grassroots level. In grassroots theology, people begin to see God act in their midst. The life of the entire church then becomes an act of their response toward this presence of God. The church needs a bottom-up theological approach. Hendriks says, "The church should follow the leadership of Christ who came into this broken world to serve and heal it by

2   D. Kimball, *They Like Jesus but not the Church*, Grand Rapids: Zondervan, 2002, p. 20.

carrying a cross and working from the bottom upwards."[3] With a missional bearing, the church must make deliberate and strategic efforts to develop theology at grassroots. Otherwise, it will be mistaken for any other NGO working merely for humanitarian purposes.

In his own humility Christ demonstrated how to develop grassroots theology. He emptied himself and became a human being (Phil. 2:5-7) in order to include the lowly in the society. This is the basis for the church in doing theology at grassroots. In the same vein, Barker writes, "When people, groups, and systems [at grassroots] start to live like Jesus, then all can have Jesus' authority to live out God's intended shalom together."[4]

Generally, the church in Africa, Malawi in particular has to learn from the history of the church in the West and be alerted to design appropriate strategies for the survival and progress of the church. It is therefore a prerequisite for the Malawian Church to develop the relevant theology that places the lay people in the church at the centre.

An Approach to Grassroots Theology

Doing theology at grassroots is a faith-seeking process that engages ordinary people in a local context to analyze and interpret their situation while discerning God's will.[5] This does not mean that the people involved in doing theology at grassroots level should detach themselves from the global understanding of their situation and the powers of the Triune God. But, the eventual achievement of such a theology should be the transformation of the theologizing community in their very context. Little known in our world today is

---

[3] Jurgens Hendriks, *Studying Congregations in Africa*, Wellington: Lux Verbi, 2004, p. 52.

[4] A. Barker, *Make Poverty Personal: Taking the Poor as Seriously as the Bible Does*, Grand Rapids: Baker, 2009, p. 129.

[5] Jurgens Hendriks, *Studying Congregations in Africa*, p.24.

the fact that everyone can be a theologian in one way or the other. When ordinary members in the church begin to apply their knowledge of God and participate in the daily life of the church, they become theologians in their own making. One does not need a theological Seminary to be a practising theologian. In his explanation of grassroots theology in a congregational situation, Bishop Kalilombe writes,

> Doing theology demands encouraging and giving room for the constant look at and careful study of the situation within which the theologising communities are immersed. Such a study entails the courage to engage in a serious analysis of society. The real life experience on which reflection and praxis are to be based must involve the whole community, and not only a few people.[6]

Essentially, this affirms that such a theology is contextual, interdisciplinary and ecumenical in nature. Although this poses a challenge to contemporary congregational leaders globally, due to denominational traditions, it is a proper starting point for realistic theological practices. Reader asserts, "A local theology will take as its starting point the stories and accounts of those who are deeply and seriously affected by the contemporary social changes."[7] As such, this means that the construction of a theology that makes sense in a community, involves listening to both Christian and secular stories, which reflect the experiences of that particular community in their own worldview. Since theology is about transformative action, Hendriks[8] points out that any practical theologian does theology by first focusing on local and particular issues with the purpose of doing something about the reality and problems that confront the faith community, as well as society. When a good and balanced, action-oriented theology is purposely and jointly developed, it is likely to

---

[6]   Patrick Kalilombe, *Doing Theology at the Grassroots*. Gweru: Mambo-Kachere, 1999, p 169. Reprinted: Mzuzu: Luviri Press, 2018.

[7]   J. Reader, *Local Theology: Church and Community in Dialogue*, London: SPCK, 1994, p. 14.

[8]   Jurgens Hendriks, *Studying Congregations in Africa*, p.32.

serve as a tool for community transformation. It is easily accepted and immediately becomes effective because the people own it.

The Place of the Laity in Doing Theology at the Grassroots

In doing theology at grassroots, the lay people in the church are not mere assistants to the clergy, who are the only labelled theologians at that level. They are participants, as well as facilitators, in the practice of theology in the society. It is clearly understood in the words of Chester and Timmis[9] that major events have a role to play in church life, but the bedrock of gospel ministry is the modest, ordinary, day-to-day work which often goes unseen. Most gospel ministries involve ordinary people doing ordinary things with gospel intentionality.

This underscores the point that the laity has the social advantage that is commonly missed by the clerical fraternity, because they read the community stories from ground level. Their analysis of the situation often reflects the ordinary common ideas that are an essential ingredient in grassroots theology. The laity is required to be exposed to the necessary skills in the process of missional fulfilment and of doing theology in their own right. Messer observes, "The challenge of the church is to encourage and empower lay persons to challenge the Goliaths in their working midst..."[10] The essence of the doctrine of the laity's ministry is that all Christians are called into ministry. So, the tasks of the laity are as valuable as those of ordained ministers in the public functions of the missional church.

It is speculated that there were approximately nine million Christians in Africa by 1900 but, by the year 2000, Africa had 380 million. It is further projected that Africa will have 633 million Christians by

---

9   T. Chester and S. Timmis, *Total Church: A Radical Reshaping around Gospel and Community*, Nottingham: InterVarsity, 2007, pp. 60-61.

10   D. Messer, *Contemporary Images of Christian Ministry*, Nashville: Abingdon, 1989, p. 67.

2025.[11] With such a phenomenal numerical growth of Christianity in Africa, the need for lay leadership skills at a grassroots level is also growing. If the laity adopts a passive role in doing grassroots theology, then the whole missionary venture is likely to collapse. For instance, in the CCAP Nkhoma Synod, Malawi, there are cases where one ordained minister is expected to preach at more than 20 locations on a single Sunday; a task that is literally impossible, so lay leaders perform such tasks locally. They fulfil God's calling of his church to be a mission in its own context.

In short, the laity's place in doing theology at grassroots is central. This is clearly evident in a simple analysis of a layman's responsibility at that level.

The Laity in the Great Commission

One of the crucial tasks of the church is to participate in the Great commission, as given by the head of the church – Jesus Christ. According to Gibbs and Coffey,[12] a missional church should have a clear understanding that it is God's mission to call, prepare and send the church, created by grace through Jesus Christ. To be a church involved in missions in its own context. This is the appropriate place of the laity to do theology at grassroots. Wherever the church manifests itself in its local context, it has to keep in mind its missionary characteristic of being sent. Every congregation has its environment and context as its missionary field. For effective participation in the Great Commission, Msangaambe[13] asserted that the laity have to be thoroughly equipped and empowered to carry out the following tasks:

---

[11] www.enwikipedia.org/wiki/Christianity_in_Africa [28.1.2018].

[12] E. Gibbs and I. Coffey, *Church Next: Quantum Changes in Christian Ministry*, Leicester: InterVarsity, 2001, p. 55.

[13] C. Msangaambe, "Laity Empowerment with regard to the Missional Task of the CCAP in Malawi," DTh, Stellenbosch University, 2011, p. 149.

(a) Compassion

Being founded on Jesus Christ's redemptive act, the church starts its missional task from *compassion*. The element of compassion stands out throughout the mission that God Himself undertook in the life and works of Jesus Christ. God demonstrated his unconditional love out of compassion - his grace - for the world, by sending his Son to redeem it. The apostle Paul indicates this missional mystery in Romans 5:8 (NIV): *"God demonstrates his own love for us [the world] in this: While we were sinners, Christ died for us."* Therefore, the church should not reach out on the basis of anything else but compassion, drawn from its foundation – Christ Jesus. Chikakuda asserts, "The church must proclaim this saving power of God in Jesus Christ to the people and to the world."[14] All sorts of suffering characterizes the church's missionary field, a situation in dire need of intervention. Compassion deals with healing, caring and reconciliation. This is the common understanding of the church's mission (task) in the African context. Oduro *et al.* remark, "It is impossible to understand AIC[15] mission of compassion apart from their emphasis on the fact that the spirit of God is able to empower, protect, deliver, purify and heal anyone seeking help."[16] A compassionate spirit that interprets the situation with divine wisdom and offers a holistic ministry is needed more than mere humanitarian services. The driving force in this should be an understanding that the church only participates in a mission that the Triune God designed and initiated through the laity.

(b) Witnessing

Along with compassion, the church should be driven into mission by its mandate *to be witnesses*. Chikakuda says, "The work of the church is to bear witness to God's love in Jesus Christ and to share this love

---

[14] W. Chikakuda, "Karl Barth's Concept of the Church for the World," DTh, Stellenbosch University, 1994, p. 74.

[15] AIC is an acronym for African Initiated Churches.

[16] T. Oduro et al, *Mission in an African Way: A Practical Introduction to African Instituted Churches and their Sense of Mission*, Wellington: CLF, 2008, p. 77.

with the world."[17] Any reasonable Bible student will encounter a clear call to witness many portions of Scripture, including Acts 1:8 (NIV), [*But you will receive power when the Holy Spirit comes on you; and you will be my witnesses in Jerusalem, and in all Judea and Samaria, and to the ends of the earth.*] Witnessing is given the right position because the Holy Spirit's coming precedes it. As a spiritual institution, the church requires the presence of the Holy Spirit to carry out its missional task of being a witness to the surrounding world. Guder says, "The witness to Jesus Christ is made by the community called and equipped for that purpose, and it entails inviting others to become part of that community to join in the obedience of witness."[18] To be a witness is an act of being obedient to God that the church has to accept without calculating the cost. The biblical sense of a witness is where the English word "martyr" gets its root meaning; where that witnessing becomes a sacrificial risky business. But the church must share the Good News and instil hope in the suffering community. The message of a perfect God who wants to make the world perfect (Mat. 5:48) is what the suffering world needs. Guder asserts, "The church as a witness does not regard itself as its own purpose, but rather as God's Spirit-empowered means to God's end."[19] The church should know the culture of its context in order to witness effectively. And witnessing has to be carried out in word and deed, focused on addressing the real needs of the context. Today, both word and deed approaches are needed for the global church in order to engage effectively. Such a task demands that the laity should proclaim the Gospel that should be packaged with a sense of care and service to the needy.

---

17 W. Chikakuda, "Karl Barth's Concept of the Church for the World," p. 124.

18 D. Guder, *The Continuing Conversion of the Church*, Grand Rapids: Eerdmans, 2000, p. 67.

19 D. Guder, *The Continuing Conversion of the Church*, p. 67.

(c) Identifying with the Context

As it witnesses to the world, another missional task of the church is *to identify itself with its context* in a practical way. The following should be noted: "The church's particular communities live in the context of the surrounding culture, engage with the culture, but are not controlled by the culture."[20] An incarnational approach to the whole missional assignment to the world is needed. The church is not an island and it does not exist in a vacuum. In many instances where a church exists as a body of elites with only a "divine" agenda, it misses an important aspect of the Great Commission (Mat. 28:20) – "*Go into the world.*" Yet, the peculiarity of this "going" of the church "into the world" is its non-conformity and humility. In a Christ-like humble style, the church is destined to display its kenotic nature. In Christ, God became a human being to reach out to human beings in a human culture. This was a gesture of selflessness that the church should emulate, especially in its style of leadership. The call to humility, as recorded in Scripture (Phil. 2:5-8), remains fresh for the church to incarnate into the world today. In doing that, the missional church should be sensitive to the culture(s) of the context in which it finds itself. Interaction of the church and the community is even necessary because it promotes the inhabitable conditions for co-existence. Guder *et al.* assert, "The calling of the church to be missional ... leads the church to step beyond the given cultural forms that carry dubious assumptions about what the church is, what its public role should be, and what its voice should sound like."[21] This missional call makes the church a sent entity into the world. As many ministries as possible should be created as means and tools to infiltrate the immediate mission field.

---

[20] D. Guder et al, *Missional Church: A Vision for the Sending of the Church in North America*, Grand Rapids: Eerdmans, 1998, p. 114.

[21] D. Guder, *The Continuing Conversion of the Church*, p. 109.

(d) Being Prophetic

Today the church has the missional task *to be prophetic* in its own environment. Roxburgh writes, "The prophet's role is about the recovery of a world. The prophet's passion is the reforming of common life around the rhythm of God's story."[22] This is what the missional church should be. It has to represent the reign of God by engaging itself with the daily problems of this world. It has to offer a biblically interpreted meaning of the conditions in which it survives and then mobilize communities into the right response. There is nothing that affects the community that cannot concern the church. The missional prophetic role of the church should be applied from individual and family issues to global, political, and economic issues. Within these issues, there is an expectation that the church will display its Christ-centred values.

A good example of this is the role that the church, through the laity, has played in the political arena of Malawi. Towards the end of Kamuzu Banda's regime in 1992, the Roman Catholic Bishops wrote a pastoral letter titled, "*Living our faith.*" On 8 March 1992 (the first Sunday of Lent that year), it was read in every Roman Catholic Church in Malawi. In this letter, the Bishops criticized the evils in Dr Banda's government and challenged the Roman Catholics and all Malawians to unite in defying the evils and to choose a better future for Malawi. This pastoral letter led to the birth of the Public Affairs Committee (PAC). This is an ecumenical and interfaith body whose constitutional objectives include encouraging religious bodies to fulfil their prophetic and religious roles, and respond to the socio-economic and political affairs of the Republic of Malawi.[23] Although decisions are made by the top clergy that form the executive governance forum, PAC is able to fulfil its constitutional mandate through the ordinary people on the ground.

---

[22] A. Roxburgh, *The Sky is Falling: Leaders Lost in Transition*, Eagle: ACI Publishing, 2005, p. 132.

[23] Public Affairs Committee, 2017 Annual Report, p. 4.

(e) Transformation

Finally, the missional church should aim at *transforming communities* through the empowerment of ordinary people. Stewart III declares, "Mission should empower people to health and wholeness by helping to see themselves as positive agents of self and global transformation."[24] Then he warns that mission should not end with just supplying foodstuffs to people. It should teach people how to develop the confidence and resources from within, and without, towards self-sustenance. Through holistic witnessing in the local context the church achieves its Christ-given mandate and its presence is felt in people's lives within their community. Well-groomed laity who are themselves members of their own communities can spearhead and experience the transformation of the community.

The Tasks of the Laity in a Missional Church

We can summarize the laity's responsibilities in the local church by using the three aspects as coined by Doohan.[25] He points out the following aspects:

The first is that, lay people have the responsibility of being the church to the world and its development through their daily work and socialization.

The second aspect is that they have the responsibility to build the foundational churches that consist of their own families or local groups.

The final aspect mentioned is that of evangelism explosion. The lay people have the responsibility to bring their Christian commitment in support of the congregation, diocese or presbytery, and universal church.

---

24 F. Stewart III, *Reclaiming what was Lost*, Nashville: Abingdon, 2003, p. 88.

25 L. Doohan, *Laity's Mission in the Local Church: Setting a New Direction*, San Francisco: Harper & Row, 1986, p. 41.

As such, the responsibility of grassroots mission entrusted to the laity does not end on the initial ground. It extends in the pattern of the Great Commission to the ends of the world. Doohan remarks, "In each case, the responsibility of the laity is to challenge themselves and the wider church."[26] This is all the more reason that empowerment of the laity, as a theological exercise within the church, is demanded.

A Theology of Empowerment of the Laity

The construction of a theology of empowerment of the laity has its direct roots implanted in biblical theology. God revealed Himself in the Bible by showing who He is and how He relates to human beings. There is more than enough evidence throughout the Bible that the Triune God is a God of empowerment. From the Genesis creation narratives to the apocalyptic projections of the book of Revelation, God is seen at work in transformative acts within the human race. The understanding that all human beings are created in God's image -- *imago Dei*[27] - is probably central to the theology of empowerment. This idea has its roots in Genesis 1:26-27. Migliore[28] contends that *imago Dei* explains human life in relation to God and other created beings. By being created in the image of God, humans are moral and spiritual creatures.[29] With us, God shares his image, his authority, as well as his responsibility for creation. He empowers his human beings for service to the created world.

---

[26] L. Doohan, *Laity's Mission in the Local Church*, p. 41.

[27] I am aware that the concept of *imago Dei* is widely debated in theology. For centuries, theologians have continued to discuss, agree and disagree on its intended biblical meaning. According to www.theopadia.com/Image_of_God, some have interpreted *imago Dei* in terms of spirituality, others in terms of original righteousness (Luther), and even sexuality (Barth). Therefore, I deliberately do not dare to go into an in-depth debate for the sake of keeping the focus on the subject matter of this discussion.

[28] D. Migliore, *Faith Seeking Understanding: An Introduction to Christian Theology*, Grand Rapids: Eerdmans, 1991, p. 122.

[29] www.enotes.com/science-religion-encyclopedia/imago-dei [13.12.2018].

God's broader empowering act within the debate of *imago Dei* is evident in his restoration of his image after the broken relationship. "The story of the image of God, then, is one of creation, loss, and what we may term the greater-than-restoration."[30] God's reconciliatory process with human beings is on-going. Migliore notes, "Being created in the image of God is not a state or condition but a movement with a goal: human beings are restless for a fulfilment of life not yet realized."[31] Theologically, God is concerned with the fallen nature of the *imago Dei* and continues to work it out towards the God-intended human status. In a human being, sin has negated the qualities of being the true image of God.

When human beings begin to discern God's will, they begin to understand God in themselves, as revealed in the Word and the world. Nurnberger[32] believes that a theology of biblical witness is meant to empower us to do, for our times, what the biblical authors did for theirs: i.e. formulate God's redemptive response to human needs. Therefore, biblical theology guides us into understanding the theology of empowerment as we reflect on what God's involvement has been with human beings. The Bible presents the story of God's work in the world, with a wide coverage of his empowering acts through creation, re-creation (redemption) and final consummation.[33] This confirms the fact that, through his Word, God empowers humans to live a life that is acceptable to Him, and to participate in his mission for the world. God empowers all his people, the church, to participate in his creative, redemptive and emancipative acts. He shares his roles with his chosen people for his own sake. In the life of the church, God does not empower only the clergy, but all the saints who are called in his name.

---

[30] See www.theopedia.com/Image_of_God. [13.12.2018].

[31] D. Migliore, *Faith Seeking Understanding*, p. 128.

[32] K. Nurnberger, *Theology of the Biblical Witness: An Evolutionary Approach*, Münster: LIT Verlag, 2002, p 3.

[33] C. van Gelder, *The Ministry of the Missional Church: A Community Led by the Spirit*, Grand Rapids: Baker Books, 2007, p. 26.

Right from the creation narrative (Gen. 2:7), God created a human being and shared his own breath (life) with him. Wanak points out,

> Even though "empowerment" is not a term used in the Bible, the concept is not foreign to the biblical material. The basic idea of setting a thing in motion is present in the Hebrew word *ruah*, which is translated as wind, breath, or spirit. The working of the spirit specifically gives people the ability and the strength to carry out special tasks. Thus, the spirit of the Lord endows individuals with strength so that they can fight the foreign oppressors of Israel.[34]

This act of empowerment demonstrates primarily God's will to enable a human being to live. Secondly, it demonstrates his willingness to relate with human beings whom He created in his own image (Gen. 1:27). Another element of empowerment attached to the creation of human beings is evident in them being entrusted with the responsibility to care for, and use, the rest of all His creation. The activities in the creation story flow from God's own character as a selfless initiator of empowerment. Migliore observes, "But to confess that God is a creator is ... to say that the free, transcendent God is generous and welcoming. God was not compelled to create the world. It is an act of free grace."[35] God's sharing of his powers is an act of empowerment par excellence, demonstrated for human beings to emulate.

In summary, the role of the laity in the theological participation of the church in the community should not be seen only as a social arrangement. In its essence the empowered laity see themselves as participating in God's act of attending to human needs.

Considering the Place of the Laity as an Integrated Subject in Theological Education

It is an open secret that Theological colleges in Malawi and elsewhere are supposed to be ministerial training centres with appropriate

---

[34] L. Wanak, *The Church and Poverty in Asia*, Manila: OMF Literature, 2008, p. 55.

[35] D. Migliore, *Faith Seeking Understanding*, p. 85.

curricula for that purpose. Unfortunately, most of them have clung to the traditional Western method, focused on theoretical principles distant from issues facing the church on daily basis. Implicitly, they fall short in addressing the real issues that require a theological engagement for our contemporary world. Hendriks points out, "Theological colleges, by and large, train pastors in the skills required by the Christendom paradigm."[36] This type of training provides much theory at the expense of the practical, grassroots churches' needs. In the analysis of theological training in sub-Saharan Africa, Wiid[37] in his thesis presented a very useful observation. He noticed that the main problem experienced by both formal and non-formal training programmes regarding curriculum, is to determine what subjects are relevant for a given student in a given context. For any training curriculum to be relevant, it has to formulate its objectives with the goal of offering the most important skills that the students need for the work in which they are being trained. The situation in the Malawian Church demands that every ordained minister has the practical skills of empowering the laity for effective participation in the grassroots theology. There is need to mainstream the empowerment of the laity in all theological subjects in the process of training ministers. Many pastors understand that equipping their members is one of their main responsibilities, but they lack the skills to do it. The absence of emphasis in allocating the place of the laity is a serious weakness of the ministerial or pastoral training curriculum in our fast-changing church context.

Therefore, it is extremely important that the theological training curricula in all training institutions, should be revised and adjusted to suit the current needs in the life of the Church – the empowerment of the laity. Just as there is a growing need for the clergy (both ordained and in training) to diversify their knowledge of the world,

---

[36] Jurgens Hendriks, *Studying Congregations in Africa*, p. 201.

[37] W. Wiid, "An Appraisal of Theological Training for Untrained Church Leaders in Sub-Saharan Africa with particular reference to the Training Programme of Veritas College," DTh, Stellenbosch University, 2002, p. 136.

such as in the fields of technology, socio-political science, economics etc., the theological curricula should consider integrating the place of the laity in the whole church ministry in our generation. All the subjects stipulated for the training of a minister should aim to answer the question: "How will the minister relate this to the laity – the congregation - at various levels of understanding?" Where needs be, some material should be organized, taught and examined in the vernacular that reflects the reality of the field experiences. The focus of ministerial training should be: helping the pastor to see his ministry in terms of equipping God's people for their ministries.[38]

Conclusion

The church which is predominantly composed of the laity is both an organism as well as an organization.[39] As an organism, it is a living body that is united around the saving work of Jesus Christ and the indwelling of the Holy Spirit no matter where each member is located. This elaborates the fact that the laity are the essential component of this organism and have to be visible in their purpose and function. They have to be recognized and empowered for the effective functioning in this living body of Christ. The church is shown as being missional, serving God's missional purpose. In its entirety, the church exists because God calls it to carry out his mission in the world. It is therefore crucial that the church should create space for a practical theological involvement of the laity. My personal experience with both rural and urban congregations in the Malawian society, has led me to the following conclusion. The success of any clergy begins in the appropriate engagement of the laity in the life of any church. I have noticed that the time has come when even the upholding of traditions in the church shall not only mean to do things the same way they were done decades ago. It has to do with the creative repositioning of the laity in the church for the sake of making

---

[38] W. Wiid, "An Appraisal of Theological Training," p. 117.

[39] Samuel Ngewa, "What is the Church?" in Tokunboh Adeyemo (ed), *African Bible Commentary*, Nairobi: WordAlive Publishers, 2006, p. 1431.

it relevant in the society. It has also been established that the involvement of the empowered laity at grassroots, manifests the presence of the Triune God in his mission to the world through the people whom he has called. Empowering the laity stirs the missionary zeal required to be God's true representative and herald in the society. From its definition, it has been established that the church is both theological and sociological. It starts and ends with God, yet it is closely connected to its worldly context. In this we see that the church and society are, and should remain, interrelated right from grassroots, with the laity as a point of contact for the part of the church. Given the right place, the laity will always have a significant role to play in doing theology at grassroots. The church in Africa today has to draw lessons from the mistakes of the western church. Every local church has to value their laity and make them missionaries in their own context.

Bibliography

Barker, A., *Make Poverty Personal: Taking the Poor as Seriously as the Bible Does*, Grand Rapids: Baker, 2009.

Chester, T. & S. Timmis, *Total Church: A Radical Reshaping around Gospel and Community*, Nottingham: InterVarsity, 2007.

Chikakuda, W., "Karl Barth's Concept of the Church for the World," DTh, Stellenbosch University, 1994.

Doohan, L., *Laity's Mission in the Local Church: Setting a New Direction*, San Francisco: Harper & Row, 1986.

Gibbs, E. & I. Coffey, *Church Next: Quantum Changes in Christian Ministry*, Leicester: InterVarsity, 2001.

Guder, D., *The Continuing Conversion of the Church*, Grand Rapids: Eerdmans, 2000.

Guder, D. et al., *Missional Church: A Vision for the Sending of the Church in North America*, Grand Rapids: Eerdmans, 1998.

Hendriks, H.J., *Studying Congregations in Africa*, Wellington: Lux Verbi, 2004.

Kimball, D., *They Like Jesus but not the Church*, Grand Rapids: Zondervan, 2002.

Messer, D., *Contemporary Images of Christian Ministry*, Nashville: Abingdon, 1989.

Migliore, D., *Faith Seeking Understanding: An Introduction to Christian Theology*, Grand Rapids: Eerdmans, 1991.

Msangaambe, C., "Laity Empowerment with Regard to the Missional Task of the CCAP in Malawi," DTh, Stellenbosch University, 2011.

Ngewa, Samuel, "What is the Church?" in Tokunboh Adeyemo (ed) *African Bible Commentary*, Nairobi: WordAlive Publishers, 2006.

Nurnberger, K., *Theology of the Biblical Witness: An Evolutionary Approach*, Münster: LIT Verlag, 2002.

Oduro, Thomas, Hennie Pretorius, Stan Nussbaum and Bryan Born, *Mission in an African Way: A Practical Introduction to African Instituted Churches and their Sense of Mission*, Wellington: CLF, 2008.

Reader, J., *Local Theology: Church and Community in Dialogue*, London: SPCK, 1994.

Roxburgh, A., *The Sky is Falling: Leaders Lost in Transition*, Eagle: ACI Publishing, 2005.

Stewart III, F., *Reclaiming what was Lost*, Nashville: Abingdon, 2003.

van Gelder, C., *The Ministry of the Missional Church: A Community Led by the Spirit*, Grand Rapids: Baker, 2007.

Wanak, L., *The Church and Poverty in Asia*, Manila: OMF, 2008.

Wiid, W., "An Appraisal of Theological Training for Untrained Church Leaders in Sub-Saharan Africa with Particular Reference to the Training Programme of Veritas College," DTh, Stellenbosch University, 2002.

Chapter 7

Changing Expectations: A Sociology of Ordination in Malawi

Blair Bertrand

Introduction

The practice of ordination in Malawi does not line up with contemporary North American or European expectations. In a country with millions of Christians there are relatively few ordained ministers. This leads to high ratios between ordained and lay. In other places such as Europe or North America you might expect to see an effort at lowering this ratio. Not in Malawi. Many Christians means there are a great number of pulpits. Many of these are filled by lay people. In other places you might expect that the church would increase the number of ordained. Again, not in Malawi. In a country with millions of Christians, few ordained ministers, and a large number of pulpits, on any given Sunday it is likely that a Christian will hear a sermon preached by someone who has not formally studied the Bible or theology. The authority of the preacher in other places rests on the community setting them apart through a strenuous education process. The fact that the preacher has been trained to interpret the Bible correctly gives them the authority to preach. But not in Malawi.

Expectations come from somewhere and in this case, each has come from the experience of the church in Western Europe and North America. In these places the expectation is that there will be a small ratio between Christians and ordained ministers, that each congregation should have its own minister, and that ordination includes a process of formal education. There is nothing sacred about these assumptions. They fit the time and place of the West. They do not however, fit in Malawi. Yet, Malawi has not adopted different expectations. Nor has Malawi taken steps to meet these expectations. Instead of training more ministers their numbers remain static. Each year the number of ordinands is very close to the number of retirees. Instead of empowering lay people to govern and organize themselves, the definition of a congregation requires an ordained moderator or priest. Instead of launching large scale lay preaching education programmes, churches create more diploma and degree-granting universities. Malawi has not shaped its own norms for Christian ministry nor does it meet the ones adopted from the West.

This chapter explains these apparent incongruities by analyzing the development of ordination in Malawi. The argument proceeds in three steps. Firstly, I argue that any practice of ordination is as much derived from context as it is from some universal theology. Secondly, after establishing that ordination is contextual, I trace the development of ordination in Malawi. I use sociologist Peter Ekeh's writings on how African societies have structured leadership in post-colonial times to understand ordination practices in the Malawian context. Thirdly, I use the rise of the charismatic church and the position of "prophets" to confirm my analysis. Finally, I conclude with some practical implications of this understanding of ordination.

Ordination as Contextual Theology

Malawians are not unthoughtful. The fact that they have not adopted different expectations or developed Malawian strategies for meeting the ones they do have, must have a good reason and an inner logic. My first contention is that it is the politics of power rather than a theology of ordination that governs the practice of ordination in Malawi. This is no different than anywhere else. As early as the book of Acts we see the church struggling to understand how to organize itself. Very quickly in the early church, a distinction between "ordained" and "lay" emerges.[1] Without ordination there is no laity.

---

[1] For a succinct but thorough review of the development of ordination from the New Testament to the early church see Darius Jankiewicz, "The Problem of

Both concepts revolve around order, control and, power. From the time of Tertullian (circa 160-220), as Jankiewicz argues, ordination "implied a movement from a lower to a higher position and from having no sacral responsibilities within the religious community to acquiring responsibilities for their performance. It represented status and ranking that did not appear to exist among New Testament Christians."[2] Both concepts also rest on an understanding of legitimate authority. Who has the power to do what with authority conferred by whom? This legitimation is always contextual.[3] Leaders must claim authority from their followers; followers legitimate leaders who have influence over their lives.

The local contrasts with the universal. On the issue of ordination, power can conflict with theology. In the world of the idealist, the Malawian church would order its life by having clear theological grounds for ordination. These grounds would authorize certain individuals to exert power for legitimate ends. For the idealist, ordination originates in theology and is somehow pure of the vagaries of time. Idealism is a kind of universalism and it denies the role played by context. The fact is, ordination arrived in Malawi from a different context, the West. The transition to independent governance happened within another context, post-colonial Malawi. We do not live in an ideal world but a realistic one. The political and sociological context has shaped the Malawian practice of ordination. There is no such thing as an ideal form of ordination, only one forged in particular contexts.

Ordination: Lessons from Early Christian History," *Faculty Publications*, no. 78 (2013), p. 30.

2   Ibid, p. 7.

3   There are a great number of studies done on the development of various ecclesial offices in the early church, perhaps best of them is Hans von Campenhausen, *Ecclesiastical Authority and Spiritual Power in the Church of the First Three Centuries*, Peabody: Hendrickson, 1997. First published in German in 1953 it was followed by an English translation in 1969 which is the edition that is available here.

To make any advance in developing a contextual theology of the laity we must first understand how the context of colonialism has shaped ordination in Malawi. Colonialism didn't arrive with a contextually free Christianity. Quite to the contrary. The Christianity that came with colonialists was steeped in Western European politics and sociologies. The practices of ordination that came with the missionaries were theological but they were also political and sociological. For reasons that Peter. P. Ekeh in his landmark study "Colonialism and the Two Publics in Africa: A Theoretical Statement" elucidates, colonial ideologies of power and authority shaped the interaction between colonial powers and the Africans they subjugated.[4] With African independence, again following Ekeh, a bourgeoisie class of Africans rejected the actual colonial administrators but adopted their ideology. This adoption of colonial ideology by the African bourgeoisie has, according to Ekeh, determined the way that power and authority has played out in post-colonial Africa.

As a sociologist, Ekeh traces the encounter between the colonialist and the colonized, along lines of power and authority in a societal context. This chapter traces that encounter specifically in the ecclesial context. Within Protestant churches in Malawi, those founded by European missionaries from Scotland, England, and the Netherlands, Ekeh's analysis explains the power dynamic that exists between ordained and lay. Following Ekeh, it is important to understand that missionaries arrived in Malawi with a theological understanding of power and authority deeply influenced by their political and sociological context. Even the best-intentioned missionaries played out the logic of power and authority inherent in their understanding of ordination. Equally as important, following independence, the Malawian bourgeoise assumed control of the missionary churches, replacing the missionaries, but not replacing the

---

[4]   Peter P. Ekeh, "Colonialism and the Two Publics in Africa: A Theoretical Statement," *Comparative Studies in Society and History,* vol. 17, no. 1 (January 1975), pp. 91–112.

European theology of ordination. Instead, what Ekeh calls the "two publics" developed within the Malawian church. These "two publics" complicate how power gets legitimated. The African leader operates in two public spheres – the primordial and the civic – with conflicting and complimentary dynamics at work. The average Malawian church goer, the lay person, legitimates and censures ways of exercising power. This legitimation of power and authority takes place within ordination thus reinforcing the divide between ordained and lay.

Power and Authority in the Two Publics

Writing in the early 1970s, Nigerian born Peter P. Ekeh wrestled with understanding political behaviours that did not fit the current sociological explanations. Years later, in describing the impetus for his study, Ekeh points to a Nigerian folktale and the apparent incongruities of morality at work in its interpretation.[5] In Ekeh's story a man witnesses a bag of money falling out of a colonial administrator's car. The man, an African, returns the money to its "rightful" owner, thus acting morally in the eyes of the colonial power who rewards him with a pittance. Meanwhile, the man's family and kin denigrate him for being foolish and immoral. For them, the man had a moral obligation to provide for his family and kin. In addition, the man capitulated to an oppressive power who only stole the fruits of another's labour. The money was not rightfully the colonial administrator's to have. The family and kin held to a strict moral code. If it had not been the colonial administrator's misfortune but instead one of theirs, then returning the money would have been the morally right thing. The moral obligation to provide for family and kin is stronger than any abstract sense of universal justice or fairness. Where some observe an immoral action, taking public funds for private use, others see a moral act, providing for one's family and kin.

---

5   Peter P. Ekeh, "Afterword: Note on 'Colonialism and the Two Publics in Africa: A Theoretical Statement,'" in Helen Lauer and Kofi Anyidoho (eds), *Reclaiming the Human Sciences and Humanities through African Perspectives*, vol. 1, Legon-Accra: Sub-Saharan Publishers, 2012, pp. 220–22.

This is only an incongruity when viewed against Western conceptions of private and public. As Ekeh argues, in the West, and by this he means Western Europe and by extension North America, "generalized Christian beliefs have provided a common moral foundation for the private and the public realms."[6] What is considered morally right or wrong in the private realm is the same as what is considered wrong or right in the public realm. Ekeh argues that in Africa, due to colonialism, there is a different relationship between private and public moralities. The private is the same. Africans have private beliefs and practices, many to do with intimate family relations and religious beliefs. These Ekeh refers to as primordial commitments. From here, the private relates to the public in two ways. The first relationship "is the public realm in which primordial groupings, ties, and sentiments influence and determine the individual's public behavior."[7] Private morality is the same as the primordial public morality. What is right or wrong privately is right or wrong publicly. The second is the public realm associated with the colonial powers and the administration of such institutions as the military, civil service, and justice system. In this realm, what Ekeh calls the civic public, there is little to no moral connection to the private. Actions in the public realm are amoral. The implications for issues such as corruption are obvious. A leader may act "corruptly" according to a Western conception of the relationship between private and public morality but in actuality, be acting morally according to the moral imperatives of the primordial public.

What is important for this chapter however are the ways in which power gets reproduced and legitimated in such a reality. Ekeh specifically uses the term bourgeoise "to emphasize the lack of firm legitimacy" on the part of two groups: colonial administrators and the African leaders who succeeded them.[8] Bourgeoise are those who have power, usually economic, but do not have concomitant, usually

---

6   Ekeh, "Colonialism and Two Publics," p. 92.

7   Ekeh, "Colonialism and Two Publics," p. 92.

8   Ekeh, "Colonialism and Two Publics, " p. 93.

political, legitimacy. They are new and therefore must find ways to justify their position both with their fellow citizens, who already have ways of legitimating power and ordering society, and with those who they have power over. Ekeh makes the case that, "In large part, the European expansion to, and colonization of, Africa must be seen as a result of the bourgeois attempt to acquire political power, via colonization, that would be commensurate with, and further consolidate, its economic power at home."[9] Colonization was a fight to legitimate a new power structure in Western Europe.

The bourgeoise constructed an ideology to fight this battle on two fronts. First, they had to convince their fellow Europeans that they had value. Colonization required a vast martialling of resources and to get these, the bourgeoise had to prove its value. In proving colonization's value for all Europeans, they legitimized their position within European society. Second, they had to convince the Africans that their subjugation was for the African's benefit. While the colonizers had certain advantages, such as technology, it was not clear that colonization would work without at least some complicity from the subjugated people. What no one anticipated, Ekeh argues, was that imposing colonial ideologies on Africans would create a new African bourgeoise who would, in time, challenge the colonial administrator's power. The very same colonial ideology that legitimated the colonial powers was turned against them and used to legitimate a new class of Africans.

The specifics of this colonial ideology are important to understanding the position of ordination. Ekeh identifies six dominant motifs within the colonial ideology: a) the backwardness of the African past, b) the lack of contributions by Africans to the building of Africa, c) inter-tribal feuds, d) benefits of European colonial rule, e) the administrative cost of colonization to Europeans, and f) native vs. Westernized.[10] Missionaries legitimated their role with their European colleagues and to the Africans with whom they worked

---

9   Ekeh, "Colonialism and Two Publics," p. 95.

10   Ekeh, "Colonialism and Two Publics," p. 97–100.

with the same colonial ideology. Africa was the dark continent filled with superstition and witchcraft (a). For millennia, Africans had not developed their own faith beyond simple animism (b). The immorality of Africans allowed for inter-tribal war and slavery (c). Missionaries can bring schools and hospitals, education and health, to ignorant and sickly people (d). The missionaries contribute so much but receive so little from the Africans (e). There are those Africans who can become Westernized, rise above their Native inclinations, and serve as able assistants to the Western missionaries (f). All of these statements are general but quite plausible. All are aimed at two targets. The first is to legitimate the position of the missionary within the Western European church. The second is to authorize their activities in Africa.

From Missionary to African Leadership

The innovation that Ekeh introduces to this relatively straightforward account of colonialism is to make sense of post-colonial power structures using the same basic ideology. Ekeh contends that for those most in contact with the colonial ideology, those Natives who could become Westernized, a similar two front legitimation process emerged. The first front was to prove that African leaders, who Ekeh calls African bourgeoise, could lead as well or better than the colonialists. The second was to legitimate their new role within African society with those who had not become Westernized. Where the colonial missionary was proving themselves to their peers, the African bourgeoise were proving themselves against the colonial missionary; where the colonial missionary authorized their subjugation of Africans, the African bourgeoise were proving that they were the legitimate rulers of their kin. In the pre-independence struggle between these two bourgeoise, the African leaders worked hard to convince both colonial powers and their fellow Africans that they met the highest standards, especially in education, that cooperation with colonial powers was detrimental to African life, and that fellow Africans could bring better results to Africans.[11] In other words, their pre-independence strategy was to adopt the same colonial ideology but argue that they could do it better.

Post-independence Africa was little different according to Ekeh. The pattern had been set by the colonialists. In essence, African leaders had colonized their own kin and family. In doing so, the African leader placed themself in an impossible position. They are both colonizer and colonized. As part of the colonized, they are resisting by taking advantage of the colonizing civic public, all the while legitimating their power through the moral performance of the primordial public. As the colonizer, they assiduously work to prove that they can perform at the standard of colonial ideological demands while creating an amoral civic public that they materially gain from.

Ekeh goes on to discuss the implications for African politics, implications that hold true for the Malawian church for it is both part of the civic culture (a participant in public politics) and of primordial culture (expressing the faith of the people). A number of times Ekeh is clear that while he has in view colonial administrators, the missionary enterprise is also part of his analysis. For instance, in relation to the construction of colonial ideologies, Ekeh will argue that, "they were wrought jointly by the colonial administrators and their close collaborators in the colonial enterprise, the Christian missionaries."[12] By extension, the African bourgeoise that replaced the colonial administration also included those who lead the Malawian church.

Education serves as a good example of how the church participates in the legitimating function of the two publics. First, the colonial administration believed that Africans were backward and unable to learn. Being educated and civilized set the administrators apart from the subjugated people. It also set colonial administrators apart from their European peers. To become a leader within the colonial regime

---

11 Ekeh, "Colonialism and Two Publics," pp. 101–104.
12 Ekeh, "Colonialism and Two Publics," p. 96.

required either peerage, something inherited, or the merit of education and work, something the bourgeoise could attain. As ministers, missionaries were no less focused on education. Ministry was changing into a bourgeoise profession in Europe, where only the brightest could stand the rigors of mission work. Upon independence, the Malawian church instituted the same educational standards for its ministers. Malawians began working towards a Bachelor's degree; attaining a PhD from a Western school was a prized possession. Curriculum at ministerial training colleges were designed and measured in relation to the standard of the United Kingdom. Because schools like Edinburgh and Aberdeen kept to Schleiermacher's four-fold division of the curriculum into Bible, Theology, History, and Practical, so too did Malawi. The adoption of English as the language for education cemented the class distinctions. While most ministers would preach in the vernacular, all of their training was in English.

All of this education served as a demarcation line between the bourgeoisie and the general public. In the church, this line was between ordained and lay. Ministers had education as good as any minister in the United Kingdom; whereas the lay were by and large ignorant and uneducated. Ministers could read and write in English; lay expressed their faith and ideas in the vernacular. Ministers were peers with the new politicians and administrators, forming a kind of political elite; lay turned to ministers as a means to make their day to day life better. The advantage that ministers had over their political peers was that they were the most closely connected to the primordial public. They presided over funerals, regulated marriages, and interpreted the myriad of spiritual forces at work in the world. Lay people gave ministers legitimated authority over them because of this. In turn, this legitimation hardened the relationship between the ordained and lay, sharpening the distinction of power and authority between the two. Those, like politicians, who were most clearly associated with the civic public, required the help of ministers, those associated with the primordial public, for their legitimation. Ministers therefore participated in the civic public realm, bringing the same

101

issues prevalent there into the church. Anyone with passing familiarity with the Malawian church knows that inter-tribal conflict, the role of NGOs and CSOs, and corruption are all pertinent issues for the church.[13]

In summary, the line between the ordained and lay in contemporary Malawi was drawn first in Western Europe by the emergent bourgeoise class. While Western Europe shared a common private and public moral foundation, the imposition of the legitimating colonial ideology in Africa created two publics. One public was related to the private and the other was amoral and associated with power. Colonial administrators legitimated their new-found status within Western Europe and over the African people through promoting certain colonial ideologies. Some Africans adopted the same ideology but turned against the colonialists. In turn, the African leaders legitimated their new position using the colonial ideology on their own people. This played into the two publics and hardened the differences between African leaders and those they led. One of the pillars of this colonial ideology was education. The church, first as a missionary enterprise and then governed by Malawians, participated in this colonial ideology because its ministers were part of the bourgeoisie. The line between ordained and lay runs along the line of a legitimating ideology. It remains so inviolate because to break it down delegitimizes the current leadership structure of Malawian society. Further, because of the two publics there is no moral imperative to change because both ordained and lay avail themselves of the spiritual benefits of the primordial public and the material benefits of the civic public.

Charismatic Power Challenges

The analysis so far focuses on missionary churches with Presbyterians and Anglicans clearly in view. The rise of the charismatic church offers a corroborating and complicating perspective of this analysis.

---

13 Ekeh, "Colonialism and Two Publics," pp. 104–105.

Early forms of charismatic churches, African Independent Churches (AIC), rejected the colonial ideology from the outset. They crafted their own form of legitimation specifically antagonistic toward missionaries. Instead of adopting a contextual theology from the West, these churches attempted to take their cues from more local contexts. Where the missionaries saw Africans as backward, the AIC saw Africa as the source for all that is good. According to their narrative, Africa had developed better and truer forms of community that were under threat from Western missionaries. The benefits of modernization were illusory because they neglected the spiritual realities at play in everyday lives. Only the AIC could effectively address the everyday encounters that Africans had with the spirit world. Fools would turn to white missionaries for protection against curses or to worship God, whereas the wise people would look to AIC leaders for help. Authority was claimed over the spiritual lives of the people and the people legitimated those who could adequately meet those needs. The AIC operated almost entirely within the primordial public, offering an alternative interpretation of important private beliefs without the concomitant legitimation within the public realm.

The fact that post-colonial Malawi was led by those from within the mission churches but not charismatic churches, AIC or otherwise, fits with this analysis. Hastings Kamuzu Banda was Presbyterian and prototypically filled Ekeh's expectations. For instance, Banda was educated in both the United States and England only to return to Malawi after decades away. He insisted on being referred to by his titles, relying on a formality that outdid colonial propriety. For the 33 years of his rule, Banda typified the bourgeoise as described by Ekeh. Upon the assumption of multi-party democracy in 1994, the ground began to shift. With the election of Elson Bakili Muluzi, a Muslim, the ideological ties with the missionaries and Christianity were strained. Still, Ekeh's analysis of the two publics and the ways that Malawian politicians legitimate their authority persists. Malawian politicians, including Muluzi, would still claim educational credentials to reinforce their legitimacy even if these credentials are academically specious or honorary. The "fight" against corruption fails because corruption assumes that private and public moralities are the same whereas in Malawi there are two publics. In post-colonial Malawi, leadership came from the mission churches and was legitimized using the colonial ideology as Ekeh has described.

Ironically, this means that the churches that articulated the most independent view of Africa and its people, the AIC, were not part of the leadership post-independence. Arguably this has begun to change with the rise of charismatic churches and their powerful "prophetic" leaders. Loosely allied with North American charismatics but modelled on prosperity preachers in West Africa, these churches and their leaders legitimate themselves using a combination of the AIC and mission churches. On one hand, the prophets/apostles/evangelists rely on their effectiveness at performing deeds of power and wonder. If a prophet can heal, they are self-evidently a prophet. They need no other form of legitimation for they bring the benefit of spiritual protection and bounty to those who follow them. This is the contra-ideology found in the AIC churches and the charismatic churches are the legitimate heirs of this legacy. On the other hand, the prophets are also self-styled business men. Part of their authority rests on the fact that they are wealthy. This wealth is tied to entrepreneurial market activities and not the public coffers but all the same, it is part of the public realm. A prophet's followers have the same expectations of them as they do of other Malawian leaders, that they will provide goods in both the primordial (signs of power and wonder) and the civic (goods and services). The prophet's wealth buys him authority with his followers and places him in conflict with those already within the existing power structures. Prophets struggle to find a place in Malawian society as they are a new class, a new kind of bourgeoise.

The implications for ordination are straightforward. Charismatic churches do not require education as a legitimating factor in leadership. They may undertake learning for pragmatic reasons but they do not inherently require it because they reject the underlying colonial ideology that supported it. Pragmatic reasons might include church growth and this is directly tied to the primordial public for it meets the religious needs of its followers. Furthermore, because prophets find their legitimacy within the civic realm through free market capitalism rather than through state funded economic projects, any wealthy person may claim authority. Followers give legitimacy to a prophet because they bring wealth to them, both in terms of the prosperity gospel which functions in the primordial public and in terms of business dealings which functions in the civic public. Therefore, anyone who is wealthy, is both blessed within the primordial and effective in the civic. Leadership comes via wealth. It follows then that the distinction between ordained and lay falls away because any lay person wealthy enough to bless the people becomes a Christian leader.

Conclusion: Changing Expectations

This chapter began by pointing to three expectations regarding ordination that the Malawi church does not fulfil: a low ordained to lay ratio, ordination as authorization to preach, and widespread lay education. My first argument was that the Malawian church took on normative views of ordination from the Western missionary context. That is, the expectations outlined are not indigenous to Malawi. Instead, like an invasive species, they have migrated here. The second argument was to explain how the practices of ordination developed from colonial to post-colonial times. Again, like an invasive species, the practices of ordination originating in the West took root and flourished in Malawi for reasons that Peter Ekeh outlined. The creation of two publics, one associated with the civic and the other with the primordial, has created a climate where the ideology of ordination as practiced by the missionaries has been able to become Malawian. Finally, I argued that even though new models of power and authority have arisen, specifically the charismatic church and the prophets that lead it, a similar power dynamic persists. Following the image of invasive species, a new strain has emerged in the charismatic churches that may appear different but continues to have the same DNA as the old.

I use the image of invasive species for two reasons. The first is that I want to be clear that there is no moral condemnation of the current ordination practices inherent in my analysis. There is moral condemnation of the invasive species, of the colonial enterprise. Missionaries could have encountered Malawians in ways that were more faithful to the Gospel they proclaimed. Any ideology that assumes an entire group of people is inferior is inherently evil and therefore deserves moral condemnation. This same condemnation does not follow through to the post-colonial context. As Ekeh demonstrates, African leaders were moral just not in the ways that were practiced or expected by colonialists. In Ekeh's tale of the money falling off the truck, there were competing moralities at work. The fact that the colonial administrator could not acknowledge the validity of the African alternative does not condemn the African but the colonialist.

The practical challenge that arises from my analysis is for the Malawian church to consider ways that it might meet the moral obligations that it does have in ways that are true to the Gospel. That is, the creation of two publics was the result of colonialism and creates a situation where the moral goods of the civic realm are sacrificed for the moral goods of the primordial realm. In what ways can the Malawian church order itself to pursue the moral goods of the primordial? Increasingly, Christians in Malawi give legitimacy to charismatic leaders. These prophets provide spiritual (primordial) and material (civic) benefits to their followers and in doing so are granted authority. A significant issue with this power structure is accountability. How can legitimacy freely given be revoked and by what criterion? On the other hand, established churches continue to rely on the post-colonial structures for their authority but they are increasingly under pressure. Prominent church leaders face serious questions from their followers. These questions are delegitimizing.

Is it possible that the future of ordination lies between these two? That is, that the established churches relinquish previous ways of legitimizing leaders through ordination. For instance, education as one of the major criteria would fall away. Instead, established churches would grant authority based on whether an individual fulfils the moral obligations of the primordial public. Education would become no less important but instead of serving a legitimating function it would equip leaders to be more effective in the performance of their duties. The charismatic churches, which already grant authority for effectively performing in the primordial public, would incorporate ways of moral accountability. Instead of an individual claiming authority, groups of people, perhaps at the local level (but more likely in larger areas), would formally legitimate a leader. Churches would need to develop polities that would create moral accountability mechanisms that lay followers would both understand and actively participate in.

The second reason I use the image of the invasive species is because I am arguing that the practices of ordination could have been otherwise. The invasive plant need not have been brought here. For instance, missiologist John Flett provides a book length argument for an alternative view of authority and power within the missionary enterprise.[14] Others such as Jurgens Johannes van Wyk have attempted to connect Western and Malawian contexts but have failed.[15] Van Wyk sets out to give a thorough historical account of how the offices of minister, elder, and deacon developed in the Reformed tradition in Scotland. As a missionary to Malawi, van Wyk believes that "exposure to the background and development of the offices in Scotland will assist the reformed [sic] and presbyterian [sic] churches in Central Africa to develop a more relevant ministry of the offices within their context."[16] Van Wyk argues that to understand ordination in Malawi today we must understand ordination in Scotland before colonialism. He further argues that understanding the historical context is critical to making improvements in

---

[14] John G. Flett, *Apostolicity: The Ecumenical Question in World Christian Perspective*, Downers Grove: IVP Academic, 2016.

[15] Jurgens Johannes van Wyk, *The Historical Development of the Offices According to the Presbyterian Tradition of Scotland*, Zomba: Kachere, 1995.

[16] van Wyk, *The Historical Development of the Offices*, pp. 9–10.

contemporary ordination practices. Van Wyk succeeds very well at developing a historical reconstruction of ordination within "a specific ecclesiastical and political context."[17] In doing so, he acknowledges that the view of ordination within the Scottish Reformed tradition is thoroughly contextual. However, Van Wyk offers very little political and next to no economic analysis of the context. He dwells exclusively on the ecclesiastical. Perhaps because of this emphasis, van Wyk does not provide an account of why this understanding of ordination was introduced into Malawi or why it persists in post-colonial times. For van Wyk there are deficiencies of theology and ecclesiology at work but not an immanently logical political and economic process that accounts for ordination in Malawi. Van Wyk's analysis lacks the conceptual tools required to connect the Scottish context to the Malawian context in a clear and compelling way. In lacking this connective tissue, Van Wyk's study remains rooted in Scotland and in history, unable to help Malawi move into the future.

If Scotland's history does not offer the clue to moving forward then another alternative put forward is a kind of retrieval of pre-colonial leadership practices indigenous to Malawi. Given the time that has passed and the insidiousness of colonialism, I have doubts that any project of retrieval has a chance of success but even more, I'm not sure it is theoretically possible. Pre-colonial Malawi had a diversity of people present and therefore a diversity of structures of power and authority at work. Given that the nation state Malawi itself is a colonial construct, how could the church adjudicate among the various leadership options present and discern the "true" Malawian alternative? By what criterion would the church decide that one or another view was more "Malawian" than another? Furthermore, the context has changed so much over the past 200 years, is it conceivable that leadership structures developed for another time could still have validity today?

The instincts inherent in both Van Wyk's and the retrieval project hold the seed for a way forward. Van Wyk demonstrates how

---

17   van Wyk, *The Historical Development of the Offices*, p. 163.

different theological understandings of authority played out in post Reformation Scotland; retrieval projects take the philosophic commitments of Africans seriously. What the above analysis moves towards, relying on Ekeh's two publics, is that ordination in a Malawian context is less about the "office" held by an individual and more about the way that individuals exert authority within a communal setting. The primordial public is deeply communal and that is easily missed by Westerners who are inherently individualistic. There is a moral priority given to the group, to family and kin. A return to the Bible with this lens in mind should reveal a more communal understanding of ordination that affirms the Malawian understanding of a moral public. On the other side, the Bible will always challenge facile understandings of community. Nostalgia for a pre-colonial past can hide or justify current day immorality. In fact, the current context with its two publics creates a trap for Malawian leaders. Two publics creates two masters. In playing to two moralities they must violate one.

Malawian ordination practices defy Western expectations. The way forward is not to meet those expectations. Malawi is not the West. Malawi does not need to prove itself to the West. Rather, the Malawian church must prove itself to God. The way forward lies in meeting a clear-eyed understanding of current practices and then a faith filled reimagining of how the Malawian church determines who has the authority to lead Christ's church.

Bibliography

Campenhausen, Hans von, *Ecclesiastical Authority and Spiritual Power in the Church of the First Three Centuries*, Peabody: Hendrickson, 1997.

Ekeh, Peter P., "Afterword: Note on 'Colonialism and the Two Publics in Africa: A Theoretical Statement,'" in Helen Lauer and Kofi Anyidoho (eds), *Reclaiming the Human Sciences and Humanities through African Perspectives*, vol. 1, Legon-Accra: Sub-Saharan Publishers, 2012, pp. 219–232.

Ekeh, Peter P., "Colonialism and the Two Publics in Africa: A Theoretical Statement," *Comparative Studies in Society and History,* vol. 17, no. 1, January 1975, pp. 91–112.

Flett, John G., *Apostolicity: The Ecumenical Question in World Christian Perspective,* Downers Grove: IVP Academic, 2016.

Jankiewicz, Darius, "The Problem of Ordination: Lessons from Early Christian History," *Faculty Publications,* no. 78, 2013.

Wyk, Jurgens Johannes van, *The Historical Development of the Offices According to the Presbyterian Tradition of Scotland,* Zomba: Kachere, 2005.

Chapter 8

Voices from the Grassroots: Meaningful Partnership

Volker Glissmann

Introduction

No review of theological education or assessment of its fitness for purpose can succeed without the contribution of the voice of the laity. This is even more true for everything that directly affects the laity like grassroots theological education (sometimes called Christian education) and ministerial theological education where there is the most direct relation and engagement with the grassroots/laity of the church. The natural inclination for institutional reviews of theological schools and theology programmes of churches is to seek input from specialists in the area of theology and theological education but unfortunately, not always from the laity. These reviews will fall short and be incomplete if no special consideration is given to pro-actively engaging the voice of the grassroots who is the direct audience and recipient of the majority of grassroots and ministerial theological discourses. This is why reflections in "Towards a Malawian Theology of Laity" is incomplete and impossible to conceptualize without giving a prominent voice to the grassroots of the church. The voices amplified in this chapter will help in moving towards formulating a Malawian theology of laity. The voices recorded here have not exhausted the voices, the contributions, the concerns and the ideas of representatives of the Malawian grassroots. Rather the opposite is true, the voices heard here show that a depth of reflection and awareness of what is good for the grassroots. However, the recorded distinct responses to very unflattering situations in very specific local church contexts also show that generalization of these initial voices of the grassroots needs to be balanced with voices from other

111

sections of the church. Yet, at the same time there are also some themes that connect across denominational backgrounds (like the relation between money and positions in the church) and the lack of explicit grassroots ministry preaching across the churches (if it would exist as a key theme in the church already than this book would have no need to be written now). It became quite quickly clear that this research can only be the beginning of giving a stronger voice to the grassroots and actively allowing them to have their voices heard. Perhaps previously, the absence of a strong and unfiltered voice of the laity can give the impression that a) the laity does not have a distinct role to play in the participation of *their* faith in the church; and that b) the laity does not have contributions to make to the direction and the theological reflections of the church itself; and that c) the contribution of the laity is irrelevant to the life and ministry of the church. Overall, the laity is for a great part not only committed to God but also committed to their local church. The importance of the laity for the church is obvious because without the laity there is no church, without the laity pastors are without ministry. The laity is not powerless when it feels that it is not served well, some though committed to a certain denomination leave and worship somewhere else, others redirect financial contributions away from Sunday offerings to helping the needy or other Christian ministries directly. And yet, at least the members of the laity interviewed here are very much aware of the deficiencies that they encounter in preaching, church teachings, clerical power games, injustices, ministerial shortcomings, laity internal politics and yet at the same time, they also recognize the inputs of clerical or denominational inputs and ministry received, opportunities for participation and ministry in the church offered and taken up by the laity as important parts of their faith journeys.

The first observation in any discussion about the grassroots is that the grassroots (or the laity) is not a homogeneous group, rather it is a diverse group of individuals who have different experiences, aspirations, characters, preferences and of course grew up in (and sometimes accumulated different) church and spiritual traditions in their lives. All of these make generalizations about the grassroots' perception of participation and empowerment untenable. Additionally, the reflection of grassroots participants about their own roles significantly depends on both their own level of reflective practice and Bible engagement, their participation in church activities and leadership as well as experience of perceived leadership shortcomings within a denominational setting as well as a congregational setting.[1] An additional factor is of course the church tradition that participants are engaged in that either explicitly or inexplicitly builds a theology of grassroots participation. This is most clearly seen in the laity reflection of members of the CCAP who generally uphold the original Presbyterian idea that the pastor is a designated teaching elder but not one of the ruling elders that make up the church session.

Research Description

The method for the research is a case study. It is a qualitative research whereby in-depth insights were collected from a small sample group (fifteen individuals) who were interviewed in February and March 2020. Unfortunately, some additional arranged interviews did not materialize which would have widened the samples. The interviews were based on a predesigned questionnaire that also included an open question which allowed participants to voice whatever they felt needed to be said without being limited in scope by the interviewer's pre-determined research questions. All interviews were in English and conducted by the researcher himself. The objective was to give a voice to the laity. Interviews were chosen here because the interview will provide more detailed answers than a questionnaire, especially in

---

[1]   Throughout this research the term "laity" and "lay person" are used as it is currently still the most familiar terminology to those interviewed, though I prefer the organic term grassroots. I use the term "grassroots" for lay theological education because of how it offers a semantic link to organic imagery. Roots support the plant. Without roots, the plant dies. Damaged or underdeveloped roots equal underdeveloped or damaged plants. See Volker Glissmann, "Grassroots Theological Education," p. 54.

a relational culture where the assumption is that the interviewees prefer to express themselves verbally. The research was designed to assess the interviewees' own views and preferences concerning lay or grassroots participation in the churches that they have or are attending. The purpose of the qualitative interview is to describe the interviewees' point of view. All the interviewees reside in urban and semi-urban centres of Zomba and Blantyre. The interviewees also represent a mixture of genders (seven female and eight male), from a variety of churches, including: Anglican, Baptist, CCAP, Pentecostal and AIC, however, there was also overlap as some interviewees had experience in more than one church tradition. Members of various CCAP congregations formed the majority of the interviewees: eleven. The researcher as well as all interviewees were lay people, though a few were elders in their respective churches. The interview findings are anonymous, all interviewees are only identified as LP (Lay Participation) and a number. The sample size of fifteen participants that were facilitated by the researcher himself provides only an initial insight that further research needs to verify and expand upon, including what role denominational backgrounds play in the self-understanding of grassroots participants, as well as if there then also differences in understanding between the urban and rural centres, between younger and older members, between man and women, between elders, deacons and women's guild members (who are laity) but different from "ordinary Christians." Four of the participants also drew on comparisons with experiences of non-Malawian churches that they attended for at least some months/years (2 in South Africa, 1 in Zambia, 1 Scotland). Additionally, 2 participants are well-experienced non-Malawians that were included to allow for a more global perspectives to also inform the reflection and to help to understand the lay voice both in its general (global) concerns as well as in its local (Malawian) concerns. Eight participants (LP4, LP5, LP6, LP7, LP10, LP11, LP12, LP13) were interviewed as mini focus groups because they are married couples. This allowed for dialogue between the two participants concerning their individual views of lay participation which resulted either in affirming a view shared by both or by acknowledging alternative experiences in order to arrive at a more balanced contribution.

Research Questions

The research presented here only includes part of the originally conducted research interviews of over eight hours of interviews (nearly 45,000 words in transcripts). The original research interview three parts to it: Part A: the grassroots view of categories of qualities in new pastor (question 1). Part A is based on research done by Jaison Thomas in India in 2006 in an attempt to create dialogue between his findings and the Malawian grassroots context. Part B: questions concerning grassroots participation; Part C: an open question thus allowing the participants to share insights independent of the research questions. The main focus of this paper is on Part B of the original research.

Definitions

The research assumes the following definition, a church leader is someone who has been ordained into the pastoral ministry and is usually addressed with a "professional" ecclesiastical title (Reverend, Pastor, Bishop, etc). The laity or the grassroots includes everyone else (including ordained elders as some traditions have them also ordained).

Question on Lay Participation

1) From listening to the preaching and teaching of the pastors in your church, what would you say does the pastor believe the role of lay people to be? Is there a distinct role?

2) What is the actual role of lay people in your church?

3) What image would you use to describe the role of lay people in church?

4) In your opinion as a member of the church, what do you think should be the role of lay people in the church be?

5) How satisfied are you with the overall role of lay people in your church?

Very satisfied (1)	More than satisfied (2)	Satisfied (3)	Partially satisfied (4)	Not at all satisfied (5)

6) How can the church improve the empowerment and participation of lay people?

Interview Findings

This section presents the key answers provides by the interviewees to the above six questions. The answers are not recorded in full length but are cut for clarity to show the main points raised. The voice of interviewees is given in verbatim and only minor stylistic changes very made to aid the readability and clarity. Each answer is summarized in a heading for easier comparison.

The Role of Lay People according to the Pastors

The first question asked was: "From listening to the preaching and teaching of the pastors in your church, what would you say does the pastor believe the role of lay people to be? Is there a distinct role?" The aim of the question was to find out what message is received from the ordained minister from the pulpit (but also possibly through other forms of non-verbal communication) about the role of the grassroots in the life of the church. Though the emphasis of the question was on teaching and preaching delivered to the laity by the pastor, there are of course other venues and in which ordained church leaders either explicitly or implicitly communicate with the laity about how the pastor views the role of the laity. These venues are: his physical presence in church when a lay person preaches, church sessions including the physical seating arrangements of the pastor vis-a-vis the laity, private conversation both privately with the pastor as a private individual but also private conversation in the church office with the pastor in his pastoral function.

The role of the grassroots as defined by the pastors was summarized as following:

Changing role of some lay people

"OK, I think that times are changing. So, I think my church is also embracing this. In the past, the lay people always were just involved in the church activities like maybe fundraising - most of those things. But things have changed, whereby church elders are now involved in preaching. But in the past it was always about the pastor, the pastor, the pastor. But they are now giving a leading role to the lay people who have knowledge in theology those who are willing to share the knowledge which they have. So with the youth ministry, the men's ministry. I think, nowadays, the role of us – lay people – has been redefined. In the past, it was just about the activities away from mainline preaching and everything." (LP1)

The laity being used by God to speak through them

"I think the pastor thinks that the laity has something that they can offer. Because there are cases where the pastor will sit in the church and there will be somebody else on the pulpit preaching. While he is there. This means this pastor has trust that God can speak even through a lay person, a lay person has value, spiritually they can also offer. [Follow up question: Does the pastor every say this?] It is not explicitly said, but seen in the action. He is there and yet he has given the pulpit to somebody else." (LP2)

The laity as district/zone shepherds

'There are different positions in the districts/zones of the church. Those ones they are more or less like shepherds as well. The minister cannot take care of everything. Like the example that I was giving you just now. They called me around 4am that there is a funeral. I had to wake up and go there. If I had no role to play, then they would have called the minster himself to go and pray. That is the way of opening the funeral ceremony. Because without the presence of one member of the church they all will just be sitting, nobody can pray and nobody can sing." (LP2)

The laity as some committed people while others just attend

"There are lay people who are heavily involved, they are more or less like pastors too. And yet there are others at the low level. Who, I don't know how I can describe this, they are just part of the team, just part of the church. I don't know if this is just being rude. They are just part of the church. And there are other lay people if you give them responsibility they will say: "no." If they take it they won't to do it faithfully, they will be busy with something else. So, it depends how dedicated you are in the church." (LP2)

The laity as servants <u>in</u> the church

"And I felt that I was a second rate church member. Because I was not showing up and doing official church things. And I always felt that I was kind of having to prove myself. And it is a very subtle message, and it often comes out with the church notices are given, because they are all about stuff that everybody should be doing mid-week. I am like ... you know, I work. I can't." (LP4)

The laity as lazy because they don't follow the pastor's vision and do what the pastor tells them to do

"I think our current pastor is very saddened by the number of lay people that he feels very seriously miss their vocation to serve Christ, they miss the call of God in their lives, not to be ordained but to serve. He thinks the church fails in its mission to be salt and light because the laity, by and large, let me be bland, I think, he thinks we are lazy." (LP5)

The laity as satisfying the pastor if they do things in church

"If you get into the Sunday School and the choir then you can do anything you want to do during the rest of the week." (LP5)

The laity as giver of money

"I think, the role of the laity is to raise funds. Sorry to say this. I think that is the major role that they want the church to dive in: to raise more and more funds. Because there is no Sunday that has gone without talking about it. And if the pastor sees that people are not giving according to his expectations, then it becomes an issue." (LP6)

The laity as audience for pastoral performances

"Lay people have a role but their role is not that much significant. Most of the times lay people they are just people who makes the service to go on. Like to have people to preach to and to attend all church services. That is the role that they play." (LP8)

The laity as giver of money

"There role [of the laity] is to contribute some money." (LP8)

The laity (ordinary Christians) as without role in church

"If there is an ordinary role, then these ones: you are going to read the Bible, pray, or you are going to be like an MC on Sundays. Those ones, but if it comes to preaching, that one has to be a women's guild, a deacon or a church elder. That is according to the pastor. So, when you talk about the lay person, not those [church lay leaders] that have positions, just an ordinary person like me. The owner of the church – the Reverend – does not recognize the lay people. [Follow Up: the owner?] Yes, because he is owner, others are just coming in." (LP9)

The laity as voiceless

"It is not through teaching but through what they say elsewhere. I think it varies from individual to individual. Like the pastor that we have now, for me, I think, he is a dictator, I would say. Whatever he thinks should go, goes. He doesn't listen to the lay people." (LP10)

The laity as giver of money, free time and free labour

"Most of the talking even on the pulpit about the participation of the lay people in the church especially now, have gone towards fundraising and the like. This is the essence of the committee work [as envisioned/promoted by the pastors] the raising of funds and the logistics of running up and down. And the women cooking. Free labour for them." (LP11)

The laity as giver of money

"Right now, the BIG ROLE of the Christians is giving and the [lay] leaders to ensure that Christians are giving." (LP12)

The laity as listeners and receivers of pastoral truth

"You should just listen to what the pastor has to say, the whole truth and nothing but the truth is with the pastor. So what the pastor says is the truth and you just have to listen and not question what he is saying. And that is the attitude of most pastors that I have met." (LP13)

The laity as giver of money

"Giving and tithing, whatever you do make sure that people are giving, and that they are giving enough, they are not defaulting, the role of a lay people is to give and support the church financially." (LP13)

The laity either as "extensions of pastoral ministry" or as "know-nothings"

"It varies from pastor to pastor. Some people's expectation is that the lay people maybe are to move on with the gospel that the pastor preaches. It is as if you are training someone and you expect that someone to be able to also mentor someone. Maybe that is the expectation of someone, of some leaders. But the challenge that comes in, the issue is that those lay people, were not trained on how to go about it. For example, I am a church elder, sometimes you don't even know what you are supposed to do. If you are not told, you don't know what you are supposed to do. So, I think that for some these are the expectations, while for others, the lay people don't know anything. The pastor has all the know-how (which is a mistake anyhow)." (LP14)

Summary

The most important finding is what was not said. No participant mentioned (even after being prompted by follow up questions) that he/she remembers the pastor explicitly preaching about the role of the laity in church. This is extremely significant, as it strongly suggested that pastors do not explicitly teach about the unique role of the laity in church. It is indicating also that lay participation is not part of the living pastoral theology of the preachers. Nevertheless, there were hints of a role of the laity along the lines of "share your faith" (or the like) but these comments were not part of a clear theological or even practical message how and why the laity should engage in these activities.

There is a positive recognition that in at least in one congregation the role of lay church leaders has improved (see "Changing role of some lay people"). Again, there is some recognition that God speaks through the lay church leaders (see "The laity being used by God to speak through them") and they, the lay church leaders, have a shepherding role within their district/zone (see "The laity as district/zone shepherds"). The laity serve within the church and that satisfies the pastor as its supports his church ministry either through ministry or through free time and free labour (see "'The laity as servants *in* the church", "The laity as satisfying the pastor if they do things in church" and "The laity as giver of money, free time and free labour"). But the laity is not a homogeneous group, beside lay church leaders the "ordinary Christians" don't feel that they have a role and reading the Bible in church is not viewed as a distinct contribution (see "The laity (ordinary Christians) as without role in church"). A further division exists within the laity, they have different commitments to participation or different time available to contribute (see "The laity as some committed people while others just attend" and "The laity as servants *in* the church"). In some churches the laity does not feel that they have any role beside being an audience for pastoral performances (see "The laity as audience for pastoral performances") and beyond that are voiceless in their church (see "The laity as voiceless"). However, one ministry is completely reserved as the domain of the laity: the role to financially provide (see "The laity as giver of money, free time and free labour" as well as four times the "The laity as giver of money.") The laity as givers of money is raised by a 1/3 of the interviewees, some of them are from the same congregation but not all. So, it seems that this is a significant issue. Another role reserved for the laity is that of listeners to pastoral truth (see "The laity as listeners and receiver of pastoral truth") and yet somehow also as (voiceless) implementing agents to extend the pastoral vision of ministry (see "The laity as lazy because they don't follow the pastor's vision and do what the pastor tells them to do" and "The laity either as 'extensions of pastoral ministry' or as 'know-nothings"). The last point is important because at the one hand the laity is supposed to receive the wisdom and vision of the pastor (without ever being properly engaged to own the vision or being trained) and yet somehow the laity is at the same time expected to implement the pastoral vision according to the pastor's ideals.

The Actual Role of Lay People in the Church

The 2nd question asked was: 'What is the actual role of lay people in your church?" The aim of the question was to see which roles are actually fulfilled by lay people in different churches as well as to appreciate the diversity of roles played by lay people in the church.

The Malawian church is blessed with gifted and very active lay people, the answers were therefore, repetitive. The following is the overall summary of what had been mentioned by the interviewees:

Lay people are taking part in the visible church Service, where they lead the service, the readings, the prayers, contribute through singing both congregational as well as music groups, worship teams or individual songs, some are given the opportunity to preach also in church. They are involved in the activities that make the church services possible, they do welcoming, they are handing out the notices sheets when you come in, greet you as you come in, preparing the church for service, help with communion, often organize the Sunday collections, manage the administration and affairs of the church through diverse committees and sub-committees, management and the executive and are (depending on church tradition) the deciding voice in session.

Outside of the church, the zones/district administration is devolved to laity in the form of elders often and there the role is often pastoral. Outside of the cities, the laity, the elders are managing all affairs of smaller congregations/prayer houses in the absence of a resident pastor. Depending on individual congregations, some have lay lead ministries or committees, like visiting or pastoral care, house or cell groups, prayer, prison, women, men, street children's ministry, charity or welfare ministry/committees.

Three reflections stand out which didn't just describe activities but take a more theological approach to the question what is the role of lay people in the church:

"To work hand-in-hand with the minister. If the minister is willing." (LP6)

"to listen to the Word of God, live by the Word and to serve." (LP7)

"So, when I say they are supposed to be partners. They are supposed to be co-workers. Co-workers in the ministry. Laymen are supposed to be co-workers. What I mean is that there should be a working relationship between the pastor and the lay people. The fact that the pastor has been trained as a pastor does not necessarily mean, that he has the capacity to do everything on his own. He needs to materialize or make use of the people that surround him. That he can be able to work with them for the effectiveness of the ministry. So, they need to be taken as co-workers." (LP14)

Summary

First of all, there are differences between denominations and churches and so not all of the above activities are found in all churches. It seems that there is a significant difference between those attending established churches (Anglican, Baptist, CCAP) and those that attend newly established churches, or it could be an issue between bigger congregations and smaller congregations. Though it seems that potentially the work of lay leaders in the established or bigger churches where some of the spiritual leadership is devolved to allow for preaching and zone/district initial pastoral leadership is distinct while ordinary Christians even in the established churches as well as members of more recently founded churches, do not necessarily play a big role as there is no hierarchy through which responsibility and opportunities are made available. Committees and sub-committees are often open to ordinary Christians not just deacons and elders. Certain roles are fulfilled by the elders and deacons which technically fulfils the requirement of laity, however, it also complicates the picture as not all opportunities are open to *all* lay people. The laity recognizes that pastors are set aside to fulfil an important leadership role within the church (no one interviewed spoke negatively about pastors in general and many recognized pastoral contributions to their faith journey). At the same time, the interviews are very much aware of the human side of the pastoral office, where the pastor cannot do everything, he cannot be everywhere, he cannot talk to everyone, he cannot minster to everyone that needs it and so the laity offers meaningful partnership and assistance under the recognition of the laity, empowered by the Holy Spirit, to join in ministry as co-workers.

An Image to Describe the Role of Lay People in Church

The 3rd question asked was: "What image would you use to describe the role of lay people in church?" The aim of the question was to hear from the laity about how they view their own role within the church but describing their role not with words but through an imagine. The use of this creative question was to challenge the interviewees to find a new way and describe their experience in one single picture or image. Some interviewees used an image to describe the current experienced role while others describe the ideal role as they perceive it.

The role of the grassroots as defined by the pastors was summarized as follows:

A) Current Experience in Images

The shepherd who goes to assist the needs of the sheep

"The biblical image that Jesus is our shepherd. He is the good shepherd. We are shepherds but not good shepherds like Jesus. You are supposed to look for the lost sheep. In our church zone/district each church elder, and each deacon is going to have certain number of families to look after. So for those families you are responsible, if somebody is sick you would be the first person to know. You should go and help spiritually and even report to others. In that case, you are also like a pastor for that small group. Though you cannot baptize them, but the pastor is far somewhere, he is relying on you. And I am

125

the one to call him to say I have a sick member within our area. He is admitted at the hospital. I am the one to let the pastor know." (LP2)

Lay people are servants to the minster

"he lay people are hands who run around. The minister is the head." (LP10)

Lay people are just a means for the pastor

"You have a pastor and the lay people are a camel. The pastor will ride on the camel when it is convenient for him and when it is not convenient for him then he will disembark. A camel, because it will do the tedious work in the desert. As long as it enables you to get to a well somewhere in the desert you are fine with it." (LP13)

Pastors as bosses

"Pastors instead of being pastors end up being bosses. The lay person is a servant or a junior who serves the boss. Pastors are supposed to be leaders, supposed to be servants not bosses. As servants we have to respect the pastor, he has all the wisdom and the lay people need to listen to this (supposedly) good person." (LP14)

Lay people with empty spiritual hands

"People who go to church in most cases, they just go there as a routine. This is just a thing that they have to do. We are talking of they are going to church empty handed, then they come back the very same way they came to church, empty handed because they did not grow spiritually in church. Sometimes the lay people are not growing because it depends on the pastor, because we are looking at some of the pastors, it looks like they are there just as an employment. Not that they are spiritual or are convicted that they have to do the work of God." (LP15)

B) Ideal Experience in Images

Jesus Christ's inclusive call to ministry

"The Ideal role is the way Jesus Christ in cooperated each and every person and was helped by each and every person and Jesus Christ could relate to each and every person, from tax collectors to prostitutes. I think that this is the ideal role. In one way or the other those helping Jesus. Look at Simon Peter who was a fisherman and, in their society, he was from the low classes and yet he rose to become a leader." (LP1)

Living Stones and Priesthood of All Believers

"'Living stones and the priesthood of all believers.' The Living stones because everybody in the church is playing their part, the arms, the legs – the body of Christ. The priesthood of all believers is about having actually a role, a fundamental calling to be Christ-like, to be priestly... whatever you do." (LP4)

Jesus using the disciples and bread and fish to address a need

"The story of Jesus feeding the 5,000. Where there was Jesus, the disciples and there was a need. And somehow one of them knew that there is a little boy with only fish and bread. Jesus said, 'Let's use that!' And that was used to multiply food for everyone. For me what that image says first of all is that those that were given responsibility were aware of the needs of the people. They were also aware of what possible could come from the people to address the needs of others. And that use of what is within the church or within that group to actually meet the needs of everyone else. So it is coming from within, it might need to be multiplied, the good that is coming out should be able to spread. And there is something coming from within, these people ... also the fact that Jesus said, okay there are people here, we cannot send them away. Let us not just look for us, because that is what the disciples were initially saying, let them go because at this

127

time and if we keep them longer than we need to feed them and we don't have that. But then, you know, Jesus was like, 'No, let's do that together, we all have this need and we address it together.'" (LP12)

Summary

As expected, the laity has different experiences which are expressed in the images given. The first experience, of the current experiences, is that of a lay church leader (an elder) who reflects about the role of lay church leaders as shepherds under the main shepherd (see "The shepherd who goes to assist the needs of the sheep"). The other experiences are less positive and describe both the experience of the laity as being overlooked by the pastoral ministry without taking something home to grow spiritually (see "Lay people with empty spiritual hands"). While the other three images describe the role of the laity as serving the needs of the pastor (see "Lay people are servants to the minster," "Lay people are just a means for the pastor" and "Pastors as bosses").

This is contrasted with the ideal images of the role of lay people which envisions an inclusive role based on Christ's calling of individuals to empower even low-class Christians to become leaders (see "Jesus Christ's inclusive call to ministry"). The second image envisions everybody playing their God-given role in the body and in reaching out with Christ's pastoral concern to the world (see "Living Stones and Priesthood of All Believers") and finally, a vision of the church and its laity responding to the needs with all the talents within them (see "Jesus using the disciples and bread and fish to address a need").

Lay Reflection on their Own Role in the Church

The 4th question asked was: "In your opinion as a member of the church, what do you think should the role of lay people in the church be?" The aim of the question was to hear from the laity about how they understand and envision their own role within the church to be.

The role of the grassroots as defined by the pastors was summarized as following:

Inclusive Role

"'I think it should be big. They should take a central role but they should involve each and every person. It seems that most people take part in the church and the administrative issues are from the English service, the other ones, they are lay, yes, but we are all lay people. But our ability like, our financial ability separates us. So, some are considered more lay than others. I would rather think that each and every one should be given an equal part. Even those that are not well educated, should at least be given a chance." (LP1)

A good working model (from the CCAP)

"I think what we have is in order. There is always a certain secrecy with each and every profession. As a lay person, I cannot demand that one day I also want to administer communion. It means that I am infringing on someone's position. So, what we do as lay people, especially at our church where I go to, because we are involved in almost everything, in financial, administrative issues, we are managing the funds on a congregational level, the minister has nothing to do with it. There is an executive, which will operate that. So, I feel what we are doing is in order. And we should continue to be around and do like that. Once in a while we can preach, teach. There are certain things reserved for the pastor only and as a member of the church I agree." (LP2)

Witness Christ where we are

"To serve others, after knowing Christ you should be able to manifest what you have learnt about Christ. To become a witness of Christ. Our role as lay people is to witness Christ. It is what Christ himself said in Matthew 28, verse 20b where he is commissioning the people, the disciples. We need to pursue that wherever we are." (LP6)

Win lost souls

"I think that a lay member he must be active in the church as to win the lost souls outside the church. Sometimes the lay members are just being satisfied in being the church members. But they are supposed to go outside to win lost souls for Christ." (LP8)

Build up the community of believers

"And those church members are supposed to know each other very well, to assist one another. If one of them falls into trouble, like he doesn't have food and all that. The lay member should assist that person." (LP8)

Evaluate critically the pastor's sharing

"A lay member must observe, he must scrutinize between the Word of God and the opinions of the pastor. Sometimes, they do not differentiate between these two things and then fall into trouble. They must like, 'This is his opinion, and this is the real word of God.' I think after doing that they will be living a good life according to the Word of God." (LP8)

The actual well-established structure defining the role of the laity in the CCAP

"'I think the role of lay people is, I have been a Presbyterian, there is a lot I would say, because you take part in the administration, you take part in the service, and you are also given an opportunity to preach. And you are given an opportunity to be in committees. And you are given an opportunity to manage the affairs of the church. So, I think the role of the lay people is well established – structurally. The structure is there. And it is well established." (LP10)

The laity running the church guided by the minster

"I think, maybe in the typical belief of Presbyterians. I think the lay people, should run the church in terms of decisions and the like but guided from a spiritual point of view by the minster. He should come in and show whether certain decisions are contrary to the Word of God. I think that is the role that I would appreciate would be the minster's guidance. Because sometimes, the lay people might take experiences from the world and transfer them into the church, to run the church from secular experiences, which have no bearing with the Word of God. I think that is where the minister must come in, to show them that the church cannot run this way. It is not a secular organization. It depends on God's guidance." (LP11)

Full deliberate participation of all God's people with orientation to help those new

"The role that they have is that they should participate in the worship in all aspects and with special orientation on how to do it. I think that as much as possible that the lay people should be involved in the service. God can use anybody and so we should be able to allow that possibility and nurture that possibility that someone who is not necessarily fitting into the different categories (deacon, elder, age) can be used by God in a specific way. There is so many roles that Christians or lay people can take up and even if it requires some sort of orientation, little orientation but that can be done without making a whole fuzz about how and why this person shouldn't be able to do it. It should be in such a way that it is deliberately moving towards letting certain roles be for lay people so that they can grow and influence the worship, even the youth and children should be given a role to play in worship." (LP12)

Influence the direction of the church

"And that the lay people must as much influence the direction of the church as those that are in leadership doing." (LP12)

Gift-based participation in ministry

"It just might be that the pastor might not have all these gifts or skills required himself. But he has some lay people that are good in those skills. Moses' father-in-law said to Moses, 'I hear that you are not resting? What is your problem? Moses said, 'I have so much on me." So, Moses' father-in-law said, 'You need to delegate!'[2] Pastors should find the ones that are gifted in certain areas. They then can be in the forefront of that particular section of the ministry." (LP14)

Participation in the direction of the church because it mainly affects them

"The role of the lay people in the church, I think, apart from listening, apart from preaching. There is also much of the lay people that can participate in the church, in decision making of the church growth, they have to take part, because sometimes, what is happening, management is coming up with something without consulting with the lay people. They just come and say we need to do this and that. Management might be advertising things by the management but not by the lay people." (LP15)

Summary

The fourth question asked the laity what should your role in church be? The role of the laith should be inclusive (not based on education and money) but on the gifts that God has the church in the form of gifted individual lay people (see "Inclusive Role" and "Gift based participation in ministry"). The ministry of the laity is both to build the church community (see "Build up the community of believers") as well as continue to reach out with the gospel (see "Witness Christ where we are" and "Win lost souls"). At the same time there is a recognition that the faith of lay people requires them to critically evaluate if the pastoral message is from the Word of God, there is a responsibility by the laity to guard their own faith and practice (see "Evaluate critically the pastor's sharing"). For others there is a recognition that the role of the laity is already well established and defined in the constitutions and faith of some denominations (like the CCAP) and that model frames their response to affirm the model

---

2   See Exodus 18:13-26.

and the division of responsibility (see "A good working model (from the CCAP)," "The actual well-established structure defining the role of the laity in the CCAP," "The laity running the church guided by the minster," "Full deliberate participation of all God's people with orientation to help those new," "Influence the direction of the church" and "Participation in the direction of the church because it mainly affects them").

Overall Satisfaction with the Role of Lay People in your Church

The 5th question asked was: "How satisfied are you with the overall role of lay people in your church?" There were five options to choose from "Very satisfied (1)" to "Not at all satisfied (5)," while "Satisfied (3)" was the positive middle ground, with two options above being satisfied: "Very satisfied (1)" and "More than satisfied (2)," and two options below satisfied: "Partially satisfied (4)" and "Not at all satisfied (5)." The aim of the question was assess the satisfaction level of the lay people with their role in their church.

Question 5 of the interview looked at satisfaction levels, out of 15: one was "more than satisfied (2)," five where "satisfied (3)" and nine were "partially satisfied (4)." The average satisfaction score $(2+(5x3)+(9x4)$ divided by 15) is: 3,53 which is below "Satisfied (3)." Statistically, it is half-way between "Partially satisfied (4)" and "Satisfied (3)."

Summary

Overall, there is definitely a need to improve the satisfaction level within the church.

Suggestions for the Improvement of Empowerment and Participation of Lay People

The 6th question asked was: "How can the church improve the empowerment and participation of lay people?" The aim of the question was to collect suggestions from lay people how to improve the empowerment and participation of lay people in the church.

Suggestions for the improvement of the empowerment and participation of lay people:

Intentionally inclusive and dedication-centred (not money centred)

"I feel like by being inclusive. And people should not be elected because how financially stable they are or how they give financial help to the church. They should look at dedication, ability of the person. We have people who have financial muscle and are dedicated. For them that is fine. But we have people who are dedicated but they don't have the financial ability. So, I think that the church can improve the participation of lay people by being inclusive." (LP1)

Introduce teaching seminars on relevant topics

"Introducing talks or seminars so that we can empower everyone with seminars on for example, financial management. Real interactive seminars not just preaching. We can have seminars on good relationship, ethics, a bit to equip each and every one with theological ideas so that everyone can understand better. I would say Jesus was mostly a teacher. He could preach but you would find that there were times when he could sit down and teach the people. Sunday is mostly preaching but call for seminars so people would come to learn." (LP1)

Improve the participation of those lay people who are not active: First, sit down with them and find out

"I think the church has to do something to improve the participation of lay people, because there are very few people who are active lay people in the church. The majority are not. So, like in my case, I was just supposed to have one position, and share the positions with other people, people are there but they don't have that passion to do something. But there are people who say: no. They will even say no

134

when you ask them to give just a short prayer. They will say: 'No, I can't pray.' Yes, there are people in the church who refuse to do anything in that role even to come and preach. You can delegate them, please, tomorrow for our *mulaga* prayer, you do the preaching. They will say, 'no.' And those ones are in the majority. Why are they refusing? So, if we could sit down with them to find out. If we know why we could be in a better position to know what to do. So that we empower them. Is it lack of knowledge? What is it?" (LP2)

Use existing grassroots courses from institutions like TEEM

"Encourage many courses from TEEM. That is very important, those laymen can do with proper courses, short courses, so that they understand at least the importance of whatever they are involved with. For instance, when I came here, I had no knowledge whatsoever, I thought if somebody is going to preach the Word of God, he has to be somebody who has dreamed up things and can be there to shout loudest and people will be able to hear him. But that is not the case, there is a way, a proper way of going about preaching, and you can only get it, assistance ... firstly, you want to preach and I am sure many people want to do it, but they lack the knowledge how to do it. So they can be assisted by these courses, I don't know how enthusiastic there are but immediately when I heard that there is a course here, I volunteered to attend even though I didn't know much about TEEM." (LP3)

Encouraging people to join discipleship and small groups

"Encourage people to participate in discipleship and engagement with Scripture in small groups." (LP4)

Publicly acknowledge with a gift those lay people serving already

"The church did a very good thing this year. I don't know if they regularly do it, but they just gave my wife a little gift just to acknowledge what she did in church. They wrote a note with a little card. That was about just simple recognizing it. I think this was disproportional powerful. It was much more powerful than being asked again and again from the announcements to do something in church." (LP5)

Leaders who listen, are humble, are accommodative and don't see disagreement as treason, then the voice of lay people is heard

"The pastor should be a good listener, because then he will be able to learn more from lay people. He should not take himself to be an 'all-knowing-person.' Because the 'all-knowing-person' is God himself. So, when you go to the people, you should not believe that everything that you are going to deliver is the most important thing and no one else has anything to say. Because they can also learn a lot from the lay people. And what they suggest, you must accommodate them. And they should not consider those who are vocal as enemies. But they should ask them, what do you mean when you are saying this?" (LP7)

Create an environment that allows for full participation of the laity

"For the church to improve you start from the Reverend itself. His thinking about lay people needs to change. Because the rules that have been put in place are prohibiting some of the lay people from taking part in the activities of the church. And if the rules have been changed, give room to other people to take part. But if not, then that cannot help. They need to start from the top, going down." (LP9)

For the CCAP: maintain that structure

"The structure is there, it is a very good structure, it is there and people participate. So the improvement could be: maintain that structure! You know, let the people do the work. And the ministers should be teaching elders and not ruling elders. They should look at the session and see a body of elders that are going to meet and make decisions together. And for them their role is simply to guide, or in this case to chair the session. But beyond that it should be the people who make the decisions, and I think that would help to empower people to participate better." (LP10)

Many lay people are knowledgeable about the Bible and Theology

"I think, I am not sure, but I would like to think that the church ministers might not be acutely aware that within their congregation are a lot of people who are very knowledgeable in terms of maybe the Bible, what the Bible says and so on and so forth. And sometimes they preach or institute things, you know almost as if they think people are ignorant. They don't know that they know. So, I think for them, it is better to have a more positive view of lay people and to be more accurate in their preaching." (LP10)

For the CCAP: Review the role of ministers to acknowledge lay leadership

"I think there is also need to review the role of the ministers. That the minister must be open to the lay leadership of the church who make decisions in running the church… And the lay leadership of the church, must also understand that they can or that they do have a final say, except in matters where their decisions are challenged by the teaching of the Word of God." (LP11)

For the CCAP: Stick with the good Presbyterian systems

"One is the orientation, right orientation on the good Presbyterian systems. So as I had said, we have agreed that what is designed on paper is actually good but with time it is losing its effect because the Reverends, the Moderators, are trying to get decisions made more, more and more by them than leave them up to the people, so if there could be that orientation and sticking with that good system. That would help." (LP12)

Offer inclusive opportunities for lay people to participate

"The other thing, I think it is opening up opportunities for people to take up different roles, whether it be on Sunday or the different activities, but also to have an attitude where there is no distinct preference. Because sometimes this is what the reaction is. That perhaps to be able to serve God, you must have certain something and this thing ... this emphasis on money and giving sometimes that could cripple someone. Because I want to serve but I don't have money, and it seems if you have money then you are doing it all." (LP12)

For the CCAP: Allow the Presbyterian system to operate the way it was designed

"The systems as they were originally designed they are very inclusive of the many people who are taking part in the decision-making or even the direction that the congregation is taking, okay, the challenge is the way it is being run now, the pastors, maybe for their own reasons, they have found ways of limiting participation. So if they can allow the systems to operate the way they were designed. I think more lay people will be involved within the church and they will be empowered." (LP13)

Minister to the spiritual life of lay people not just giving and tithing

"Lay people's participation should not be restricted to giving and tithing. I mean they can also participate in other areas, but the focus has tended to be giving, you go and approach people, and sometimes we even pressure leaders to approach people 'There is a fund raising,' we approach people they give but we are not ministering to people, their spiritual life. So, one area that they could be doing well is to take the time, to minister to them spiritually, their spiritual needs." (LP13)

Use the different abilities of the laity

"I think that the best way would be for the church to recognize the different abilities of people in the church and harness them to build a congregation that really is a fellowship-based congregation that takes into consideration the different abilities of people." (LP13)

A laity that is spiritually self-supported

"But also to build a church that is very vibrant, Christians who on their own can read the Word, study the Word, understand and apply it but now to a certain extent I think maybe even the teaching is not geared towards making the people to understand or even take an active role in the church." (LP13)

Organize deliberate training for lay people using outside expertise

"I think that nowadays, unlike in the past, nowadays we have so much that is on the table that even the church can deliberately organize training for the lay people within the church. For example, in our setup where they have selected the church elders, like in Zomba we have TEEM, Zomba Theological College, we need to utilize those institutions. Whereby you can organize a training, so that they are trained." (LP14)

Provide appropriate training for the lay people

"There should be a training for the lay people. There must be, there has to be something in place, in order to make the lay people, there has to be some sort of training which includes lay people as participants. By doing so, people will understand their role in the church and how to participate and what to do and what they is expected of them. Yes, that would it good. I think for somebody to be at that catechumen class for six months, then you can be baptized. But there should be follow-up training since spiritual growth as a human being is important." (LP15)

Summary

The final question asked "How can the church improve the empowerment and participation of lay people?" The practical suggestions collected here are reflections on how lay people could be empowered and participate more in the life of the church. The suggestions range from how to empower dormant lay people through meaningfully engaging them where they are (see "Improve the participation of those lay people who are not active: First, sit down with them and find out"), to publicly and meaningfully acknowledge those that already serve and thereby creating an incentive through public recognition of service (see "Publicly acknowledge with a gift those lay people serving already") to creating and intentionally inclusive environment where gifts, talents and abilities of lay people are encouraged to be used (see "Intentionally inclusive and dedication-centred (not money centred)," "Create an environment that allows for full participation of the laity," "Offer inclusive opportunities for lay people to participate" and "Use the different abilities of the laity.") An important part of empowerment is to focus on the spiritual development of laity through appropriate small groups so that individuals grow in maturity (see "Encouraging people to join discipleship and small groups" and "A laity that is spiritually self-supported"). Some ministers might re-think their attitude that treats lay people as spiritually active individuals who maintain a spiritual life independent of the pastoral ministry and yet are part of the church community (see "Leaders who listen, are humble, are accommodative and don't see disagreement as treason then the voice of lay people is heard," "Many lay people are knowledgeable about the Bible and Theology," "Minister to the spiritual life of lay people not just giving and tithing") in the way existing structural role of the CCAP should maintained as designed (see "For the CCAP: Maintain that Structure," "For the CCAP: Review the role of ministers to acknowledge lay leadership," "For the CCAP: Stick with the good Presbyterian systems" and "For the CCAP: Allow the Presbyterian system to operate the way it was designed").

Finally a good number of interviewees pointed to the need for further training (not just Sunday preaching) that will empower the laity to participate in an informed way in the life of the church (see "Introduce teaching seminars on relevant topics," "Use existing grassroots courses from institutions like TEEM," "Organize deliberate training for lay people using outside expertise" and "Provide appropriate training for the lay people").

Conclusion

Those interviewed have over years even centuries shown that their commitment to God and their commitment to the church (in some case even to the same denomination where they highlight shortcomings) and that reflects the importance of their voices being heard and incorporated into the discussion about the role of lay people. A significant obstacle for the empowerment of the laity in the Malawian church comes from the very clergy-centred view of ministry and the mediative role between the divine and human world role ascribed to the ordained ministry. Let me share my personal experience as someone who is not ordained. I was asked by an ordained friend some time ago, when I finally will be ordained so that the Holy Spirit can fully use me? There are significant theological issues with that question especially coming from a Presbyterian. But it shows that an underlying hindrance to the full participation of lay people in the church, namely, the belief that divine wisdom exclusively is with the ordained ministers and the Holy Spirit is only active in a limited capacity in the laity. I personally cannot imagine how such a view could be sustained or supported from the New Testament. This seems to be part of the background to some of the concerns raised by lay people of issues surrounding the negative experience with some ministers who deny the laity a distinct role.

One participant summarizes the overall picture about grassroots participation in the Malawian context poignantly, when she reflected about church life that she experienced in Scotland. "Every Sunday only the pastor was preaching. I asked myself, does that mean that no one else can preach? Such a scenario is nearly unheard in Malawi. The pastor needs also a break and also needs to hear what a grassroots preacher can share. In most churches in Malawi the ordained pastor give room to lay people to speak what God has put in their hearts" (LP2). One clear identifiable quality and strength of the Malawian church is that grassroots participation in the life of church is the norm. However, pastors (most of those that were reflected upon by the interviewees) do not explicitly elaborate or teach about the participation of the grassroots in church. This misses an important chance to further empower the grassroots by offering theological and biblical justification for the full participation in the life and ministry of the church. Furthermore, the church urgently and thoroughly needs to develop comprehensive and clear theological guidance on issues surrounding finances.

God's calling is God's choice how best to use his servants to build his kingdom, it is not an endorsement or rejection of the spirituality of one group over the other. "Most serious Christians have, I think, at some point considered the question should I get ordained or not?" (LP5). The majority of theological educators here in Malawi are members of the ordained clergy and their chosen path frames and references their own experiences of positively responding to being called by God into the pastoral ministry. However, there is an equal valid and important alternative path and that is recognizing that one is not called by God into the ordained ministry. But this does not mean that one is not called to participate in the mission of God, instead one is called is to serve in a different area and not exclusively within the church context. The grassroots experiences a call by God to a predominantly "secular" ministry within the context of also being called to participate in certain specific ministries within the church. Yet, the grassroots engagement within secular society and the workplace is the place of calling for the grassroots and thereby an extension of the ministry of the church. These days, during the Covid-19 crises, we should also ask ourselves if a Christian nurse or a Christian doctor are not equally important gospel witnesses for the church, the same is generally true for Christian teachers who can model the incarnate Christ to their pupils much more effectively than a minister can. One specific way to look at grassroots reflection is to recognize that the grassroots is the pool out of which every minister is not only chosen but in which he/she learns to participate in the activities of the church.

Throughout the research the "definition" of the laity or the grassroots includes everyone who is not an ordained minister. The definition is basically used to distinguish between the clergy and the laity. Importantly, however, this semantic distinction also hides a difference within the laity group, namely that some lay people are "lay church leaders" (elders, deacons, woman guild, etc.) while others are lay people without a distinct role or function or influence in the church. A widely used title for them is "ordinary Christians" which is also used here until a better and more accurate title can be found. There is more to the issue of the participation of lay leadership vs ordinary Christians in the Malawian context, as the saying goes "there are no poor elders in the church." The issue of elevating financial assistance to the church as a "criterion" for the selection (be it intentionally or unintentionally) of lay leadership is one factor that undermines wider lay participation. LP1 describes it as follow, "… we are all lay people, but our ability like, our financial ability, separates us. So the other ones are considered more lay that others." There is no question about the dedication of most of the lay church leaders, however, the concern is about being inclusive and "should look at dedication and ability of the person" (LP1). These "ordinary Christians" are potential huge untapped ministry sources for the church. LP1 describes it as follows, "the real local person is always left behind. They are only considered as the person coming to church, attending the service, going home. He is just in their books. I don't think he is valued that much by the church leadership. This lay leadership-ordinary Christian divide also informs, in at least some churches, who is allowed to preach in church or in other words who is allowed to spiritually contribute to the church. For the rest there the 'ordinary' roles, you are going to read the Bible, you are going to be like an MC for the service and pray" (LP9). The reality that LP9 further lamented was "these ordinary lay people could contribute to the growth of the church," but they are not asked. One of the reasons is potentially that for the church leadership, some Christians are "considered lazy" (LP5) because they don't involve themselves in the activities of the church. So, they are considered "second rate church members" (LP6). Because "church activities count for more" (LP5) This could be the result of a lack of consideration by the church leadership that secular work within "secular society is valued as part of the church's board ministry" (LP4). Additionally, the time commitment to the church is not a sign of the lack of the commitment of members, "some of them are riddled with so many responsibilities. Some of them are looking after orphans, something that they completely never expected to fall on them. But they have to do it, maybe because their brother passed on and they have taken hold of the family to be looking after them. And it calls for quite a lot. They have to see to it that the children also go to school. It's a role that God has given them. Their role is not only in the church. So, we must be very much mindful about these things" (LP6).

Part of the research design that informed the interview questions was to find out if any of the interviewees, when asked about what image they would use to describe the role of lay people in the church (question 5A) would mentions the image of the "priesthood of all believers," or mentioned the theological terminology (like "*missio Dei*" or any alternative expression that could point to an awareness of the ideas) that is used in the first part of this book to theologically anchor lay participation in the theology of the Old and New Testament. Within the Malawi church context (and the reflection of the contributors of this book) the idea of the priesthood of all believers is central to the reflection. In theory the Protestant Malawian churches should be strong on this image. If the idea of the "priesthood of all believers" (or alternative terminology) is mentioned in the interviews, that would indicate that the theological concept is expanded, used and understood among the grassroots. However, out of the 15 interviewees only one person (LP4) mentioned the "priesthood of all believers" idea. On further inquiry it turned out that the individual reads a lot of theological material. When 1 person out of 15 mentions the idea, this strongly suggests that the theological bases of the lay participation reflection is not part of the living theology of the church. It seems that this idea is not communicated in any meaningful way from the pulpits. In the same vein, I personally, do not remember hearing the issue mentioned in church even though the idea is central to Christian discipleship and ministry participation. I teach an OT grassroots course to the laity and in my experience when the idea is highlighted in the text for the first time in Exodus 19:6, people do not seem familiar with it. I do not experience that there is a conceptual recognition of the words or of the idea which should have happened if that central idea is communicated as part of the living theology of the church. This seems to be a key failure of the church to properly and theologically teach the full participation of all of God's people in ministry of the kingdom. This is missing in the lived theology of the people here in Malawi but actually worldwide too.

The laity does not seek to overthrow the system but looks for a meaningful partnership to be allowed and encouraged to play the role that God has given them, which is to work in a meaningful partnership with pastors to work towards the realization of the Kingdom of God on earth.

Chapter 9

Lay People and Caring for the Widows

Gertrude Aopesyaga Kapuma

Introduction

Lay leadership is key and plays an important role in the life and work of a congregation /church. Depending on the setup of the church, these could be elders who may include men, women, the youth, deacons and the women's guild. Lay leaders are the ones that know members of a particular congregation very well, including some who are their family relations. For a minister to know the area in which he/she operates and the challenges facing the people will depend on the information they get from the lay leadership. Lay leaders have the responsibility of visiting the members who are sick by cheering them and giving them hope. They do this in people's homes or when they are sick in hospital. When death occurs, they are the first people to be informed so that proper procedures can be followed with regard to funeral arrangements. They make sure that the minister is informed and if he/she lives far, arrangements can be made to allow the minister to come and conduct the funeral service.

Whilst doing this commendable service to the Christians, there are some areas that are not taken care of holistically because of a lack of proper training. The care of widows when they lose their husbands through death becomes a challenge and raises many questions. Widows experience quite a number of problems and need someone who can help them with some of the issues they encounter in their journey of widowhood. Many widows feel that the church is only present to conduct the funeral service and bury their husband. What happens thereafter seems not to be the concern of the church according to the widows themselves. When the funeral service is over at the grave, the church would say that; "The part of the church in

146

this funeral ends here." This may mean that what happens after is not the responsibility of the church. It brings different meanings, such as the idea that it is now over to the family and or the traditional chiefs to take over and do the cultural practices.

This chapter will look at some of the challenges faced by widows, which would be an opportunity for lay leaders when empowered to holistically understand their role of care so that they can help and stand with the widows in their plight and challenges. Lay people have an advantage, the fact that they live with the people and understand some of the traditional practices and customs in a particular area, make them to be unique. Through training and empowerment, the lay leaders will understand that their role is very important in helping and caring for members of the church who need them. By so doing the church will be able to reach out to people, help them grow and heal from many dimensions. A critical look at some of the issues faced by widows will be highlighted in order to help people understand the magnitude of the problem.

Widowhood Experiences

One experience that married women fear is the experience of becoming a widow. They fear because of what they see happening to some of their friends. "Losing one's partner is traumatic, but this trauma is compounded by the societal and cultural expectations of widows."[1] Widowhood experiences vary from one area to another. There are also many similarities with regard to the pain and challenges experienced by them. In the olden days, widowhood was associated with older people, but recently widowhood is across the board. There are young widows as well as older widows. With the spread of HIV and AIDS, widowhood has become even more common, many women are becoming widowed at a young age. Nkhoma and Kirwan further comment that; "Widowhood is not a situation experienced

[1]   Gertrude Kapuma, "A Story of Pain, a Need for Healing," in H.J. Hendriks, E. Mouton, L. Hansen and E. le Roux (eds), *Men in the Pulpit, Women in the Pew? Addressing Gender Inequality in Africa*, Stellenbosch: Sun Press, 2012, p. 61.

only by older women. There are many early marriages in Malawi and it is common to find widows in their early 40s with more than seven children and some grandchildren."[2] These young women will need someone to journey with them in their grief. To help them understand, come to terms with the loss and move on with life. Kapuma further comments that; "Despite the trauma suffered by widows and despite the fact that this status is becoming more common, widowhood remains an issue people are hesitant to speak about. Death and the dead are topics that are avoided and people are hesitant to address and confront traditional cultural practices.

> This hesitation is also present with higher institutions of theological learning. Ministers are not trained on how to support women who have lost their partners, nor are they shown how to confront cultural practices that discriminate against widows. On the contrary, ministers often do not even see what is wrong with such cultural practices.[3]

This, then shows that widows are not supported in their time of need and the church which is supposed to accompany them, plays no role in helping them to heal.

The widow is seen not to be in a position to make decisions on the arrangements of the whole funeral. Very few women will be asked for their decisions, but many decisions are made by the relatives of the deceased husband, together with male relatives of the widow. So many changes happen within a short period of time. Her title changes, she becomes "the widow." Nkhoma and Kirwan add that;

> The death of a husband brings about major changes in a woman's position in the extended family and in the wider society. Her husband's death does not automatically remove the widow from the family, but her position

---

[2] H.M. Nkhoma and M. Kirwan, "Social Change and Widowhood: The Experience of the Tonga People of Northern Malawi," *Religion in Malawi*, no. 7 (1997), p. 14.

[3] Gertrude A. Kapuma, "A Story of Pain, a Need for Healing," p. 61.

becomes the subject of discussion and decision-making by her late husband's relatives.[4]

Cultural Practices

Each family grouping/clan has their own traditional practices that they follow during and after the burial of their family member. In these practices, rituals/rites may be practised. In the case of the death of a husband, the person who has to go through the rituals is the widow. Rituals to be performed have meaning to the family, and it is expected that these have to be followed in order to respect the spirit of the departed. Rituals vary from one grouping to another. It can be a simple practice, but at times it can involve harmful ritual practices. All these are done at the expense of the widow.

Widowhood Cleansing

The practice of ritual cleansing is present in many traditional African societies. The practice is based on the belief that the person who is most affected by the death of a husband is the widow who is unclean. Rituals are performed after the death to cleanse or purify the affected person and in this case the widow. They do this in fear of the evil spirits that are regarded as agents of death, and if she is not cleansed by this ritual, the spirit of her deceased husband will haunt her. In this case a widow is regarded as being ritually unclean, because of her husband's death.

She goes through many hazardous experiences in order to appease the spirit of the departed husband. Even though Malawi as a country is trying to educate communities through their traditional Authorities about the dangers of practising such rituals, because of HIV and AIDS, some families continue to practise cleansing rituals secretly.

White et al clarify cleansing as follows:

> Cleansing literally means making clean what was dirtied and/or defiled. This implies that the death of her husband makes the widow dirty. This is

---

4   H.M. Nkhoma and M. Kirwan, "Social Change and Widowhood," p. 15.

disempowering in itself because a dirty person is looked upon with contempt in society. A widow then cannot be fully accepted as a woman in the society until she is 'cleansed.' The cleansing ritual is therefore directly linked to property dispossession because in her state, the widow is not expected to take part in important discussions including that involving property.[5]

Those who still follow this practice feel that mourning the deceased is complete when the wife performs the required rituals. Perry et al continues to explain that;

Among the Luo community of Kenya, according to tradition, after a woman's husband dies, she must engage in a sexual intercourse without a condom with a "cleanser" often a non-relative of the deceased husband, to remove the impurity she is believed to have acquired from the death of her husband.[6]

This practice is practised in some parts of Africa and leaves the widow in danger. In Malawi, this harmful ritual is what they call *kupita kufa or kuchotsa fumbi* (which means, taking away dust after death). In performing this ritual, the family and community believes that they are cleansed from the evil spirit that causes death. The family is protected from the calamities that could have happened after the death of the brother and now they are safe. Manala further asks the following; "The practice undoubtedly exposes all involved in the sexual cleansing act to the risk of HIV infection. Where is the compassion, respect, dignity and solidarity in such practices?"[7]

---

[5]   S.V. White, D.K Kamanga, T. Kachika, A.L. Chiweza and F. Gomile-Chidyaonga, *Dispossessing the Widow: Gender Based Violence in Malawi*, Blantyre: CLAIM-Kachere, 2002, p. 63.

[6]   B. Perry et al., "Widowhood cleansing and Inheritance among the Luo in Kenya: the Need for Additional Women Centred HIV Prevention Options," *Journal of the International AIDS Society*, No 17, Issue 1 (2014), p. 1.

[7]   M.J. Manala, "African Traditional Widowhood Rites and their Benefits and/or Detrimental Effects on Widows in a Context of African Christianity," *HTS Theological Studies*, vol. 71 no. 3, p. 7.

She does not just lose a husband, she loses her integrity, her identity, dignity and her property. She is seen as someone without a right to be heard. This may happen in a Christian family and the church, through the lay leaders may be aware of it and do nothing to protect her. The family and community reinforce this practice instead of protecting and respecting the widow.

If this is the understanding of *ubuntu* and is applied by members of the community, it means that the widow in this case can be protected by the community and will not allow harmful practices to be imposed on her. Manala further cites Emeritus Archbishop Desmond Tutu's words of wisdom, "when I dehumanize you, I inexorably dehumanize myself."

> According to this insight, it is unthinkable for people who take *ubuntu* as their point of departure to treat others in impolite, painful and dehumanizing ways as believed to be the case with African mourning rites practices.[8]

Part of the problem we are facing is globalization which has changed the mindset of Africans.

Widowhood Inheritance

Inheritance should be looked at from two perspectives. The first one where she is inherited together with the property by the in-laws and the second one where the widow is dispossessed of her inheritance by her in-laws, be it she is from matrilineal culture or patrilineal cultural practices. People have become greedy, such that they eye the property of their relatives, and when they die they are quick to grab it without considering the widow and the children.

This suggests that women are only honoured and respected by the in-laws when the husband is alive. When he dies anything can happen to her. The widow suffers after many years of working in the home and having acquired property together with her husband, then all is taken away and she is left with children without money to survive on.

---

8 M.J. Manala, "African Traditional Widowhood Rites," p. 7.

Moyo narrates an experience of a widow she interviewed who says; "My husband was a retail shop businessman...After his death his brother locked up the shop and he would not allow me to access money from it. After six months, I went to confront him. He told me that if I am interested in the benefits of the shop then I should cooperate with him. I said I was willing to work with him. He told me he would come to my house later on after closing the shop. He came and that is when I realized what he meant by cooperating with him. He allows me to have cash whenever I cooperate with him."[9] The woman is a victim after years of working together with her husband. She does not just lose a husband, she loses the property, she becomes a sexual object and is abused, in order for her to access the money she worked for alongside her deceased husband, the money that belongs to her.

Ownership of property in both cultural settings largely belongs to men. Since men have power and control, they are able to determine who gets what. Even in situations where the woman is a bread winner, the property is labelled male. The family does not even care to understand who was doing what in the family, and how they accumulated what they have. In so doing their interest is to distribute the property even if it means to distant relations. The absence of a will and ignorance of the law has left many widows with nothing in their possession. The church should know what happens to the widow after burial, to be able to follow up on how property was distributed and how she is settling and coping after the loss. There are other challenges that they need to explore. For example, issues of children and how she is managing them.

Issues of widowhood are of great concern because these women are members of not only the community, but the Church also. Anything concerning the members should not be taken lightly; they should be

---

[9]   Fulata L. Moyo, "A Quest for Women's Sexual Empowerment through Education in an HIV and AIDS Context: The Case of Kukonzekera Chinkhoswe Chachikhristu (KCC) among Amang'anja and Ayao Christians of T/A Mwambo in Rural Zomba, Malawi," PhD, University of Kwazulu-Natal, 2009, p. 155.

a concern of the church. "Christ loves his church and the church is called upon to listen with love to the many cries of people in and outside of the church."[10] The above experiences and stories of widows speak for themselves as to how much work has to be done to address them. There are issues of poverty, abuse of rights, ignorance of the law and gender-based violence that widows experience. These issues should be understood well by the church leadership so that proper care can be provided.

Poverty

Poverty is a serious concern among women in Malawi. Women become poor due to many reasons, such as being deprived of the basic necessities of life or disadvantaged because of their status. Those who are not able to obtain a minimal required standard of living may be seen to live in poverty. Many widows live in poverty after all their possessions are taken away by the in-laws. In Malawi the condition of poverty may be seen as lack of a productive means to attain basic needs of life such as food, water, shelter, health and education. The plight of widows is when they have no means to start a new life again. Everything may have been taken including land, which she could cultivate, and help her to get food. The land she may have cannot produce anything without applying fertilizers and manure.

The experiences of some widows will make them fall into this category of poverty not by choice but because of selfish in-laws who do not take into consideration her upkeep in the long term. Chebet and Cherop further comment that, "Gendered poverty and the right to human dignity have been recognized as the central challenge to the development of humanity. Poverty is a dehumanizing condition for everyone. It violates the human rights of the affected, whether

---

10 Gertrude A. Kapuma, "Gender Based Violence and the Church? Malawian Women speaking out," in E. Mouton, G. Kapuma, L. Hansen, and T. Togon (eds), *Living with Dignity: African Perspectives on Gender Equality*, Stellenbosch: Sun Press, 2015, p. 266.

women or men. Poverty subjects an individual to a state of powerlessness, hopelessness and a lack of self-esteem, confidence and integrity."[11] For those widows living in the rural areas where the land has become degraded, management of such will be difficult and this will lead to malnutrition and continuous illness. She may not even have proper shelter which will affect her living condition. In such cases poverty may include lack of clothing, lack of beddings so that they sleep in the cold and basic necessities like soap to wash and bathe to mention a few.

Human Rights and the Law of Malawi

Women are supposed to live with dignity as those created in the image of God. They are supposed to be treated as human being's that have rights. As much as we talk about "African culture," the culture is not static but dynamic. Things have to change with time. Women have to be recognized as people having their own rights to exist. Baloyi further comments that, "Cultural widowhood rituals clash with the rights of individuals involved in the act. Despite the widow's tears, many African women continue to instigate this practice even if it threatens someone's life. A culture that disregards one side of human individual rights but promotes the other, fails to acknowledge what it means for God to have created a human being as complete. It fails to recognize that human individual rights are essential steps towards reaching full development for women."[12]

It should be noted also that women would want to have a good quality of life and live happily even after the death of a husband. Their rights should not be violated and it should not be taken for granted

---

[11] D. Chebet and B. Cherop, "Gender and Poverty: Rereading Proverbs 31 in Pursuit of Social-economic Justice for Women in the Reformed Church of East Africa," in E. Mouton, G. Kapuma, L. Hansen, T. Togon (eds), *Living with Dignity: African Perspectives on Gender Equality*. Stellenbosch: Sun Press, 2015, p. 195.

[12] G.T. Baloyi, "When Culture Clashes with Individual Human Rights: A Practical Theological Reflection on the Dignity of Widows," *Verbum et Ecclesia*, vol. 38, No 1, (2017), p. 4.

that they will abide with the violation of these rights. Chitando further says, "Personhood in African cultures has been construed and constructed in a hierarchical manner, with men enjoying full and privileged status... Expunged of its patriarchal underpinnings, *ubuntu* can socialize boys and men to fight sexual and gender-based violence. Currently African men committing violence are not exuding *ubuntu* (particularly in its refined form). *Ubuntu* can empower men to realize and accept the full humanity of women."[13] When men are empowered to understand issues of oppression and dehumanization of women, they will be able to protect women and give them the dignity they deserve.

Malawi has signed many protocols on human rights and these are not supposed to be only written on papers. These are laws must be followed to protect the lives of innocent people, women included. The church should take this seriously to educate and empower lay leaders with knowledge of the Malawi law so that they are able to assist in times of need. The law says:

All human beings are born free and equal in dignity and rights:

- Both men and women are entitled, without any discrimination, to equal protection by the law.
- Everyone has the right to own property alone and/or in association with others.
- No one should be arbitrarily deprived of his property.
- Everyone has a right to a standard of living and a right to security in the event of ... widowhood.[14]

As a person a widow needs protection. The lay leaders can help in this to make sure that she is protected in all areas by being there for her. The Church as part of the community should make herself

---

13 E. Chitando, "Do not tell the person carrying you that s/he stinks": Reflection in Ubuntu and Masculinities in the Context of Sexual Gender-based Violence and HIV," in E. Mouton, G. Kapuma, L. Hansen, and T. Togon (eds), *Living with Dignity: African Perspectives on Gender Equality*, Stellenbosch: Sun Press, 2015, p. 276.

14 S.V. White et al, *Dispossessing the Widow*, pp. 31-32.

available to assist and journey with the widow. Nyangweso strongly says that,

> Although indigenous practices and attitudes are culturally legitimate and meaningful in social units which they are found, it is imperative that moral principles remain a fundamental responsibility of Africans. Recognizing that some of what is upheld, as culture is incompatible with the welfare of significant members of African communities, ought to be central to efforts to promote human rights in Africa. It is particularly important that the rights of women be centralized in the moral discourse of African virtues.[15]

Ignorance of the Law

The above incidents that women found themselves in, is a clear indication that they do not know the law. As a result of this ignorance they are taken for granted and deprived of the things that belong to them. Women can inherit property without other people interfering. But the cultural practices have made them believe that they have no rights to fight against the injustice done to them. The ignorance of the law is from the family to the institutions that help to distribute property. Because of grief and lack of support women keep quiet and accept whatever is done to them. White et al explain from the Malawian perspective that;

> Property dispossession takes many forms. These include grabbing, seizing, diverting or disposing of deceased property. Of these, property grabbing is the most widely used term and is sometimes used to entail all forms of property dispossession. There are however problems with the term "property grabbing" because it is incorrect term to use to define taking of property from widows. The term is androcentric because the act is perpetrated against women because they are women. It is a term for circumventing the act of theft since the grabbers take what does not belong to them against the property rights of the widow. The term also fails to describe the aspects of violence that occur when property is taken from the widow...The injury perpetrated against the widow

---

[15] M. Nyangweso, "Religion, Human Rights, and the African Widow," *Peace Human Rights Governance*, vol. 1, no. 3, (2017), p. 387.

transcend to physical injury and in some it is hidden because of socio-legal norms and the vulnerability of women.[16]

Such ignorance of the law, and what it means to an individual has made many widows lose what belongs to them. They have also not done anything about it because they do not know what to do and where to start from. In this case the presence and knowledge of the church in these laws can save the widow from being exploited by greedy in-laws.

Gender Based Violence

Violence targeted at women happens everywhere even in places like the home, where one would expect to get maximum security. It is a conduct intended to show the other person that those in control have power and can do anything. It is also intended to undermine a person's humanity, identity and dignity. It encompasses acts of physical as well as emotional abuse. The act of making widows go through difficult ritual practices and stripping them of their possessions is a violation of one's rights.

> Violence against women should indeed be viewed as a form of gender-based violence directed at women because of their gender. Violence, therefore, is an engine for the maintenance of unequal power relations between men and women in society…neither can it be limited only to the physical aspect. It extends beyond the physical to include emotional, psychological and sexual abuse.[17]

The ritual of widowhood cleansing and dispossession of property are acts of violence that affect the widow both physically, emotionally and psychologically. Zulu alludes to this by stating that;

> Despite the fact that this cultural practice applies to both men and women, it is in most instances the women who are subjected to it in practice. This is so because in most situations the woman would be dependent on her husband for her livelihood. One also sees that this gender-based prejudice

---

16 S.V. White et al, *Dispossessing the Widow*, p. 24.

17 S.V. White et al, *Dispossessing the Widow*, p. 24.

or treatment of women is linked with other culturally legitimized forms of discrimination - in some contexts, with a woman's inability to inherit from her husband, or a woman's inability to own land...Men would often use her fellow women to subject her to all sorts of practices in the name of culture.[18]

The problem at hand is that gender-based violence issues are there in the communities and there seems to be no one to address these. The fact that society is patriarchal in nature, and that power resides with men, men will not risk challenging their own privileges to favour women. Patriarchy will make sure that men are benefiting at the expense of women even if they don't deserve it.

Issues of violence should be at the heart of the church because it deals with humanity. There should be ways that can help restore the dignity of women so that they live a life that has meaning. Le Roux suggests that;

The challenge is thus to find a way of challenging culture and the cultural practices which empower men at the expense of women, and which enable and lead to VAW [Violence against Women], while at the same time not denying or denigrating the importance of culture.[19]

What this means is that culture that is oppressive and exploits people in this case women cannot be accepted. Nyangweso comments that;

The major moral concern with regard to widowhood rites is that they violate many basic principles contained in all key international human rights conventions. A culture that undermines one's health, freedom of

---

18 Zulu, "Masks and the Men behind them: Unmasking Culturally-sanctioned Gender Inequality," in E. Mouton, G. Kapuma, L. Hansen, and T. Togon (eds), *Living with Dignity: African Perspectives on Gender Equality*, Stellenbosch: Sun Press, 2015, p. 93.

19 E. le Roux, "'Telling Stories': Talking about VAW within Church and Seminary," in E. Mouton, G. Kapuma, L. Hansen, T. Togon (eds), *Living with Dignity: African Perspectives on Gender Equality*, Stellenbosch: Sun Press, 2015, 239.

choice and general welfare is a violation of the basic human rights and should be considered problematic.[20]

Culture is dynamic and there is a need to look at all the positive elements of culture that makes us who we are and get done with those practices that are inhuman and dangerous to women. The hope is in the church to bring back *ubuntu* to reality.

Christian Teaching and Prophetic Role

The Christian teaching is centred on love. That is to love one another and to be there for each other. These are the values that many Christians have, but one wonders why it is not shown in practice. Some of the teaching known to all Christian members in Malawi is: *Kulewa miyambo yonse yoyipa ndi zonse zotsutsana ndi mau a Mulungu* (To avoid all harmful cultural practices which are against the teaching of the Good News). If this is so, why is it that some members of the church are forced to go through harmful cultural practices when those in the forefront are also members of the Church? Are the rituals that widows go through not seen to be harmful? What widows experience is not from the outside. Those forcing the widow to be cleansed belong to the same church and can be in leadership, but will defend and say it is culture. Where is the boundary between cultural practices and Christian practices? Aren't people practising both at the expense of other people, who are seen to be vulnerable during their time of loss? The Church may have relaxed in its teachings giving chances to those that would want to maintain their harmful cultural practices.

The Church teaches also of the Ten Commandments that should be followed to keep the Christian values of how one should be living. How can this be justified when a widow is forced to have sexual intercourse with an in-law or a stranger and say she was being cleansed? Is that ritual more important to prevent bad calamities from happening to the deceased family, than the values that she may want

[20] M. Nyangweso, "Religion, Human Rights, and the African Widow," *Peace, Human Rights, Governance*, vol. 1 no. 3 (2017), p. 374.

to keep. In other words, the widow is forced to commit adultery by her in-laws. How are the Christian practices different from those of non-Christians? The Church is called to be present in the midst of people's situations. How can she continue with the prophetic role if there so much that is compromised?

The Bible is very clear in its teachings of love and caring for others. It is also very clear on how God cares for widows. If this is the case, what stops the church from sticking to its teachings other than following that which is not accepted. If through marriage a husband and wife become one flesh, it means that this union extends to the two families making them one family. If this is the understanding, then there is no reason the other family would want to harm a widow who is flesh of their deceased son. In this case one may start questioning the roots of our Christian faith if we have double standards like this.

Many people continue to become Christians because they want the church to be present when they die. They want their funeral to be a Christian funeral where the clergy will come in their attire and the women's guild will wear their uniform. The church is partly present at funerals, but the rest of the time decisions are left to the family members, which are unable to protect the decisions made by the member when she joined the church.

The Minister may come from a distant place and cannot stay to oversee all the procedures, but there are elders within the area who can stand for the church. The problem is that it is the very elders who are the custodians of cultural practices and would want to see that all the rituals are followed. The church is not strict enough on the use of harmful cultural practices. It does not bring the culprits forward for discipline, nor take a prophetic stand against that practice as such and or violation of other people's rights. There are several challenges that take place in her life within a short period of time, and these may continue for a longer period if not attended to. The community and the church take it for granted that she is going through her grieving period and handling it well, little do they know of the actual pain she

160

is going through at that time, and what will need attention. The shock of losing a beloved one and to begin a new life and the trauma that follows because of the traditional rituals that the widow will go through, is a challenge to the church today. The church's presence should be felt throughout her grieving period and should be giving her a helping hand.

The story of Mwangi from Kenya gives us an example of how she missed the presence of the church at a critical time of need. She says,

> I had lost my husband, my child and my dad and now I was sent away by the church. The recent experience made me reflect on the situation of widows even more, especially the humiliation they go through both in the church and society. You may think people sympathize with you till the end … I was left as a nobody in the church and in the society. It was not easy to cope with this.[21]

Mwangi is an ordained church minister but she suffered under the church's authority due to the fact that she was a woman. The church failed to journey with her at a critical time of her life, instead she was pushed away.

The Church is seen as unavailable, which makes the widow feel that they do not exist anymore. The church will go ahead to organize activities for different groups in the congregation but has never organized anything for widows. Instead they are asked to assist in those other activities and do many voluntary activities in the church because it is thought that they are available, they have nothing much to do at home. Oduyoye comments that,

> Women would agree that to be caring and helpful, to share with, provide for and minister to the needs of others is to be truly human. But to be made to do it, to be taken for granted when you do it is to be treated as less than…The lack of respect for women's feelings and perspectives

---

[21] M. Mwangi, "My Life Can be Meaningful," in E. Mombo and H. Joziasse (eds), *If you have no Voice just Sing: Narratives of Women's Lives and Theological Education at St. Paul's University*, Limuru: Zapf Chancery, 2011, p. 78.

should be seen by theologians as lack of recognition for women's humanity.[22]

Women are human beings created in the image of God and this has to be seen and emphasized by the church.

The Role of the Church

The church is the body of Christ called to care for God's people and to bring human dignity to all. People join the church for different reasons. The common reason is that people want the church to care for them when they are in need. The church is seen as a safe place where people can go to without being harmed or discriminated against. "We, as a faith community, can be the safe place that people are intuitively searching for."[23] Unfortunately the church has been too slow to offer such support. She has allowed culture to control the wellbeing of her members, making them suffer. Widows suffer because the church is far from them. As a place of safety, the church is called to holistically look at some of the cultural practices that widows go through and see how these can be changed. Those harmful practices that leave the widow a victim with no one to turn to for support. Shisanya agrees that the church has not been able to address some of the critical issues that affect its members and in this case widows. She comments that,

> The Church as a major liberating agent should show practical commitment to the oppressed and work for their fruitful future. In this regard, the Church needs to address itself to various issues that affect (Abaluhyia) women in the event of death.[24]

---

22 Mercy Amba Oduyoye, *Introducing African Women's Theology*, Sheffield: Sheffield Academic Press, 2001, p. 74.

23 P.R. Holmes and S.B. Williams, *Church as a Safe Place: A Handbook Confronting, Resolving and Minimizing Abuse in the Church*, Colorado Springs: Authentic, 2007, p. 13.

24 C.R.A. Shisanya, "Death Rituals" in M.R.A. Kanyoro and N.J. Njoroge. (eds), *Groaning in Faith: African Women in the Household of God*, Nairobi: Acton, 1996, p. 192.

This means that the church should empower lay leadership to assist and help those in need of care.

Widows live among Christians who see what is happening to them but have very little to offer or give support to a sister who is in need. As a result of this, widows live without hope, surrounded with people who are not caring. Kabonde poses a critical question to the church with regard the cries of widows in our communities. She says;

> How do we, as a church or circle, restore hope and intervene in the sufferings of other women today? What cries do we hear? We hear cries of women who are oppressed, exploited and totally helpless, unable to make ends meet because all their money, in the name of tradition or ritual, has been taken by the relatives of the deceased. We hear cries of mothers whose children have no hope for the future because the person who is responsible for supporting them is gone. Just as we would offer food and comfort to crying children, so, as Christians, we are bound to show and express our support and sympathy to all those in need.[25]

This poses a challenge to the Christian church that so much has been left unattended to and women have continued to suffer.

> It is the church's responsibility to liberate women from the unjust experiences they go through in the community. The church is a critically important agent in achieving a society in which women's equality and dignity is recognized. If the dignity and importance of women is not recognized, the plight of widows cannot be addressed. The church has to identify and side with women, not only in order to improve the situation of widows, but because it is their Christian duty to be in solidarity with those who are in pain.[26]

The call is that the church must be Christ like. To love and care for all people. Holme and Williams add, "What we are describing here is more than just a polite, smiley kind of love. Christ suggests that we

---

[25] M.P. Kabonde, "Widowhood in Zambia: The Effects of Ritual," in M.R.A. Kanyoro and N.J. Njoroge (eds), *Groaning in Faith: African Women in the Household of God*, Nairobi: Acton, 1996, p. 201.

[26] Gertrude Kapuma, "A Story of Pain, a Need for Healing," p. 69.

are all capable of loving one another as an act of human will, hence his command to love (Lk. 10:27)."[27]

The church has a responsibility to make herself available and listen to the stories that widows go through. It is through listening to these stories that the church can understand the plight of widows and be able to offer the needed help. To provide practical pastoral care that can help widows appreciate the presence of the church. Nwachuku suggests that:

> There are many issues in the present lives of African Christian widows that clearly call pastoral counselling as an essential service from the church. Properly organized counselling sessions are needed in which the widow is taught to appraise her new situation realistically and is equipped with new skills in order to avoid being disappointed by having undue expectations of the community members...The widow also needs help in acquiring strategies for handling grief without getting hopelessly broken. She needs strategies for handling loneliness and desertion, and techniques for decision-making in her new role of leadership for herself and the family.[28]

This means that the church should be in a position to provide mechanisms or especially skilled people who can help the widow in her healing process and empower her to handle the unfortunate and negative experiences of widowhood.

Women are created in the image of God and their issues should be handled with dignity because they are human beings. The Church can stand for widows and bring back the lost hope. This can be done by empowering the lay leaders with knowledge that will help them in their call of caring.

---

27 P.R. Holmes and S. B. Williams, *Church as a Safe Place*, p. 17.

28 D N. Nwachuku, "*The Christian Widow in African Culture*," in M.A. Oduyoye and M.R.A. Kanyoro (eds), *The Will to Arise: Women, Tradition, and the Church in Africa*, Maryknoll: Orbis, 1992, p. 70.

Recommendations

The church is called to give support to widows who are members of their church and community, this could be done by:

- Empowering the Women's Guild to understand the issues of widowhood and to be able to support the widow through pastoral visits. They should be encouraged to report back to the church any negative experiences the widow may be going through.
- Elders and Deacons should be helped to understand their role of leadership at times like this. To be encouraged to support the widow after burial, to understand the challenges she may be going through and be in a position to assist.
- The church should teach and encourage both male and female members about death and dying so that people are prepared when such a time arises.
- The theology should be able to address the realities and problems faced by widows. This could be achieved by including in the Theological training a curriculum that would address pastoral issues such as that of widowhood. Refresher courses could also be done to raise awareness of this burning issue and such should include lay leaders.

Conclusion

The church has the responsibility to liberate women from the unjust experiences they go through in the community. Its responsibility includes pastoral care for their members, that by extension includes widows, in order to restore their lost dignity. This should be done by empowering the lay leaders with counselling skills to effectively care for widows. Widows are women created in the image of God and their dignity has to be preserved.

Bibliography

Baloyi, G.T., "When Culture Clashes with Individual Human Rights: A Practical Theological Reflection on the Dignity of Widows,"

Verbum et Ecclesia, vol. 38 no. 1, 2017, pp. 1-5, (https://ver bumetecclesia.org.za/index.php/ve/article/view/1599/3105).

Chebet, D. and B. Cherop, "Gender and Poverty: Rereading Proverbs 31 in Pursuit of Social-economic Justice for Women in the Reformed Church of East Africa," in E. Mouton, G. Kapuma, L. Hansen, T. Togon (eds), *Living with Dignity: African Perspectives on Gender Equality*, Stellenbosch: Sun Press, 2015, pp. 193-218.

Chitando, E., "'Do not tell the person carrying you that s/he stinks': Reflection in *Ubuntu* and Masculinities in the Context of Sexual Gender-based Violence and HIV," in E. Mouton, G. Kapuma, L. Hansen, T. Togon (eds), *Living with Dignity: African Perspectives on Gender Equality*, Stellenbosch: Sun Press, 2015, pp. 269-283.

Holmes, P.R. and S.B. Williams, *Church as a Safe Place: A Handbook Confronting, Resolving and Minimizing Abuse in the Church*, Colorado Springs: Authentic, 2007.

Kabonde, M.P. "Widowhood in Zambia: The Effects of Ritual," in M.R.A. Kanyoro and N.J. Njoroge (eds), *Groaning in Faith: African Women in the Household of God*, Nairobi: Acton, 1996, pp. 195-203.

Kapuma, G.A. "A Story of Pain, a Need for Healing," in H.J. Hendriks, E. Mouton, L. Hansen and E. le Roux (eds), *Men in the Pulpit, Women in the Pew? Addressing Gender Inequality in Africa*, Stellenbosch: Sun Press, 2012, pp. 61-70.

Kapuma, G.A., "Gender Based Violence and the Church? Malawian Women Speaking Out," in E. Mouton, G. Kapuma, L. Hansen and T. Togon (eds), *Living with Dignity: African Perspectives on Gender Equality*, Stellenbosch: Sun Press, 2015, pp. 253-268.

le Roux, E. "'Telling Stories': Talking about VAW within Church and Seminary," in E. Mouton, G. Kapuma, L. Hansen, T. Togon (eds), *Living with Dignity: African Perspectives on Gender Equality*, Stellenbosch: Sun Press, 2015, pp. 235-252.

Manala, M.J., "African Traditional Widowhood Rites and their Benefits and/or Detrimental Effects on Widows in a Context of African Christianity," *HTS Theological Studies* 71 (3), 2015, Art. #2913, pp. 1-9.

Mwangi, M., "My Life Can be Meaningful," in E. Mombo and H. Joziasse (eds), *If you have no Voice just Sing: Narratives of Women's Lives and Theological Education at St. Paul's University*, Limuru: Zapf Chancery, 2011, pp. 77-79.

Moyo, Fulata L., "A Quest for Women's Sexual Empowerment through Education in an HIV and AIDS Context: The Case of Kukonzekera Chinkhoswe Chachikhristu (KCC) among Amang'anja and Ayao Christians of T/A Mwambo in Rural Zomba, Malawi," PhD, University of KwaZulu-Natal, 2009.

Nkhoma, H.M. and M. Kirwan, "Social Change and Widowhood: The Experience of the Tonga People of Northern Malawi," *Religion in Malawi*, no. 7 (1997), pp. 12-18.

Nwachuku, D.N., "The Christian Widow in African Culture," in M.A. Oduyoye and M.R.A. Kanyoro (eds), *The Will to Arise: Women, Tradition, and the Church in Africa*, Maryknoll: Orbis, 1992, pp. 54-73.

Nyangweso, M., "Religion, Human Rights, and the African Widow," *Peace Human Rights Governance*, vol. 1 no. 3 (2017), pp. 365-391.

Oduyoye, M.A., *Introducing African Women's Theology*, Sheffield: Sheffield Academic Press, 2001.

Oduyoye, M.A., "Transforming Power: Paradigms from the Novels of Buchi Emecheta," in N.J. Njoroge and M.W. Dube (eds), *Talitha cum! Theologies of African Women*, Pietermaritzburg: Cluster, 2001.

Perry, B. et al., "Widowhood cleansing and inheritance among the Luo in Kenya: the need for additional women-centred HIV prevention options," *Journal of the International AIDS Society*, vol. 17, no. 1:19010 (2014),; p. 1-7. (https://onlinelibrary.wiley.com /doi/10.7448 /IAS.17.1.19010).

Shisanya, C.R.A., "Death Rituals," in M.R.A. Kanyoro and N.J. Njoroge (eds), *Groaning in Faith: African Women in the Household of God*, Nairobi: Acton, 1996, pp. 186-194.

White, S.V., D.K. Kamanga, T. Kachika, A.L. Chiweza, and F. Gomile-Chidyaonga, *Dispossessing the Widow: Gender Based Violence in Malawi,* Blantyre: CLAIM-Kachere, 2002.

Zulu, E., "Masks and the Men behind them: Unmasking Culturally-Sanctioned Gender Inequality," in E. Mouton, G. Kapuma, L. Hansen and T. Togon (eds), *Living with Dignity: African Perspectives on Gender Equality,* Stellenbosch: Sun Press, 2015, pp. 81-95.

Chapter 10

The Fragmentation of Theological Education and its Effect on the Church, Grassroots Theological Education in Malawi and TEE

Volker Glissmann

Introduction

The context of theological education in Malawi is predominantly church-owned institutions who operate under the assumption that they mostly train ministers.[1] There are also two Theological and Religious Study Departments at the University of Malawi and Mzuzu University. I will not be undertaking to establish how many theological Colleges/Schools operate within Malawi, but it is fair to say that beside the well-established institutions, there are a huge number of small denominational, independent or mission-funded institutions that offer a variety of imported (accredited or not-accredited) courses or their own formal as well as non-formal theological/biblical education programmes. The fragmentation of theological education is not limited to the well-established institutions that offer formal theological education, but it also affects smaller institutions and even the non-formal theological education.[2] The reason is that among graduates of formal theological education here in Malawi, there is a (perceived) standard theological curriculum

---

[1]   Though over the last number of years there has been an increase in non-ministerial (fee paying) students in theological institutions, this has thus far not yet led to a theological rethinking of the training paradigm.

[2]   A clarification: I do not subscribe to the linguistic fragmentation of theological education into Christian education and theological education. For me this is a sign of fragmentation whereby the ability to engage and inform between these silos is lost.

and content, a way of delivering theological education that influenced both established as well as the smaller theological educational institutions. Surprisingly, this also affects grassroots theological education, though it operates under less academic accreditation requirements. Much has been written about how the fragmentation of theological education affects theological institutions and its current learners as well as its graduates.

However, in this chapter the focus is on how fragmentation affects both the laity and the church, as well as ministerial and grassroots theological education here in Malawi.[3] Finally, a model of integration, namely the founding of Theological Education by Extension (TEE) in Guatemala in 1967 will be discussed in order to show a positive example of the integration of theological education.[4]

An Illustration/a Parable/a Story

A story like the following is often shared by way of assessing how successful the church is in training future ministers. The story is told of a village, somewhere in Africa, that had sent their pastor to the city to study theology. They villagers had desired to know more about God and wanted their pastor to be better prepared so he could the help the church grow spiritually stronger. Initially, the pastor only studied theology in the nearest city, but when the opportunity arose he was offered a scholarship to study his theological PhD in America. The local church was very pleased and proud of their pastor and looked forward to the time when he would return to empower them.

---

[3] For the distinction between academic theological education, ministerial theological education and grassroots theological education, see Volker Glissmann, "Grassroots Theological Education," *InSights Journal for Global Theological Education*, vol. 5, no. 1, 2019, pp. 53-67.

[4] Within our Malawian context, TEEM, which stands for Theological Education by Extension in Malawi is widely known especially for its accredited programmes through the Board for Theological Studies/University of Malawi. However, this chapter highlights a different form of TEE which is like TEEM's grassroots training programmes here in Malawi.

Many years later he finally returned, now as a graduate with a Doctorate in theology. The local church was delighted to receive him back and after celebrating his return they took him to a child in their community that suffered for many years from a mysterious illness that prevented the child from speaking properly. Upon seeing this child our pastor exclaimed, "No, no, you got it all wrong. I am not that kind of Doctor. I studied theology not medicine. You need to take the child to the Health Centre." Astonished the church members replied, "But the child is not physical handicapped, the child is possessed Pastor! After your ten years of study, surely you will be able to drive out that demon! You studied so much, you must be very spiritually strong. Pray and deliver the child!" The whole community shouted, "Amen!" Nervously, the pastor looked around and said, "But this is not what I studied." The church members looked at him confused and puzzled. And inquired, "but you studied theology? – the knowledge of God and his ways, didn't you?" "Yes, I did," he replied." I achieved a *distinction* in my Bachelor in Theology, a *distinction* in my Master in Theology and even finished a PhD in New Testament Studies in *one of the best theological universities in the world*," said the pastor with some satisfaction. "Great," replied the church members, "Then, drive out the evil spirit, now that you have prepared yourself in the best university in the world and studied under spiritual giants." To this the pastor replied impatiently, "But this is *not* what I studied, I studied Bultmann and Moltmann and did a PhD on the economy of the Trinity." "So, you say that you can't help us?" inquired the church members confused. Without a word, the pastor turned around and slowly walked away, leaving the village behind.[5] He mumbled to himself while leaving, "I even tried to return. How

---

5   For a similar parable see John Mbiti, "Theological Impotence and the Universality of the Church," in Gerald H. Anderson and Thomas F. Stransky (eds), *Mission Trends No 3: Third World Theologies*, Grand Rapids: Eerdmans, 1976. Similarly, see also Perry Shaw, "'New Treasures with the Old': Addressing Culture and Gender Imperialism in Higher Level Theological Education," in Allan Harkness (ed), *Tending the Seedbeds: Educational Perspectives on Theological Education in Asia*, Quezon City: Asia Theological Association, 2010, pp. 47-74.

many of my colleagues are still in the city or never returned from studying abroad ..."

The Fragmentation of Theological Education

Though this story is made up, many of us recognize the essential truth that ensured that the narrative, in one form or another, is repeatedly retold in different contexts. The sad tale above ends with a disillusioned pastor as well as a disillusioned congregation, neither of the two is able to fulfil its missional role within the economy of God. The education that the pastor in the parable received unfortunately did not empower him to be a good minister of the local congregation. Ministerial theological education surely has one main and overarching aim: to train ministers to serve congregations effectively. But this was not the case here. This story highlights that something is not aligned between the pastoral and spiritual needs of the community of God's people, and the kind of theological education that theological institutions offer. In the story, the pastor is ill-equipped (through the theological education that he received as it did not nurture his initial pastoral skills), he is ill-equipped to pastorally care for the needs of the people, he is ill-equipped to understand and respond to these needs to teach and guide the congregation, he is unable to provide leadership in the situation. The story illustrates a fundamental misalignment between the needs of the grassroots church and skills that the pastor learned at a tertiary level theological education. In the story, the pastor walks away from the situation but in a real-life situation the pastor would stay and minister even though he/she unfortunately lacks the essential skills. This is a not-satisfying situation either for the pastor or the grassroots church. Yet, realistically, a pastor who studied to degree level would probably seek a more prestigious city job, even a secular job, rather than live in the village again. Once pastors were trained in the city or overseas, few wanted to become village pastors.

One solution to the misalignment highlighted above could be to dismiss tertiary level theological education entirely. Yet, higher theological education has surely helped the church in its reflection and has produced outstanding contributions to the wellbeing of the church and our understanding of God. Secondly, deep theological thinking (which is nurtured in higher theological education) is, by its very nature, worship of God and should be part of the church's theology of worship through learning. The problem above manifests itself to the people as a problem of misalignment, however, within theological education the issue is not simply misalignment of purpose, but the fragmentation of theological education.[6] Theological educators use fragmentation to describe an underlying course for the misalignment of purpose. Fragmentation also refers to the breaking into fragments and the partial shattering of an initially united content. This fragmentation also implies an essential loss of usefulness of theological education. Yet, the call for the renewal of theological education and the need to overcome the fragmentation is an issue that has been raised for many years. The way forward is for the church, in its twin expression of clergy and grassroots, to engage with its theological training institutions, thus determining what kind of theological education is required for the current time and for each of the two target groups of theological education.

In doing so, the question also needs to be asked whether in all circumstances of theological education: higher theological degrees are the only way forward or, if theological training institutions, are also required to provide both for clergy and the grassroots, the access to vocational skill-based training as well as training which is based on non-formal education (like gaining an expertise in preaching through supervised practice and feedback, rather than through written academic essays or through Sunday-School Teacher Training). This

---

6   Max L. Stackhouse describes the fragmentation as misalignment of focus of theological education; he writes about theological education that, "it is beset by a rather vague discomfort, a sense that what we and others do is really not so bad, but that it also does not have an overwhelming and fully compelling focus." Max L. Stackhouse, *Apologia: Contextualization, Globalization and Mission in Theological Education*, Grand Rapids: Eerdmans, 1988, p. 15.

would encompass everything that can be summarized as "Life-Long Learning." It is often claimed that higher and higher degrees are necessary for an effective urban ministry, though the issue would benefit from further reflection.[7] The danger is that it is too exclusively focused on academic qualifications for ministerial candidates, thereby limiting the choices that the Holy Spirit is allowed to bring forth for the selection of ministerial candidates.

The objectives of academic/higher theological education and the objectives of ministerial theological education are not the same.[8] A shift from ministerial theological training to an exclusively academic training can actually hinder effective ministry (yet, the opposite can also be true, that the lack of any form of theological education significantly hinders the pastoral ministry). The above example illustrates the imbalance that can occur in theological education well, where one stream (subject area) of theological education is more consistently developed while other subject areas remain underdeveloped. The same imbalance can occur when theological knowledge is not consistently integrated into the main professional objective in ministerial theological education. Traditional academic theological education emphasizes the four historical disciples (biblical theology, systematic theology, historical theology and practical theology).[9] Thirty years ago Hough and Cobb already highlighted the

---

[7] A PhD in theology is not automatically a hinderance to being a good minister in a congregational setting. I would be very interested to see how important ministers with degrees are for the grassroots church. My initial feeling would be that the church values spirituality more than degrees. But degrees per se are not eliminating factors for exquisite theologically-sound and vibrant spirituality. The question should be how do degrees help in fostering this kind of spirituality?

[8] See Volker Glissmann, "Grassroots Theological Education," pp. 55-57 also, Victor Babajide Cole, "Toward Integration in the Theological School Curriculum," *Evangelical Review of Theology*, vol. 23 no. 2, April 1999, pp. 141-162.

[9] Though of course the theological educational landscape in Malawi is still highly influenced by three of the four historical disciplines: biblical theology, systematic theology and historical theology as they predominantly formed the first theological curriculum at the University of Malawi and the adjunct Board for Theological

problem of theological education as, "theological education is torn between academic norms, defined chiefly as excellence in the historical disciplines, and modern professional norms defined in terms of excellence in performing the functions church leaders are expected to perform."[10] The underlying question partially is whether or not the role of the minister is an academic role or a vocational role. Again, Hough and Cobb are helpful in providing a real important historical corrective to such a binary choice. The same question was actually present when the first modern research university in Berlin opened in 1810. Friedrich Schleiermacher was tasked to justifying the inclusion of theology as one of the distinct subjects in the new-found university. Schleiermacher argued for the inclusion of theology based on a distinct and recognizable methodology but also that pastoral ministry is the overarching unifier. In that regard, Schleiermacher argued, theology is like law, medicine, architecture or engineering. All three disciplines are integrated subjects that rely not only on contemporary academic research as well as practical-vocational skills and expertise. All of them clearly belong into Higher Education.[11] Farley reminds us that Schleiermacher actually made the point that theology is a "positive science," as opposed to an exclusive scholarly

---

Studies. The non-emphasis of practical theology (with the common exception of ethics) in the theological curriculum is indeed a significant shortfall of the curriculum that was explicitly designed to empower ministers of the church (see Board for Theological Studies, *Diploma in Theology*, p. 3, where the emphasis of the Diploma in Theology is highlighted as "expressly designed to meet the needs of those who are in training for the ministry of the Church in Malawi").

10 Joseph C. Hough, Jr. and John B. Cobb, Jr., "Christian Identity and Theological Education," Chico: Scholars Press, 1985, pp. 16-17. It is important to note that the Hough/Cobb book is the result of a major evaluation of theological education within the ATS (American Theological Association). The evaluation itself was the second major evaluation within the ATS in the second part of the 20th century. The first was conducted in 1955-56 by Richard Niebuhr et al.

11 Here is it of course noteworthy for theological education that both law and medicine have a practical focus while at the same time not every doctor and lawyer is believed to be an academic in the way that sometimes the argument is made that all pastors are theologians.

enterprise that looks at Christianity as a religion but is detached and looks at it from the outside. Theology is a "positive science" because the focus is on a particular social community and their concerns and leadership needs.[12] From the mid-nineteenth century onwards the four-fold division of theology (as a science) were: biblical theology, dogmatics or systematic theology, historical theology (Church History) and practical theology.[13] This change also brought a fragmentation in the relationship and responsibility of the church towards theological education as it was now administered from within a theological training institute.[14] This then lead to a crises in theological education as universities do not view personal, spiritual and moral formation of the trainee pastors as their responsibility.

In the beginning of the history of the church, theological education was done mainly through apprenticeships, where trainee ministers learned as apprentices under an experienced minister. The emphasis was on practical and ministerial skills as well as the formation of the individual through prayer and Bible reading. Later, especially in the middle ages an additional form of theological training emerged: Monastic and Cathedral schools. Where trainees lived, studied, prayed and served together in a community. These schools of theological learning were designed to expose the learners to more systematic learning, especially in relation to the classical texts of the church fathers. A significant change happened in theological

---

[12] Edward Farley, *Theologia: The Fragmentation and Unity of Theological Education*, Eugene: Wipf and Stock, 2001, p. 103.

[13] Farley, *Theologia*, p. 10.

[14] Ester Mombo makes the important point that though the theological lecturers in government universities are theologically astute and are theologically able to address contextual issues, nevertheless, these lecturers do not hold a position within the hierarchy of the church. She also makes the point that in her observation some denominational Colleges, which are closely aligned with their respective churches can sometimes suppress innovative contextual theological engagements. See Ester Mombo, "Theological Education in Africa," in Andrew C. Wheeler (ed), *Voices from Africa: Transforming Mission in a Context of Marginalization - An Anthology*, London: Church House, 2002, pp. 127-133 [128-129].

education with the rise of the universities, especially the scientific research universities. Friedrich Schleiermacher wanted to ensure the continued relevance of theology in an increasingly modern (enlightened) society that emphasised the rigorous methods of scientific enquiry. Scientific enquiry builds upon scientific, repeatable observations, inquiries and methodologies. The new proposed emphasis of theology was to produce new knowledge and not to apply new knowledge to concrete contexts. It was a quest for knowledge creation for the sake of advancing human knowledge. All of this, Friedrich Schleiermacher applied to the study to an unseen God and to theology. Schleiermacher succeeded in convincing the authorities to include theology as a subject in the newly founded universities.

The consequences of studying theology in the university setting had far reaching consequences still felt today: the division of the four-fold curriculum into four distinct areas of biblical, historical, philosophical, ministerial/practical studies as separate, individual disciplines with different methodologies, approaches and terminology. However, Schleiermacher ultimately envisioned that the field of practical theology would "relate the scholarship of the other theological disciplines to the work of clergy and congregation."[15] This is the classical shape of most curricula. This division is often explained through the agricultural image of silos. Silos are storage units in which farmers store foods crops in order to keep the crop pure and not contaminated by other crops. The changes introduced by Schleiermacher also resulted in a shift to the professional clericalization of the ministry as well as the raise of critical methodologies in the reading of the Biblical text. It also separated (to differing degrees) the theological inquiry and training from the affairs and concerns of the church. Character and Moral formation were replaced with the enlightenment notion that cognitive knowledge will

15 Richard Osmer, *Practical Theology: An Introduction*, Grand Rapids: Eerdmans, 2008, p. 234. See especially the chapter: "Epilogue: Teaching Practical Theology in Schools of Theology."

automatically lead to individuals becoming more cultured who then will promote the welfare of society at large.

Yet, early on – and as a result of the tension of theology being defined as a science and not as a religion or a professional vocation, – the academic paradigm increased the fragmentation of theological knowledge, by removing a unifying purpose and centre that could hold differing objectives together. Other aspects also contributed to the fragmentation, namely the decontextualization of theological education in its removal from the church setting, and in Africa especially, from the cultural setting. Within the context of the establishment of theology as part of the first modern research university, the understanding was that theology serves a clearly defined purpose, namely the preparation of ministers for congregational service.[16] The "science" approach to theological learning also resulted in the specialization of theological teachers which lead to a specialization into distinct and often unrelated academic sub-fields of study. This then accelerated the fragmentation and a loss of the unifying centre of theological education. It is not uncommon that even in related fields in one discipline like the Old Testament and New Testament courses in Biblical Studies, they are taught nearly without reference to each other. The underlying assumption is that *somehow* a graduating student who has studied fragmented theology and who has very limited positive examples of purposeful theological integration will somehow be able to integrate multiple theological fragments of learning into one consistent whole.[17] This of course is not the norm. It is then perhaps not

---

[16] The American seminaries are highly influenced by the Berlin model as faculty members from institutions like Andover and Princeton studied in Berlin and introduced this model of theological training back home (see also Farley, *Theologia*, p. 10).

[17] See also Shaw who makes the same point, when he says, "in the traditional approach to theological education, students are trained through a relatively fragmented curriculum, the assumption being that it is the students' responsibility to bring the pieces together once they graduate." (Perry Shaw, *Transforming*

surprising that theological education is not always seen as essential for the wellbeing of the church.

The call for the renewal of theological education has been repeatedly voiced for over 100 years, both for the Western context as well as for the mission context.[18] Numerous credible suggestions concerning the renewal of theological education as well as suggestions for partially or fully overcoming the fragmentation by identifying *the* unifying centre and purpose of theological education.[19] Farley et al. have voiced the following concerns about the fragmentation of theological education: divisions into specialized sub-fields, thus losing the ability to engage across disciplines in the quest for theological knowledge;

Theological Education, Carlisle: Langham Global Library, 2014, p. 4). Unfortunately, only quite gifted students are evidently able to do this well.

[18] See Christine Lienemann-Perrin, *Training for a Relevant Ministry: A Study of the Work of the Theological Education Fund*, Madras: The Christian Literature Society, 1981, pp. 4-5 who highlights the need to re-align theological education to the discussions at the 1910 World Mission Conference in Edinburgh. See also Robert W. Ferris, *Renewal in Theological Education*, Wheaton: Billy Graham Centre, 1990, especially pp. 7-20. Ferris highlights a call for renewal that arose out of the 1938 International Missionary Council's conference in Tambaram, Madras, India, which stated, "Almost all the younger churches are dissatisfied with the present system of training for the ministry and with its results. In many reports received from different parts of the world, it is stated that there are ministers of a poor standard of education, who are unable to win the respect of the laity and to lead the churches, that some are out of touch with the realities of life and the needs of their people, and are not distinguished by zeal for Christian service in the community." The International Missionary Council Report, pp. 188-189 cited in Robert W. Ferris, *Renewal in Theological Education*, p. 7.

[19] See the works of Edward Farley, *Theologia* (1983, reprinted in 2001), Robert Banks, *Reenvisioning Theological Education* (1999), Bernhard Ott, *Beyond Fragmentation* (2001), Linda Cannell, *Theological Education Matters* (2006), Ross Kinsler, *Diversified Theological Education* (2008), David Kelsey, *Between Athens and Berlin* (2011), Perry Shaw, *Transforming Theological Education* (2014). As well the two *Handbooks on Theological Education in World Christianity* (eds Dietrich Werner, David Esterline, Namsoon Kang, Joshva Raja, 2010) and the *Handbook of Theological Education in Africa* (eds Isabel Apawo Phiri and Dietrich Werner, 2014), which take stock of where we are in theological education in the beginning of the 21st century.

the growing dissonance between ministerial preparation and an emphasis on the intellectual and philosophical skills of higher education (the academic paradigm seems to be one consistence throughout this – but is it helpful?); the replacing of personal (spiritual and moral) formation with critical methodologies due to the pressure of attaining academic excellence. Further, limiting our understanding of theological education to the accredited intellectual education attained through a degree or diploma programme exacerbates the fragmentation. An emphasis on clergy education while ignoring the essential training needs of the grassroots church.[20] The fragmentation is often not addressed as theological educators see themselves primarily as theologians rather than teachers and educators whose emphasis is on ensuring that adequate learning takes place. Finally, the fraying of the relationship between the church and its theological training institutes and the resulting overreliance on tuition-fee paying students coupled with the diversification of non-theological degrees offered by theological institutions.[21] All of these elements contribute to the fragmentation of theological education not being adequately addressed in our context.

The continuation and acceleration of fragmentation is predominantly driven by the recognized custodians of theological learning: the

---

[20] Dieumeme Noëlliste in "Toward a Theology of Theological Education" makes the same point that the focus of theological education is on the people (*laos*) of God. However, "this emphasis on the people as the target of theological education does not make redundant the singling out of a smaller group within the wider body of the *laos* for special attention." See Dieumeme Noëlliste, "Toward a Theology of Theological Education," *Evangelical Review of Theology*, vol. 19, no. 3, July 1995, pp. 307-313 [309-311].

[21] The introduction of non-theological degrees in theological schools is not necessarily negative, it could help students relate faith and theology to other fields of study and get a wider perspective. Yet, this kind of integration needs to be done intentionally. However, if the purpose is to subsidize the theological school by diversifying income, then this will fail. A much better way to deal with fragmentation and cost is often to amalgamate colleges and work together.

theological colleges.[22] Therefore, the discussion about overcoming the fragmentation starts with the delivery of theological education through theological trainings institutions. And of course, the conversation needs to be owned ultimately by all stakeholders of the theological enterprise which includes the church. The church but not only as the institutional church through its leadership but also the grassroots church as a key recipient of graduates of theological education. Theological education has a tendency to emphasize abstract, theoretical and philosophical-theological arguments over quantitative and qualitative scientific research which is in its essence is repeatable and which tests hypotheses to see how applicable they are. Theological education is fundamentally an educational enterprise that is informed by theological thinking. The foundation of theological education is pedagogical while its purpose is theological. An interesting as well as illuminating empirical research was carried out a few years ago in India. Jaison Thomas researched the ideal "graduate profile" or in other words the priorities of characteristics that people look for in a minster.[23] He then asked three groups: church leaders, theological educators and students who had just joined a theological College. These three groups of people were asked to arrange certain theological educational objectives in order of their priority. These priorities are roughly grouped as Academic Formation, Spiritual Formation and Ministry Formation. Here is a summary of the finding:

The Students consistently prioritized Ministerial Formation (Inspiring Preacher, Successful in Church Growth and Evangelism, and Skills in interpersonal relationships), while Leaders of the Theological Institutions prioritised Academic Formation (Theologi-

---

[22] The term Theological Colleges encompasses here all institutions that offer formal and non-formal theological education using residential or decentralized forms of theological education.

[23] Jaison Thomas, "Church Ministry Formation in Protestant Theological Education: The Contemporary Debate in Kerala, India," PhD, Queen's University of Belfast, 2008, p. 190.

181

Characteristics of an 'Ideal Minister' Listed according to Priorities for Graduates by Church Leaders, Seminary Leaders and Students.

Church Leadership's Priorities for Graduates		Seminary Leadership's Priorities for Graduates		Priorities of Students	
Person of Prayer (1)	Spiritual Formation	Theological Knowledge (1)	Academic Formation	Inspiring Preacher (1)	Ministry Formation
Character (2)	Spiritual Formation	Administrative Ability (2)	Academic Formation	Successful in Church Growth and Evangelism (2)	Ministry Formation
Role Model (3)	n/a	Leadership (3)	Academic Formation	Skill in Interpersonal Relationships (3)	Ministry Formation
Successful in Church Growth and Evangelism (4)	Ministry Formation	Skill in Interpersonal Relationships (4)	Ministry Formation	Theological Knowledge (4)	Academic Formation

Loving Concern for People (5)	Spiritual Formation	Inspiring Preacher (5)	Ministry Formation	Leadership (5)	Academic Formation
Inspiring Preacher (6)	Ministry Formation	Successful in Church Growth and Evangelism (6)	Ministry Formation	Role Model (6)	n/a
Skill in Inter-personal Relationships (7)	Ministry Formation	Character (7)	Spiritual Formation	Administrative Ability (7)	Academic Formation
Leadership (8)	Academic Formation	Person of Prayer (8)	Spiritual Formation	Character (8)	Spiritual Formation
Administrative ability (9)	Academic Formation	Role Model (9)	n/a	Person of Prayer (9)	Spiritual Formation
Theological Knowledge (10)	Academic Formation	Loving Concern for People (10)	Spiritual Formation	Loving Concern for People (10)	Spiritual Formation

cal Knowledge, Administrative Ability and Leadership Skills) and church leaders prioritized Spiritual Formation (Person of Prayer, Character, Role Model). Jacob's research basically confirms the anecdotal evidence of the first story I told, namely, a huge gap exists between the priorities that students (and by extension the local church) values, compared to those of church leaders and leaders of academic institutions. All of this points to the fragmentation of priorities exist between the church members, church leaders and theological institutions.[1] All of this exemplifies that significant fragmentation exists.

Effects of Fragmentation on the Church and Grassroots Theological Education

Theological Educators have summarized the fragmentation into three interrelated issues,

> First ... the meaning of theology has been distorted – that the unifying principle in theological education has been lost. The second issue ... the seminary's curriculum, without adequate definition of the nature and purpose of theology, devolves into a collection of specialized subjects. The third issue derives from specialization: a fragmented curriculum, organized generally into theory and practice divisions, leads to a distorted understanding of that which theological education addresses.[2]

And I would like to add a fourth one which develops from the previous three, namely, fragmentation of ministry. Or in other words the professionalization of ministry (of which clericalism is one prominent expression) which is too often understood as implying that church ministry is the exclusive domain of the professionally

---

[1] It would be very interesting to repeat this research here in Malawi in order to establish to what level the same differences in priorities exist (as someone working in grassroots theological training, I would suspect that Malawi will not be different from India).

[2] See Linda Cannell, *Theological Education Matters*, p. 36. See also Banks, *Reenvisioning Theological Education*.

trained minister.[3] Good ministerial theological education addresses the question of the self-identification of the minster in relation to ministry and in relation to the empowerment of the congregations for independent spirituality and ministry.[4] This is the essence of the educational enterprise, to achieve the independence of the learner. This purpose of the theological enterprise sets Christianity apart from some of the African Traditional Religions in which the "priests" are the only and exclusive custodian of secret divine knowledge and power. This leads to pastors clinging to power and knowledge, with less desire to share what they have learned. Post-Pentecost Christianity enshrines this democratized theological vision to demand the full participation of God's people both of access to the divine as well as to source of divine power. This is one of the reasons for its extraordinary appeal and success in Malawi.

Schleiermacher had envisioned that the three disciplines of biblical, historical and philosophical theology would thoroughly and critically investigate, while practical (or ministerial) theology would assemble and reunite theology into a unit which is used within the church. However, this did not happen. Practical Theology did not become the unifying force, rather it followed the lead of the three other disciplines to critically engage. Institutions affiliated to the University of Malawi through the Board for Theological Studies, offer Diplomas

---

[3] The other element of clericalization is the minister as gate keeper to the empowerment of his/her congregation, as Jey J. Kanagaraj poignantly puts, "The pastor's leadership style, the quality of his interpersonal relationships, and his professional competence are critical factors in enhancing or blocking the empowerment of lay involvement in the church's ministry." See Jey J. Kanagaraj, "The Involvement of the Laity in the Ministry of the Church," *Evangelical Review of Theology*, vol. 21 no. 4, October 1997, pp. 326-331 [329].

[4] Is the minister primarily the leader of the church? The shepherd leading his (stupid) sheep? the teaching elder? Or could the pastor be a priest of priests, the washer of feet (the servant), the one who steps into the river carrying the ark, the trainer of trainers, the father leading his children to maturity? (adopted and expanded from Dorothy McRae-McMahon, "The Formation of the Laos" in John Pobee (ed), *Towards Viable Theological Education*, Geneva: WCC, 1997, pp. 109-119).

in Theology mainly in the complete absence of Practical Theology. Perry Shaw rightly highlighted a strange theological practice, where institutions expect students themselves to reassemble their fragmented theological learning once they have graduated. It is a non-starter to expect students to unify their theological learning by themselves if they have not been taught at the Theological Institution. The same difficulty exists in the transfer from general to particular, from one culture to another culture, from theory to practice and even from one language to another language, including from English into one of the Malawian vernaculars.[5]

The loss of the clearly defined unifying centre of theological education may result in individual subjects lacking a clearly stated purpose, part from transfer.[6] Additionally, the presentation of theological knowledge as an academic abstract or theoretical discipline results in a fragmentation of theoretical and applied practical and spiritual knowledge. The lack of a curriculum-wide integration results in the compartmentalization of theological knowledge which then results in compartmentalized application of theological knowledge. Therefore, Theological knowledge is detached from wisdom and the ability to live wisely and in harmony with the community. This can be seen in the difficulty that preachers

---

[5] In 2014 TEEM, as part of a promotion of grassroots church-based theological education, spoke to around 400, and one repeated appreciation of TEEM's vernacular course books by the theologically (Diploma/Bachelor) trained pastors was that it gave a vernacular expression of theology.

[6] Recently, the TEEM Academic Staff met to discuss plans for a contextual preaching course. One of the findings was that our staff observed that preaching in the churches mostly does not connect the Old Testament to the New Testament which means that the relation between the two testaments is not clear and also that the Messianic fulfilment of Old Testament prophecies are not explicitly made to the grassroots. This is a significant sign of the fragmentation of the theological curriculum as the Old Testament courses are not connected to courses on the Gospels and the Later New Testament Writings as well as Christology from Systematic Theology is not integrated into a theological practice like preaching of theological graduates.

who are asked to preach about an Old Testament passage or even a gospel passage have, where they only provide a moral reading of the text rather than a theological reading of the text. Theological knowledge is often about contemporary academic in-house theological discussion rather than driven by the need of the grassroots church, for example, every female minister who visited my office looked at TEEM's grassroots marriage course. Why is this? Because, it is an important ministry subject that is not thoroughly discussed in most theological curricula in Malawi. Furthermore, in the absence of a contextual curriculum, theological graduates will not have been empowered to address contextual challenges in a meaningful and biblical/theologically informed manner. It must be said, that it is actually impossible to expect contextual issues to be addressed if they have not been thoroughly discussed during the theological studies.[7] Even historical theological studies prefer to address theological issues that have been discussed for hundreds of years, where a vast amount of literatures exist and where the theological (perhaps denominational) position is settled.

One area in which the impact of the fragmentation is highly visible is in lay training or grassroots theological education. The overall impact on the church is nearly equivalent to the impact on grassroots theological education, this is because the contextual needs of an audience are rarely explicitly reflected in theological education. Grassroots Theological Education is ultimately done (either in denominational offices or in para church organizations) through graduates of local theological institutions. The questions and concerns that drive contemporary academic or higher-level theological education are not the questions that usually concern the

---

[7] It would be wise in that regard, to move towards a greater use of dialogue education (even better a flipped classroom approach) to engage theological students more thoroughly while at the same time including plenty of practical case studies, open-ended stories, and simulations to promote discussion and application of theological principles. These work much better than purely theoretical discussions.

grassroots in their day to day spirituality. This includes the day-to-day reading of the biblical text where a significant gap exists in reading the text between the usually untrained and uninformed grassroots and theologically trained ministers. This observation cannot be underestimated as it shows that biblical literacy is not a skill that has been transferred to the grassroots church. Theologically, spiritually and pastorally there cannot be a justification that the grassroots do not have ownership and the level of biblical literacy to read their own holy text in a unified theological way.

The fragmentation of the unity of theory and practice as well as fragmentation between theology and discipleship/spirituality results in a miscommunication between what the minister perceives as the grassroots challenges (it is unfortunately misleading to assume that because a minster many years ago was part of the grassroots, that the minister is today able to understand, in its entirety, the grassroots). A high percentage of evangelical sermons are within the sphere of philosophical-spiritual monologue discourses (or alternatively a moral discourse about a threatening God) this seems to be the direct result both of discipline fragmentation whereby biblical passages are not looked at with the additional aim to produce a sermon – the gap is between exegesis and sermon (this is also the result too often of academic either actual or perceived standards which should inform academic theology).

The fragmentation of the audience of theological education in a training emphasis on ministerial theological education results in a significant under-investment in grassroots theological education as the majority emphasis in theological education is on ministerial theological education. Ministerial theological education is important, but so is grassroots theological education for the wellbeing of the church. The way forward would be to include grassroots theological education as an integrated subject in the ministerial theological curriculum. The grassroots are a key recipient of pastoral ministry, therefore the concerns, challenges and worldviews, as well as the spiritual growth of the grassroots is essential in fulfilling the pastoral ministry

Integration, Please!

The answer to the persistence of fragmentation lies in the consistent and planned integration of the different streams of theological education into one constituent unity. If theological education is fragmented, then it seems logical to deduct that the individual subjects are fragmented as well and thereby deprived of their full contribution to the whole. The unity of ministerial theological education (in contrast to fragmentation) should balance academic excellence with spiritual (personal, moral) formation to equip students for appropriate ministry. Academic excellence also applies to grassroots theological education though it has to take an appropriate grassroots friendly form but it should not exclude appropriate insights arising from academic theological studies. An integrated grassroots curriculum on biblical studies would then integrate: biblical content with appropriate and selective hermeneutical (or Bible study) tools in order to empower the grassroots to theologically and meaningfully read the text on their own. The development of expertise and comprehension skills is a learning objective therefore, the hermeneutical exercises should be repeated and practised continuously. At the same time the course should be consciously and painstakingly related to the context which is the wider story of God's people in the two-testament Scripture along an appropriate theologically-sound theme (purpose). Additionally, open questions that focus on personal and discipleship application are included. Preferably, especially within grassroots theological education, the context is addressed through communal dialogue education (or in other words: TEE) and not through monologues.[8] An integrated ministerial curriculum on biblical studies would be twofold: a replication of the grassroots curriculum as

---

8   See Volker Glissmann, 'Grassroots Theological Education, pp. 60-61.

described above followed by special set of questions and tasks that are centred around the four main areas of ministerial formation (preaching, teaching, pastoral care and leadership). Other subject or topics areas might seek the integration along slightly different lines.[9]

Fragmentation affects the whole curriculum as well as the design purpose behind the curriculum, therefore, there cannot be a simple "we will change one thing" or the "add one course" approach but the integration between the purpose of the institution and the purpose of the curriculum both in its theological approach, content and overarching purpose, as well as a pedagogical integration that is aimed at assisting in developing deep comprehension. A *theological integration* is needed that centres theological learning around a valid and theological justifiable central outcome (like "preparing God's people to participate in the mission of God"). Additionally, a *pedagogical (or educational) integration* is needed that designs theological content and theological curricula in a deliberate integrative way as to actively link ideas together, concepts and models that in the life of the church exist in a pedagogical union (including a theory-practice integration). The pedagogical integration also asks the pedagogical question of how to effectively integrate content delivery that aids best contextual learning practice; as well as a *theological purpose (or audience) integration* which asks the questions if the training is directly or are trainers of trainers trained (training the church, training the grassroots, training academic theologians or training leaders of the church or training for a specific ministry). Finally, a *grassroots theological education integration* which recognizes that the empowerment and understanding (cultural exegesis) of the grassroots is integral to theological educational enterprise (either directly or indirectly).

---

[9] For the innovative integrated curriculum of the Arab Baptist Theological Seminary (ABTS), see Perry Shaw, *Transforming Theological Education*, pp. 8-9.

Fragmentation of Theological Education and Theological Education by Extension (TEE)

What strikes me as a TEE practitioner and someone interested in the renewal of theological education, is the similarity between the identified issues resulting in fragmentation and the underlying reasons that led to a development of TEE as a theological renewal movement.[10] TEE developed through a process of developments and adjustments that culminated in its start in 1963. The process involved conceptual, theological and pedagogical adjustments to address a local training challenge that faced one small Guatemalan Protestant denomination. TEE's founding vision has a lot to do with both equipping God's people for mission,[11] as well as the ministry by the people[12] overall, the idea was the decentralized extension of seminary education to those unable to attend full-time residential studies.[13] TEE was not founded to be a method of grassroots theological education but rather initially focussed on ministerial theological education but, due to the need to train pastors without sufficient secondary schooling, the TEE Guatemala experiment taught immediately at a variety of academic levels in order to empower the

---

[10] For an introduction to TEE, see also Volker Glissmann, "What is Theological Education by Extension (TEE)?" in *The Theological Educator*, 28.11.2014, under www:thetheologicaleducator.net/2014/11/28/what-is-theological-education-by-extension; or Volker Glissmann, "The Role of Community in Theological Education by Extension (TEE)" in *The Theological Educator*, 10.4.2015, under www.thetheologicaleducator.net/2015/04/10/the-role-of-community-in-theological-education-by-extension-tee.

[11] "Equipping God's People for Mission." This is the title of the 1982 volume of *International Review of Mission*, vol. 71, no. 282 (pp. 129-253) April 1982 which features numerous reflections about TEE.

[12] "Ministry by the People" is a landmark documentation about global developments within TEE. See Ross Kinsler (ed), *Ministry by the People: Theological Education by Extension*, Maryknoll: Orbis, 1983.

[13] The journal that initially was founded bears witness to the extension idea as it was called, "Extension Seminary."

pastors which the church felt were called to the ministry but did not finish primary or secondary school education. The Evangelical Presbyterian Church in Guatemala in the 1960s observed that their Theological College did not produce pastors that stayed in the ministry.[14] Over a period of a few years, the Seminary was moved first from the capital to a city closer to where most of the church was located. Then it moved by extension to seminaries even closer to the rural pastors as they should be trained on-the-job as this pedagogically improves the integration of theory and practice. The students were given reading material but then it was discovered that it was essential there was discussion on their reading and their comprehension of the material while trying to apply it to the ministry. This was the process of re-conceptualizing for a local context what theological education could look like.

That TEE is often, nearly exclusively in some contexts, used for grassroots theological education is an affirmation of the need for providing appropriate levels of theological engagement for the grassroots. Numerically it seems inevitable that once theological education is extended geographically and is available in the vicinity, that the grassroots church members want to fully participate in theological learning. The TEE focus was on increasing access: geographical, economic, cultural, ecclesiastical, gender, race, class, pedagogical and spiritual access.[15] This is built on a vision of a theological educated church community whereby access to theological education is provided. Another emphasis has been on on-

---

14 A 1962 inventory disclosed that after 25 years, only 10 of the more than 200 students who had enrolled in the Seminary were still functioning as pastors. Once accustomed to urban life, many students of rural background did not return to the agriculturally rich but unhealthy and economically depressed areas from which they had come.

15 This is how Ross Kinsler summarizes the extension of access, see Ross Kinsler, "Preface," in Ross Kinsler (ed), *Diversified Theological Education: Equipping All God's People*, Pasadena: William Carey International University Press, 2008, pp. 7-14 [8-9].

the-job training rather than pre-job training and the shifting of content delivery from the classroom to home-study thereby freeing the class time for a communal dialogical pedagogy. Home-study then enables learners to come prepared to class, including time for reflection on the learning content. Human beings are social communicating beings in our essence and a communal dialogue-based learning experience suits us, but is also the essential ministry medium. These two elements of TEE are self-study material and the TEE group discussion, nowadays (outside of TEE) this approach is rediscovered and called: flipped learning or flipped classroom.[16] The flipped classroom approach uses self-study material for content delivery and then replaces the classroom with tutorials.[17] Tutorials are usually small, less formal interactive discussion-based groups to deepen and apply course content. The flipped classroom approach is also practised within residential institutions and it is there to help especially the learners with comprehension as well as the integration of seemingly unrelated abstract proposition into a unified learning experience. Or in other words: tutorial-based theological education (which also abbreviates as TEE!). This was the process of theological and pedagogical re-conceptualization for a local context on what theological education could look like.

TEE is an interesting case study, partly because it offers a valuable blueprint that integration of theological learning is not just a utopian

---

[16] One of my best classes as an undergraduate was a course on Contemporary Theologians at Union Theological College in Belfast because of the intensity of engagement with the material. Only three students signed up for the course, but Professor Williamson did not cancel, instead he proposed that he give us the readings beforehand and then we will meet in his office for a discussion about what we read during the week. The students were supposed to argue the same case that a famous theologian made and Professor Williamson would argue against it.

[17] For an introduction, see https://elearningindustry.com/blended-learning-vs-flipped-learning-can-tell-difference. See also Perry Shaw, *Transforming Theological Education*, pp. 196-197.

vision but– if desired – can be done.[18] Alternative models of theological education are available. Theological education does not need to exclusively rely on a standardized form of higher education whereby most content is orally delivered through a field expert which is then tested for recollection through a standard written test.[19] Theological Education should open access to the training of the grassroots church as an integral part of the theological vision. TEE practitioners very early on sought pedagogical advice on how to improve the delivery of their education which is important as theological education can only strive if it is utilizing sound pedagogical methodologies as well as sound theological paradigms. Theological Education exists in a variety of contextual forms and all of them – jointly – are at the disposal of theological educators but of course not every method is suitable for each context.

Conclusion

The fragmentation of theological education is not just an issue affecting the preparation of clergy but actually an issue that affects the whole church. Outside of Malawi, there is a discussion going on about how to overcome the fragmentation and integrate the theological education into a consistent theological, pedagogical and contextual approach. Too often the discussion is solemnly focused

---

[18] Other important blueprints can be found in the curriculum changes done in the Arab Baptist Theological Seminary (ABTS) in Lebanon as explained in Perry Shaw's book *Transforming Theological Education*. Not surprisingly, there is overlap between the two approaches, though they are not the same. ABTS also stresses the need for reflection in community through discussion (or dialogue) in relation to ministry reflection.

[19] A surprising consistency among the fragmentation is the singularity of the schooling method for theological education. For a criticism see, Allan Harkness, "De-Schooling the Seminary: An Appropriate Paradigm for Effective Pastoral Formation," in Allan Harkness (ed), *Tending the Seedbeds: Educational Perspectives on Theological Education in Asia*, Quezon City: Asia Theological Association, 2010, pp. 103-128.

on clergy education or on theological education in the abstract. What needs to be considered is to address and litigate the effects of theological education on both the grassroots and on grassroots theological education. One of the visions of theological education has to be the learned church and that can only be done if the concerns, challenges and worldview of the grassroots church play a significant role in theological education. The origin of TEE speaks of a renewal movement that is conceptually tried to seek a conceptual, theological and pedagogical approach and trying to seek a greater integration of theological learning. Overall, many things could be overcome through an integrated theological curriculum or an interdisciplinary approach driven by the contextual needs of theology graduates who serve the grassroots church.[20]

Acknowledgements

I would like to thank Patricia J. Harrison for her useful comments on an earlier version of this chapter.

Bibliography

Banks, Robert, *Reenvisioning Theological Education: Exploring a Missional Alternative to Current Models*, Grand Rapids: Eerdmans, 1999.

Board for Theological Studies, *Diploma in Theology*, Zomba: Kachere, 2007.

Cannell, Linda, Theological Education Matters: Leadership Education for the Church, Newburgh: EDCOT Press, 2006.

Cole, Victor Babajide, "Toward Integration in the Theological School Curriculum," in *Evangelical Review of Theology*, vol. 23 no. 2, April 1999, pp. 141-162.

---

[44] See Richard Osmer, "Toward a Transversal Model of Interdisciplinary Thinking in Practical Theology," in F. LeRon Shults (ed), *The Evolution of Rationality: Interdisciplinary Essays in Honor of J. Wentzel van Huyssteen,* Grand Rapids: Eerdmans, 2006, p. 328.

Farley, Edward, *Theologia: The Fragmentation and Unity of Theological Education*, Eugene: Wipf and Stock, 2001.

Ferris, Robert W., *Renewal in Theological Education*, Wheaton: Billy Graham Centre, 1990.

Glissmann, Volker, "What is Theological Education by Extension (TEE)?" *The Theological Educator*, 28.11.2014, under www: http://thetheologicaleducator.net/2014/11/28/what-is-theologi cal-education-by-extension.

Glissmann, Volker, "The Role of Community in Theological Education by Extension (TEE)." *The Theological Educator*, 10.4.2015, under www.thetheologicaleducator.net/2015/04/10/the-role-of-community-in-theological-education-by-extension-tee.

Glissmann, Volker, "Grassroots Theological Education," *InSights Journal for Global Theological Education*, vol. 5 no. 1, 2019, pp. 53-67.

Harkness, Allan, "De-Schooling the Seminary: An Appropriate Paradigm for Effective Pastoral Formation" in Allan Harkness (ed), *Tending the Seedbeds: Educational Perspectives on Theological Education in Asia*, Quezon City: Asia Theological Association, 2010, pp. 103-128.

Hough, Joseph C., Jr. and John B. Cobb, Jr., *Christian Identity and Theological Education*, Chico: Scholars Press, 1985.

Kanagaraj, Jey J., "The Involvement of the Laity in the Ministry of the Church," *Evangelical Review of Theology*, vol. 21, no. 4, Oct. 1997, pp. 326-331.

Kinsler, Ross (ed), *Ministry by the People: Theological Education by Extension*, Maryknoll: Orbis, 1983.

Kinsler, Ross, *Diversified Theological Education: Equipping All God's People*, Pasadena: William Carey International University Press, 2008.

Kelsey, David, *Between Athens and Berlin*, Eugene: Wipf and Stock, 2011.

Lienemann-Perrin, Christine, *Training for a Relevant Ministry: A Study of the Work of the Theological Education Fund,* Madras: The Christian Literature Society (in Association with The Programme on Theological Education of The World Council of Churches), 1981.

Mbiti, John. "Theological Impotence and the Universality of the Church," in Gerald H. Anderson and Thomas F. Stransky (eds), *Mission Trends No 3: Third World Theologies,* Grand Rapids: Eerdmans, 1976.

McRae-McMahon, Dorothy, "The Formation of the Laos," in John Pobee (ed), *Towards Viable Theological Education,* Geneva: WCC Publications, 1997, pp. 109-119.

Mombo, Ester, "Theological Education in Africa," in Andrew C. Wheeler (ed), *Voices from Africa: Transforming Mission in a Context of Marginalization - An Anthology,* London: Church House, 2002, pp. 127-133.

Noëlliste, Dieumeme, "Toward a Theology of Theological Education," *Evangelical Review of Theology,* vol. 19, no. 3, July 1995, pp. 307-313.

Osmer, Richard, "Toward a Transversal Model of Interdisciplinary Thinking in Practical Theology," in F. LeRon Shults (ed), *The Evolution of Rationality: Interdisciplinary Essays in Honor of J. Wentzel van Huyssteen,* Grand Rapids: Eerdmans, 2006, pp. 327-345.

Osmer, Richard, *Practical Theology: An Introduction,* Grand Rapids: Eerdmans, 2008.

Ott, Bernhard, *Beyond Fragmentation: Integrating Mission and Theological Education,* Carlisle: Regnum, 2001.

Phiri, Isabel and Dietrich Werner (eds), *Handbook of Theological Education in Africa,* Oxford: Regnum, 2013.

Shaw, Perry, "'New Treasures with the Old': Addressing Culture and Gender Imperialism in Higher Level Theological Education," in Allan Harkness (ed), *Tending the Seedbeds: Educational Perspectives on Theological Education in Asia,* Quezon City: Asia Theological Association, 2010, pp. 47-74.

Shaw, Perry, *Transforming Theological Education: A Practical Handbook for Integrative Learning*, Carlisle: Langham Global Library, 2014.

Stackhouse, Max, *Apologia: Contextualization, Globalization and Mission in Theological Education*, Grand Rapids: Eerdmans, 1988.

Thomas, Jaison, "Church Ministry Formation in Protestant Theological Education: The Contemporary Debate in Kerala, India," PhD, Queen's University of Belfast, 2008.

Werner, Dietrich, David Esterline, Namsoon Kang and Joshva Raja (eds), *Handbook of Theological Education in World Christianity*, Oxford: Regnum, 2010.

Chapter 11

Lay Empowerment and Mission for the Malawian Church

Watson Rajaratnam

Introduction

My first mission trip to Africa in 2010 opened my eyes to the fact that Africa is an untapped gold mine for World Missions. One of the greatest resources in Africa is human resource. Thus, I arrived at the conclusion that Africa including Malawi, has potential and all the necessary human resources for world missions. If Malawi continues to depend only on missionaries from the West or Latin America or Asia, it can never be turned from being a mission field into a mission force. Malawi does have gifted preachers and teachers of the Word. It has not only missionary candidates who are ready to go and serve as missionaries in other parts of the world, but also has enough mission-minded laity who are ready to pray, send and support them. Further, Malawian churches have enough financial resources to equip and send their missionaries to serve among the unreached people groups. From my personal interactions with Malawian churches I have come to the conclusion that the Malawian laity are willing to give generously and support their missionaries. But church leaders have failed to realize their potential and understand their responsibility of empowering their laity in order to tap their resources positively for World missions. Thus, many of the Malawian churches have failed to progress in their mission of partnering with God in bringing the Gospel to the unreached groups of people in Africa and in other parts of the world.

An introductory observation and interaction with churches and church leaders in Malawi, will help us to come to the conclusion that churches here roughly fall into six categories. The first category of churches are the "struggling churches" which are fighting for their survival. They are neither able to attract new members nor able to keep their old members, thereby constantly losing members to other denominations. They are just surviving because they still have some so called "'faithful old members" who are just keeping the church activities going on. But with the passing of their older generations they may slowly become extinct or continue to survive with very few members. The second category of churches are the "sleeping churches" which have very little appetite for spiritual growth. They are surviving because of their attractive programmes and activities but with very little interest in church growth, outreach, evangelism or mission. "It is simply an empty shell of a consumeristic, self-satisfied cultural Christianity, gathered in a respectable Sunday ritual called "Church."[1] The third category of churches are the "stagnant churches" which are clergy centred. They are interested only in liturgical worship and rituals, and they neglect the ministry of transforming the laity into disciples and co-labourers in God's vineyard, the church. The fourth category consists of "self-centred churches" which are busy with a variety of activities to cater to the multi-faceted needs of their own growing congregations. They are glaringly distracted from their core mission of seeking the lost but only keen to serve the needs of their own members. Serving the needs of their own congregation members includes resolving deep conflicts in the wake of strife and divisions within the church. In the midst of their "fire-fighting" they lose sight of the mission of seeking the lost for the Kingdom of God. The fifth category of churches are the "seemingly spiritual churches" which focus more on prosperity doctrines, signs and wonders. They use all kinds of secular marketing methods to draw the crowds and motivate them to be successful in their lives. Members in such churches are discipled by the world instead of by the "Word." They attract also the poor and needy and

---

[1] Edmund Chan and Tan Lian Seng, *Discipleship Missions*, Singapore: Covenant Evangelical Free Church, 2016, p. 40.

those who are keen to become materially successful and prosperous. The last category of churches are the "spiritual churches" which are awakened by the clarion call to disciple their congregations and to bring the gospel to the lost and the least, the reached and the unreached.

It is really sad to discover that "struggling churches," "sleeping churches," "stagnant churches," "self-centred churches," and "seemingly spiritual churches" are in the majority in Malawi. They seem to be satisfied with maintaining their status quo without focusing on discipleship and seriously involving their members in evangelism to bring more souls into the church. But the "seemingly spiritual churches" which appear to be experiencing spiritual renewal are very keen only to have more members. But such churches merely focus on their quantitative growth, neglecting the key ministry of discipling their members or their laity. What I mean is that their DNA is not "discipleship and disciple making." The main cause of this negligence is, pastors and leaders who lead such churches have failed to understand the need to turn their lay members into disciples of Jesus Christ. Pastor and founder of Sarang Presbyterian church in South Korea, Dr John H. Oak, while talking about the revival and spiritual renewal among churches says that churches while focusing on the quantitative growth, sacrifice or neglect spirituality and qualitative growth of their members. "By contrast, the Scripture reveals that revival consists of both aspects of quantity and quality. There cannot be true revival when this balance is lost. True healthy revival is possible only when quality determines quantity. We must realize that we have already deviated from the essence of Christianity when we allow quantity to determine quality."[2] The "spiritual churches" which have clearly understood the critical need of discipleship are struggling to identify the right methods and curriculum to disciple their members and lack the passion to introduce intentional discipleship training programmes to turn their

---

[2] John H. Oak, *Called to Awaken the Laity,* Fearn: Christian Focus, 2006, p. 18.

members into disciples, who can in turn make a positive impact on the Malawian society.

Current State of Affairs

In the backdrop of the above conditions of Malawian churches, we are looking into the key topic of lay empowerment and the mission of the Malawian church. According to *Operation World*, around 76 percent of Malawian population is Christian. "Freedom of religion exists; the various confessions of Christianity and Islam as well as smaller faiths co-exist peacefully."[3] But the influence of the Christian faith has very little impact on the society of Malawi. The main reason for this is that the faith of many here is divorced from their life style. People's knowledge of God has no bearing on their everyday life therefore, it cannot produce a tangible effect on the spiritual climate of the nation. There is definitely a huge gap between Christian profession and Christian practice. If the Christian faith is largely a sentimental Sunday affair which does not radically influence daily life, how can we expect the society to be transformed by the Gospel or the message to be preached by the Malawian church?

A. Malawian Society

It is true that the Malawian society has become an easy target today for foreigners as well as for Malawian Christians to blame for all the social evils like degeneration of moral values, corruption, breaking of marriages, crime and poverty. It is really sad and painful to see this condition deteriorating day by day. But often Malawian church leaders fail to realize that such evils exist in the society due to the failure of Christian influence in society. They fail to understand that God has placed His people in various positions in the society to fulfil His purposes. But when lay members of churches take their professions in the society for granted and fail to use them to glorify

---

3   Jason Mandryk, *Operation World*, Downers Grove: InterVarsity, 2010, p. 552.

God, society will definitely suffer due to lack of spiritual influence. Quite a number of those appointed as senior government officials are products of the Malawian church. In spite of the so-called Christians occupying key positions in the market-place, if the society is still going from bad to worse, should the church not take the moral responsibility for the current state of affairs? It is really unfortunate and shocking that market-place leaders who are key elders and deacons of churches are sometimes even mentioned in massive scandals. Does not this point to the fact that churches are failing to produce credible men and women who can influence the society positively? It is really sad to see churches often not being perceived to be different from the rest of the society. When Christians fail to function as the salt and light and become ineffective and lukewarm, the society will naturally suffer. Thus, if the Malawian society has to see a positive change, the laity of the church needs to put their faith into practice. "Many Christians fail to live out their faith. The key to Christian faith is the transformation of one's character and life. Therefore, having faith implies actions."[4] For this to happen lay members of churches need to be scripturally and spiritually empowered.

B. Malawian Churches

Sunday attendance in most of the Malawian churches is pretty high, yet many are like the crowds that gathered around Jesus only to have both their physical and spiritual needs met. Most of the laity who feel that they are not spiritually fed have learnt to live with it. Churches have too many programmes and activities which are not at all aligned to the churches' mission. Not every member of the church participates in those programmes but only the same few participate in most of those programmes. Another cry of the Malawian church is that there are too few volunteers and leaders to run church ministries as members are not properly discipled and equipped to

---

[4] John H. Oak, *Called to Awaken the Laity*, p. 20.

serve. As there is often a conscious effort on the part of the clergy to maintain the hierarchical order in the church most of the ministries of the church revolve around the clergy, that members or laymen and lay women fail to realize their key roles in church growth. As most of the members are not really motivated to serve, favourites are often forcibly volunteered by the clergy. Another big challenge of the Malawian church is that its members are not growing spiritually. "Members feel that they are not spiritually fed. Sermons lack depth. But the same members also do not feed themselves spiritually. The congregation is full of pew warmers, sermon tasters and spiritual consumers, but few are disciples and disciple makers."[5] It is sad to see churches almost turning into cooperatives or companies and pastors almost functioning like chief executive or chief operating officers (CEO, COO) providing "spiritual goods and services" like baptism, confirmation, solemnization of weddings and burials for the "spiritual tax" that members pay through their tithes and offerings. Only few are disciples who grow spiritually and help others to grow. But churches are often led by so called leaders who are not even disciples. How can churches led by spiritual dwarves grow and be productive in the community and the country?

C. Malawian Clergy

Among many of the Malawian independent churches it is quite common to see the clergy being referred to as "Men of God" and projected as "celebrities" who exercise immense power and authority over their congregations, church properties and finances. The belief that the congregation is existing for the welfare of the clergy is not from the Bible. But the real truth is that the clergy exist for the congregation. "Even if a clergyman is ordained and becomes a leader in the church, his authority is not to dominate or control the church,

---

5   Edmund Chan, *A Certain Kind,* Singapore: Covenant Evangelical Free Church, 2013, pp. 80-81.

but to submit to the entire church, including the laity."[6] Though the ministry of the Word grants spiritual authority to the clergy, it is also understood as a way of serving the laity. Thus, the Biblical teaching is very clear that the clergy belong to the laity whom they have been called to shepherd and serve for the glory of God. There seems to be a misunderstanding among the Malawian churches regarding the biblical basis of the clerical system and the exercising of authority by the clergy. The current understanding of the role of clergy is that since they are ordained by God they have complete authority to dominate or even control the church. But the Apostle Paul in his farewell address to the elders of the church in Ephesus clearly summarized his pastoral ministry this way:

> I served the Lord with great humility and with tears and in the midst of severe testing by the plots of my Jewish opponents. You know that I have not hesitated to preach anything that would be helpful to you but have taught you publicly and from house to house. I have declared to both Jews and Greeks that they must turn to God in repentance and have faith in our Lord Jesus. (Acts 20:19-21)

From Paul's example we can conclude that the spiritual authority of the clergy arises from their humility and commitment to serve the laity. We can also conclude that the true service of the clergy consists of helping the laity know their rightful place and helping them to fulfil their God given role in the best way possible. But if the clergy fail to do that, then they are failing to exercise their spiritual authority positively for the empowerment of the laity. Rev John Oak says, "Pastors are servants appointed by God to serve the church and do their utmost to help the laity to mature according to God's will. There is a need for the pastors in the contemporary church to humble themselves as servants of God."[7]

Further, very few of the Malawian clergy have realized that their core ministry is to make disciples and to equip them to produce disciples

---

6   John H. Oak, *Called to Awaken the Laity*, p. 43.

7   John H. Oak, *Called to Awaken the Laity*, p. 46.

too. Most of them seem to be quite satisfied with the Sunday attendance and the various activities that take place in the church throughout the week, to keep their members engaged. But they have miserably failed to realize that everything in the church ministry has to revolve around the intentional purpose of disciple making. Jesus's last words, "Therefore go and make disciples of all nations, baptizing them in the name of the Father and of the Son and of the Holy Spirit" (Matthew 28:19), make this truth very clear. When the clergy fail to make disciples in churches, members fail to grow in their right relationship with God and in spiritual maturity.

Leadership mentor and Discipleship expert Rev Edmund Chan says, "Disciple making is the process of bringing people into the right relationship with God, and developing them to full maturity in Christ through intentional growth strategies, that might multiply the entire process in others also."[8] Thus when the Malawian clergy fail in their responsibility of producing disciples, they inadvertently and unconsciously produce "politicians" within their churches. Things turn messy in the churches when such "politicians" who are not even disciples, take on leadership roles in churches. Such so called leaders instead of leading the churches in the ways of God, mislead the churches in the ways of the world. Another serious problem that the Malawian clergy is facing is, most of them seem to be lacking godly vision. When the clergy lack vision, they are unable to lead their churches effectively with a clear sense of direction as to where their congregations are and where they should be headed to. Vision is the ability to see the world as God sees it. As the Malawian clergy fail to see the world as God does, they are not able to respond to the needs of the world as God wants them to respond. Visionless clergy are often like the blind leading the blind. When such clergy lead the laity we cannot expect the Malawian church to fulfil God's perfect will and purpose of its existence.

---

8 Edmund Chan, *A Certain Kind,* p. 51.

D. Malawian Laity

Though lay leaders do provide support to the Malawian clergy in churches, it is an undeniable fact that the potential of the Malawian laity has not been strategically maximized for the growth and wellbeing of the church. The majority of the laity feel satisfied in being silent guests or mere spectators in churches. This majority of the laity is known for its lack of spiritual growth, hunger for the Word, passion for the lost, and understanding of their critical role in building God's Kingdom on the earth. The Malawian church is yet to clearly understand and utilize its laity's potential as witnesses for Christ in the contemporary challenging society. Did John Wesley not say, "Give me one hundred preachers who fear nothing but sin, and desire nothing but God, and I care not a straw whether they be clergymen or laymen; such alone will shake the gates of hell and set up the kingdom of heaven on Earth."

While talking about Martin Luther's reformation and the spiritual renewal that followed, Rev John Oak says, "Reformation and revival were usually characterized by the restoration of lay people to their rightful place in the church, and the times of stagnation and corruption were usually characterized by the tyranny of the clergy."[9]

This is definitely a very hard-hitting statement about the failure of the clergy to restore the laity to their God called place in the church, but there is truth in it, though very painful. It is sad that most of the Malawian clergy have failed to regard the calling and role of lay people as a biblical mandate. At the same time, it is also partially true that the Malawian laity themselves are responsible for their passive state in churches. There are lay leaders who make lame excuses by saying that they don't have time, whenever the clergy seek to teach and train them. They also think that discipling, evangelizing and teaching are only for the clergy with theological qualifications. Many excuse themselves from active involvement in church ministries by saying

---

9   John H. Oak, *Called to Awaken the Laity*, p. 27.

that their work in the market places and responsibilities at home are so demanding that they would just like to do what they are told to do and rather play a more passive role. Often, even the Malawian church elders and deacons fail to be committed in attending key board meetings and Sunday services. But they fail to realize that by doing so, they are giving up the most fulfilling responsibility that God has given them in building God's Kingdom on the earth. The stern warning to heed is that God would hold the clergy mainly responsible for neglecting the ministry of motivating or mobilizing the lay people and for the laity's current state of spiritual sickness. At the same time the laity cannot be totally excused for shirking their responsibility of making themselves available to fulfil their roles in the church.

Creating an Unhealthy Distinction between Clergy and Laity

Another challenge that Malawian pastors encounter as they lead churches is the struggle to consciously recognize the laity as their equal partners and co-workers in God's vineyard. The key reason for that is some of the denominational structures in Malawi that give pastors the exclusive right to the administration of the sacraments and key ministries of the church. As a result, respecting the laity and treating them as equals becomes difficult to them. In 1 Corinthians 12-14 the Apostle Paul clearly teaches that God has given every Christian a manifestation of God's Holy Spirit for the common good of the church. He explains that the gifts of the Holy Spirit are given not exclusively to the pastors but to each and every Christian. It is true that the actual gifts will differ from one to the other but the church will need everyone's help and cooperation in order to grow and mature. Rev Conrad Mbewe, my Zambian pastor friend and preacher who is often referred to as the Spurgeon of Africa, says that any attempt to portray pastors as a special class of church officers is unbiblical. While addressing fellow pastors he cautions by saying, "But we must go further and assert that pastors have not been called to perform any duty that no one else is allowed to perform. We have a privileged position but not an exclusive one. Brethren, I have a suspicion that our insistence on calling ourselves by certain titles may be due to an unhealthy effort to keep ourselves different from the laity."[10] Rev Conrad Mbewe says that one of the clear evidences of a pastor's calling will be the laity who mature under his ministry to take up areas of responsibility in the church. He advises pastors to willingly give the laity their due recognition as it is the Lord who has given them as co-workers to build His church. "Delegate responsibilities to them as the church grows. As they are exercising their gifts in those areas, the church will more easily see who is eldership material. This will also enable you to concentrate on the more important things - prayer and Word."[11] This reminds us of what the Apostles in the early church told the lay disciples to do when a problem cropped up due to the distribution of food to widows of the Hellenistic Jews in Acts 6:1-4.

Critical Need of the Hour

History indicates that when the church is led by the Holy Spirit and when it takes Jesus' Great Commission seriously, the Lord of the harvest is bound to enable it to become a movement writing the future history. Thus, the problem lies not with God or His ability to empower the Malawian church to fulfil His Great Commission, but with the Malawian clergy who have been failing in their entrusted responsibility of discipling and mobilizing their congregation to fulfil the task. "Chronic spiritual infancy is the ecclesiastical norm. Superficiality, immaturity and carnality characterize many Christians. Many church members don't grow towards spiritual maturity, much less reproduce spiritually. The focus of the Church has shifted from making disciples to merely making converts."[12]

---

10 Conrad Mbewe, *Foundations for the Flock: Truths About the Church for All the Saints,* Hannibal: Granted Ministries Press, 2011, p. 110.

11 Conrad Mbewe, *Foundations for the Flock,* p. 159.

12 Edmund Chan, *A Certain Kind,* p. 76.

Thus if the Malawian church desires to fulfil its purpose of existence and progress in its mission of bringing the Gospel to those who are living and dying without hearing and knowing Jesus, it needs to focus on the following five areas.

Transforming lay members into Disciples

The only way to awaken the Malawian laity is to turn them into Christ-like disciples. It is very sad and disappointing to see that most of the Malawian Churches are forgetting and neglecting the Great Commission of our Lord Jesus Christ which is, "Therefore go and make disciples of all nations, baptizing them in the name of the Father and of the Son and of the Holy Spirit" (Matthew 28:19). When Jesus commanded His disciples to "make disciples" he was not referring to merely adding members or converts to the church. Just as He himself had His twelve disciples to follow Him He wanted his disciples to transform those who turned to God from darkness to be transformed into true followers who would submit to His teachings and His ways. According to Rev Edmund Chan, "Disciple making is all about a certain kind of person who is radically committed to a certain kind of purpose and who through a certain kind of process reproduces a certain kind of product."[13] Neither church Pastors nor congregation members in Malawi have realized the need for discipleship in their churches. When the Malawian laity is not discipled by the Word, they are unconsciously discipled by the world. Many do not know how to disciple others as they themselves have not been discipled. Churches are too busy with programmes and mere activities at the expense of focusing on discipleship. Many churches do not have good role models to motivate the laity to become true disciples of Jesus. It is surprising to see most of the Pastors and church leaders are complacent and satisfied with the current state of the church in Malawi. But,

---

13 Edmund Chan, *A Certain Kind,* p. 36.

God's primary plan for the church is for disciples of Jesus to develop other men and women into disciples! There is probably no other more primary matter of negligence in the church today than our failure to follow the Lord's command to develop disciples. Because of this gross neglect, many Christians think of themselves as an audience to be entertained rather than an army ready to march... Discipleship must function as the heart of church ministry.[14]

I think that when seminaries, theological institutions and Bible Colleges fail to produce effective future pastors who are themselves disciples, we cannot expect them to transform their lay members into disciples in their churches. The saddest thing is most of the Malawian Pastors and leaders are not really conscious of the fact that their churches will be evaluated one day by the Lord of the church on the basis of their focus on their key mission of turning their lay members into disciples. Church planter Neil Cole says, "Ultimately each church will be evaluated by only one thing, its disciples. Your church is only as good as its disciples. It does not matter how good your praise, preaching, programmes or property are. If your disciples are passive, needy, consumerist, and not moving in the direction of radical obedience, your church is not good."[15]

Training the Laity to become Disciple Makers

The second key mission of the Malawian church is to turn their lay disciples into disciple makers. Jesus' principle during his lifetime on the earth was to equip His disciples first and then to give them tasks to do. His success in ministry was determined by His efforts to equip or train His disciples. "This is the basic principle of discipleship. Christ's way is to put people first before work and action. In other words, a strategy that assigns ministry or work to someone without

---

[14] Bill Hull, *New Century Disciple Making: Applying Jesus' Ideas for the Future*, Grand Rapids: Fleming H. Revell, 1997, p. 10.
[15] Quoted in J.R. Briggs and Bob Hyatt, *Eldership and the Mission of God: Equipping Teams for Faithful Church Leadership*, Downers Grove: InterVarsity, 2015, p. 32.

prior preparation of the person is not a strategy that Jesus taught."[16] Failure in raising the Malawian laity to their fullest potential in regard to their identity, role and calling, leaves them poorly equipped to serve the Lord effectively. This seems to be one of the major failures of the contemporary Malawian church. The two key questions that Malawian clergy need to ask themselves are, "Are we accepting our laity as active ministry partners and are we providing concrete spiritual training for them so that they can in turn become disciple makers? The reason why the Malawian clergy is failing in this responsibility is that they have not recognized the spiritual identity and priesthood of all believers in the New Testament. Apostle Peter while writing to new believers and lay people says, "But you are a chosen people, a royal priesthood, a holy nation, God's special possession, that you may declare the praises of him who called you out of darkness into his wonderful light" (1 Peter 2:9). Many of the Malawian pastors function like the priests of the Old Testament and fail to recognize the priestly call of the laity. "This overemphasis on the importance of the clergy has instilled a class distinction between the clergy and the laity, thus nurturing a dualism that separates spiritual life from the rest of the life. It has also cultivated an inferiority complex in many lay members, causing them to think that they are somehow less holy than the clergy"[17] Furthermore, the majority of the Malawian clergy have come to the conclusion that their sermons are enough to satisfy the laity and as a result they have neglected the task of training their laity to become powerful and productive equal partners in God's ministry. Thus, awakening the Malawian laity and providing them with adequate systematic training to become effective disciple makers is the only way the Malawian church can become the salt and light in the coming age of uncertainties.

---

[16] John H. Oak, *Called to Awaken the Laity*, p. 104.

[17] Ibid, p. 38.

It is the responsibility of the current generation of Malawian Christians to pass on their faith and wisdom to the next generation. But the question is, are Malawian Christians really passing on their faith to the next generation? "The genius of multiplication is potential for rapid growth. If one person disciples two people a year, the law of multiplication quickly reaches exponential proportions."[18] But the tragedy is, the Malawian laity have neither been adequately equipped to pass on their faith to the next generation nor to disciple others. Unless the Malawian clergy trains and equips its laity to disciple others, Christianity in Malawi will remain merely as an organized religion and not become a movement impacting the next generation. The laity needs to be consciously and consistently developed and empowered through intentional growth strategies so that they can take others through the same process of authentic discipleship and disciple making. When the laity is empowered in the area of disciple making, their lives will be impacted for Christ and transformed in Him. "There is a healthy appetite for authentic discipleship. Moreover, spiritual multiplication is actually taking place. People are investing their lives in others and seeing them grow to maturity in Christ so that they too, can pass the teaching on to others."[19] Thus disciple making needs to become the DNA of the Malawian church in order to transform lay church members into Christ like disciples who through systematic training could be turned into disciple makers.

Turning Lay Disciples into Lay Leaders

Leadership is vital for the church and the priority of leadership development within the Malawian church can never be overstated. When lay members are effectively discipled and mentored, they will be equipped to serve as lay leaders who will disciple others and the chain effect will automatically continue. One thing which is clear in

---

[18] Michael B. Pawelke, *Disciple: A Catalyst to Disciple Making*, Winnipeg: Word Alive Press, 2010, p. 143.

[19] Edmund Chan, *A Certain Kind*, p. 59.

the Gospels is that our Lord Jesus developed leadership through the mentoring of lay disciples. But before mentoring His disciples, Jesus, prayerfully selected those with kindred spirits and then invested his life in them intentionally. His discipling and mentoring of the twelve was not one of a task-oriented supervisor, but rather of a person-oriented mentor. Jesus took great care for the personal well-being and spiritual development of his disciples. "Mentoring is the empowering life-investment, in an accountable relationship, through which knowledge, skills and attitudes are effectively modelled and imparted so that lives are transformed."[20] Thus one of the current key needs of the Malawian church is leadership development. Churches here often lack coherent strategies for leadership development. Mentoring the discipled laity is definitely the key to leadership emergence in the Malawian churches. Godly lay leaders are developed through strong inter-personal relationships. "We must raise a generation of Christian leaders who are spiritually vital, biblically competent and relationally authentic. We must produce spiritually qualified leaders who understand the times and make significant difference in it."[21] Thus Malawian pastors need to take this key responsibility of mentoring their discipled lay leaders so that they can reproduce more disciples and leaders, through spiritual multiplication to change the Malawian society.

Tapping or Using Lay Disciples' Resources for Ministry and Mission

Christian life is not just about attending Sunday services and growing in holiness at a personal level. That's the reason, Apostle Paul while writing to lay Christians living in the city of Rome, said,

> We have different gifts, according to the grace given us. If a man's gift is prophesying, let him use it in proportion to his faith. If it is serving, let him serve; if it is teaching, let him teach; if it is encouraging, let him

---

[20]   Ibid, 142.

[21]   Edmund Chan, *A Certain Kind*, p. 86.

give generously; if it is leadership, let him govern diligently; if it is showing mercy, let him do it cheerfully. (Romans 12:6-8)

One of the biggest responsibilities of pastors and leaders is to identify the hidden potentials and resources of lay disciples and use them for the building of the church and progressing in Mission. Rev Conrad Mbewe while writing about the commitment of the laity and disciples to Christian service and ministry says, "When you become a Christian you also become a soldier- a soldier in the Lord's army. Hence, you need to find your position in the ranks and start fighting for the Lord in this world of sin and darkness."[22] But, in spite of being blessed with many spiritual gifts, talents and skills, most of the lay members of the Malawian churches have completely left the ministries within and without the churches to their pastors and other full time paid staff of the churches. Why? Because they have not been made aware of their spiritual gifts or have not been helped by their pastors to identify their gifts or they have not been given opportunities to exercise their spiritual gifts. Further the clergy have not gone the extra mile to motivate their laity and tap their spiritual resources for evangelism and mission. "Motivation is the key to human behaviour. If you want to persuade people to do something, or do something faster or more effectively, you must motivate them. Intuitively, this has been understood from the earliest times."[23] Without motivation, the laity of the Malawian church and their resources cannot be mobilized for mission by which I mean bringing the Gospel to those who are living and dying without hearing Gospel. A layman made this appeal to the leaders who attended the Lausanne Conference:

> What do lay people want? We want to participate in important ministries. And the clergy need to show us how to study the Bible, how

---

[22] Conrad Mbewe, *Your Discipleship Manual*, Zambia: Evergreen, 2006, p. 106.

[23] Tissa Weerasingha, *Motivating for Evangelism*, Colombo: Calvary Press, 2005, p. 1.

to pray, how to love, how to evangelize, and how to become like Christ... We need the clergy to lead and challenge us.[24]

I hear this as the cry and sincere appeal of the majority of the Malawian laity too. Thus the time has come for the Malawian clergy to awaken the Malawian laity and reinstate them to their rightful position in the churches. The more the clergy delay to do that, the more the Malawian lay members will continue to slumber and degenerate into a powerless flock who cannot do anything for their master and Lord Jesus Christ.

Try Jesus' Ways to Empower the Laity

It is very important to observe the different ways Jesus empowered his disciples to achieve His objective of reaching the world with the Gospel. Disciple maker and Evangelist, Dr Robert E. Coleman, lists eight key ways Jesus empowered his disciples (Adapted from Robert Coleman's book *Master Plan of Evangelism*).

   a.   Selection (Identify)

It all started when Jesus called a few men to follow him. He did not choose everyone he met but He took the selection of the men he trained very seriously. Rather than focusing on the multitude, he only chose twelve. The reason for his selectivity was intentional. He chose twelve men and a number of women to instruct and train. They would in time reproduce themselves in others. A few good men and women were Jesus' master plan of reproducing disciples. In the same way, the Malawian clergy must be very selective in identifying those they wish to disciple and empower. They should look for people who are faithful, willing, and able to reproduce their discipleship in others. Disciple making does not require a degree or Bible college education; rather they should seek to find men and women who have a passion

---

[24]   Quoted in J.D. Douglas, *Let the Earth Hear His Voice*, Minneapolis: World Wide Publishing, 1975, p. 458.

and a hunger for Christ. Willingness to answer the call to follow Jesus is the only requirement to be a disciple of Jesus.

b. Association (Build relationship)

Secondly, Jesus was intimately involved in the lives of his disciples as they followed Him. His training method was spending time with His disciples. Discipleship and empowering happens as the clergy spend time with the laity. In a similar way the Malawian clergy should be ready to spend time with their chosen laity in order to build a close relationship with them as Jesus did with his disciples.

c. Consecration (Assist to obey)

Jesus expected His followers to obey Him. He sought to create in His disciples a lifestyle of consecrated obedience. The Malawian clergy should prayerfully help their laity to submit and obey God's word and plan for their lives as God can only use men and women who are willing to obey Him.

d. Impartation (Share and guide)

Jesus gave himself away to His disciples by imparting to them everything that the Father had given Him. He imparted not only Himself, but also spiritual truth about life and ministry. Just as Jesus imparted Himself to His disciples, the Malawian clergy must seek to give themselves to the laity who are identified to serve. This transfer of godly wisdom and character will happen when trued discipleship takes place.

e. Demonstration (Set an example)

Jesus demonstrated how the disciples should live a Christ centred life. He was the message and the method. He lived the life that He wanted to reproduce in His disciples. It is important that the Malawian clergy practices what they preach because the people they are empowering and training will follow their life and examples. It is not enough to preach the gospel, but they have to practice it. Their personal walk with God is one of the most important factors in developing godly lay disciples and leaders.

f.   Delegation (Involve)

Jesus assigned His disciples work. He developed His disciples by delegating ministry responsibilities to them. The Malawian pastors must delegate ministerial responsibilities to their chosen laity and walk them through a yearlong process of training before they can serve in any capacity in the church.

g.   Supervision (Hold them accountable)

Jesus supervised His disciples. Supervision is an important part of leadership development, especially when dealing with the laity and new believers. Even as Malawian pastors attempt to delegate and empower people to act, they must closely supervise them in order to make sure that they stay on track. Often lay people get into trouble without proper supervision by the clergy.

h.   Reproduction (Encourage them to disciple)

Jesus expected His disciples to reproduce His likeness in others. He imparted His message and mission to His disciples so that they would reproduce themselves in others and make disciples of all nations. The Great Commission implies that the followers of Jesus will reproduce themselves and "make disciples." Reproduction is how the Christian movement was born. Thus, the Malawian clergy need to rediscover the reproductive nature of the Malawian church. They need to realize that they have been called to select, train, and send missional disciples of Christ out into the world who will, in turn be able repeat the process of discipleship in others.

Topics for Discipleship Training

Systematic and Bible-based teaching materials are necessary in order to provide effective discipleship training for the laity. Thus, after closely studying the Gospels (especially the Sermon on the Mount recorded in Matthew chapters 5, 6, and 7) and Epistles, I arrived at the following key disciple making topics to empower the Malawian church so that it could advance in its mission.

  a. Critical need of Discipling the Laity

  b. Concise definition of Disciple making

  c. Curriculum for Discipling the Laity

  d. Call of Laity as Disciples

  e. Character of Laity as Disciples

  f. Choices of Laity as Disciples

  g. Cost of Discipleship

  h. Commitment of Laity as Disciples

  i. Core values of Lay Disciples

  j. Commission of Laity as Disciples (Soulwinning & Evangelism)

  k. Commission of Laity as Disciples (Involvement in Cross cultural and cross border Missions)

  l. Consistent ways Discipled Laity can Disciple others

Conclusion

If we sincerely go back to the Bible, we will clearly find out that discipleship truly empowers the laity to become Christ-like disciples and like the laity of the first century church. Intentional Disciple making is a ministry introduced by Jesus Christ himself to make the laity into a people with a calling, and a process which can transform them into those who can inherit the ministry of Jesus. Dr John H. Oak says, "Discipleship training is that which makes a person do his or her best as one called to glorify God's name, to fulfil God's will, regardless of one's occupation and surrounding circumstances."[25] Thus lay empowerment in discipleship is definitely the secret of

---

[25] John H. Oak, *Called to Awaken the Laity*, p. 171.

inheriting the ministry of Jesus and the advancement of Malawian church in its mission. The reason is, discipleship contains all the important principles of producing people whom God is seeking to fulfil His plan and purpose on this earth. The Malawian laity is a sleeping giant whom the Lord is waiting to empower and use to establish His Kingdom on this earth. It is my prayer that God may open the spiritual eyes of the Malawian Church leadership to see what He would do if it would focus on empowering the laity in discipleship and advancing His Kingdom and His mission on the earth.

Bibliography

Briggs, J.R. and Bob Hyatt, *Eldership and the Mission of God: Equipping Teams for Faithful Church Leadership*, Downers Grove: InterVarsity, 2015.

Chan, Edmund and Tan Lian Seng, *Discipleship Missions*, Singapore: Covenant Evangelical Free Church, 2016.

Chan, Edmund, *A Certain Kind*, Singapore: Covenant Evangelical Free Church, 2013.

Coleman, Robert, *Master Plan of Evangelism*, Westwood: Revell, 1964.

Hull, Bill, *New Century Disciple Making: Applying Jesus' Ideas for the Future*, Grand Rapids: Fleming H. Revell, 1997.

Mandryk, Jason, *Operation World*, Downers Grove: InterVarsity, 2010.

Mbewe, Conrad, *Your Discipleship Manual*, Zambia: Evergreen, 2006.

Mbewe, Conrad, *Foundations for the Flock: Truths About the Church for All the Saints*, Hannibal: Granted Ministries Press, 2011.

Oak, John H., *Called to Awaken the Laity*, Fearn: Christian Focus, 2006.

Pawelke, Michael B., *Disciple: A Catalyst to Disciple Making*, Winnipeg: Word Alive Press, 2010.

Weerasingha, Tissa, *Motivating for Evangelism*, Colombo: Calvary Press, 2005.

Chapter 12

Theological Training in Malawi: The Case of CCAP Blantyre Synod

Paul Mathews Louis Mawaya

Introduction

This account presents personal responses from participants and practitioners of theological training done by a few congregations of the Church of Central Africa, Presbyterian (hereafter CCAP) Blantyre Synod. In the description, the problems affecting theological training are underlined. Among other issues, the report emphasizes on the effects and benefits of theological training. In addition, the critical role of church leaders is highlighted in order to underscore its importance in sustaining theological training at the grassroots.

The description also deals with how the highlighted problems as proposed by the participants and grassroots practitioners may be resolved. Out of this, the statement provides recommendations to those who are either implementing or planning to implement theological training, although this may be applied in a Presbyterian context that shares similar circumstances with CCAP Blantyre Synod. Nonetheless, the recommendations may also be generally appropriate to a third world church.

Nature of Theological Training in CCAP Blantyre Synod

The CCAP Blantyre Synod Missions, Evangelism and Training (hereafter MET) Directorate and its subordinate structures provide oversight and guidance in the implementation of any theological training usually done in partnership with related church agencies who share CCAP Blantyre Synod's reformed and evangelical theology. In this light, the CCAP Blantyre Synod both adopts and implements several theological training courses or modules. These include and are not limited to Theological Education by Extension in Malawi (hereafter TEEM) Certificate in Basic Theology (hereafter CBT – 15 Modules) and Certificate in Ministry (hereafter CM – 15 Modules), VERITAS College Course (4 Modules), Timothy Leadership Training (hereafter TLT) Course (8 Modules), and Dynamic Church Planting International (hereafter DCPI) Course (3 Modules).

The Nature of the Abstract

This chapter provides an abstract of a broad appraisal made in relation to the implementation of TEEM CBT modules and VERITAS College modules done between 2014 and 2018 in two out of the 18 presbyteries of CCAP Blantyre Synod, namely Blantyre City Presbytery and Shire Valley South Presbytery. The evaluation used personal interviews. The personal interviews were done either through the telephone or through personal meetings.[1] The same questionnaire consisting of a set of six questions was used for each interviewee and their responses were analyzed based on the six focused questions to generate material for this chapter. In total, the chapter is a contribution made by seven key respondents who not only successfully participated in the theological training but also effectively facilitated a cohort of students who have successfully graduated.[2] The congregations were sampled because they have a

---

[1]   The interviews were conducted between 23 and 25 February 2019.

[2]   These are: Rev. Misheck Mkumbadzala who facilitated TEEM CBT at Mpasa CCAP Congregation under Shire Valley South Presbytery located in Nsanje District; Elder Lloyd Tepani of Mount Sanjika CCAP Congregation in Chilomoni Segerege; Elder Michael Richard Jere and Elder Anthony Chirambo of Michiru CCAP Congregation in Chilomoni; Elder Hastings Phale, Elder Diana Gausi and Elder Diana Jackson Sangala of Kachere CCAP Congregation in Ndirande under Blantyre City Presbytery in Blantyre District. Interview done between 23 and 25 February, 2019.

track record of operating a class of either VERITAS College Course or TEEM CBT course within the stated period.[3]

Context

Vision Statement

CCAP Blantyre Synod desires to see at the end of year 2021 "A God fearing community that is spiritually and physically transformed, economically empowered and self-reliant."[4] In this light, theological training plays a critical role in achieving spiritual and physical transformation, economic capacity and self-confidence.

Mission Statement

CCAP Blantyre Synod is committed "to proclaim the Gospel for the salvation of mankind, discipleship, fellowship, preservation of the truth and provision of social services."[5] As such, theological training fits into the Synod's concept of discipleship and preservation of the truth.

Synod Objectives related to theological training

CCAP Blantyre Synod supports theological training. The constitution of the Synod as stipulated within the mandate of MET Directorate shows that it has duties and functions that include development of training initiatives for members to become more effective in their

---

[3]   Note that Mpasa CCAP Congregation has been running TEEM CBT Course only while Mount Sanjika CCAP, Michiru CCAP and Kachere CCAP Congregations are still running both TEEM CBT and VERITAS College Courses.

[4]   *Church of Central Africa Presbyterian Blantyre Synod Strategic Plan 2016-2021*, Blantyre: Blantyre Synod Management Team, 2015, p. 3. It was financially supported by the Presbyterian Church in the United States of America (PCUSA).

[5]   Ibid.

Christian occupation and witness.[6] Besides, the MET Department provides capacity building for Christians in Presbyterian faith and system of worship to ensure Christians are fully equipped and are firmly grounded in their faith.[7] These two objectives mandate the department to implement theological training within the jurisdiction of the church. As such, the MET Department, in cooperation with stakeholder agencies, empowers and certifies a trainer of trainers for each theological training course in order to replicate the trainings in the presbyteries and their respective congregations.

One of the four strategic focus areas pursued by CCAP Blantyre Synod, which remains the main focus of the MET Directorate, is spiritual growth and evangelism whose main goal is "to enhance spiritual growth and evangelism."[8] Theological training forms one of the many intervention projects undertaken by the MET Department in order to "increase the number of transformed Christians in communities served by CCAP Blantyre Synod."[9] Additionally, theological training strengthens the Christian family as well as enabling effective proclamation and propagation of the Word of God to the public.[10]

General Observations on theological training

So, in the case of TEEM CBT, all ministers were oriented at the start of the training in 2013 so that by their virtue as trained theologians, ministers became automatic facilitators who were expected to replicate the task of facilitation among trusted elders in the congregations for sustainability purposes. To this end, the

---

6 *Church of Central Africa, Presbyterian Blantyre Synod Constitution*, Blantyre: Blantyre Synod, p. 44. This is based on the constitution adopted by the 2013 CCAP Blantyre Synod Biennial Assembly.

7 Ibid.

8 *CCAP Blantyre Synod Strategic Plan 2016-2021*, p. 4.

9 Ibid.

10 Ibid.

observation has shown that very little progress has been made especially seen with the low sales of TEEM CBT books.

In the case of VERITAS College courses, Michiru CCAP, Mount Sanjika CCAP and Kachere CCAP Congregations were the only piloted congregations to have successfully undertaken the course with great success since 2014. The Synod plans to replicate this theological training to all presbyteries and all congregations with financial and technical support from Gereformeerde Zendingsbond (hereafter GZB) of the Netherlands.

While VERITAS College course has registered success in the piloted congregations and TEEM CBT course has not been administered by the majority of ministers and congregations, the chapter explores its bottlenecks and how interested ministers and congregations can successfully manage and sustain theological training.

Problems

Problems that affect the Outcome

Theological training is a vital strategy for building the capacity of both the lay leadership and communicants for either discipleship or mentorship purposes. The training brings inevitable transformation to the lives of the participants as well as to the development of the church. However, this and many positive outcomes arise from the difficulties as has been discovered from the participants and practitioners at the grassroots. Such difficulties affect the outcome of theological training.

Leadership Support

Church leadership plays a critical role in ensuring that theological training is sustainable. CCAP Blantyre Synod congregation leadership is made up of the Church Management Committee and Church Executive Committee. The Church Management Committee consists of the Church Moderator and all Session Clerks while Church

Executive Committee incorporates all members of the Church Management Committee and other members like Congregation Treasurer, Pledge Treasurer, and leaders of strategic committees. The inclusion varies from congregation to congregation as dictated by the nature of leadership style adopted within the Presbyterian tradition.[11]

According to CCAP Blantyre Synod, a congregation is formed by presbytery granting status of a congregation to a prayer house which has a membership of more than 200 communicants among others.[12] Further, the prayer house must have adequate competent leadership that can maintain a responsible session.[13] Moreover, the prayer house must be able to accept the responsibilities of being a congregation in their own right.[14] The responsibilities include but are not limited to the following: maintaining regular worship, meeting financial targets set by the Presbytery and Synod for the central funds of the Synod, looking after the welfare of the Church Minister in accordance with minimum standards set by the Presbytery and exercising spiritual leadership in the community. Impliedly, church leadership, at all levels of the strata of the CCAP Blantyre Synod, which specifically includes the congregation, is central to the rise and fall of church.

As a result, the commitment of ministers and elders in the Church Management Committee and Church Executive Committee towards theological training determines the progress of theological training at a congregation. When the ministers and elders are not committed to theological training, it is expected that theological training will either dismally fail in the congregation or face insurmountable strains.

With the absence of clear policy at Synod level to ensure that all lay evangelists are procedurally certified after undergoing an acceptable

---

11   *Malongosoledwe a Mapemphero: Church of Central Africa, Presbyterian Synod of Blantyre*, [undated], p. 164 and interpret this in light of the *CCAP Blantyre Synod Constitution*, p. 56 section 9.15.2.

12   *CCAP Blantyre Synod Constitution*, p. 17.

13   Ibid.

14   Ibid.

basic theological training, most lay evangelists undermine the critical role of theological training. As such, many congregants depend on lay evangelists who may hold theological positions different from the accepted reformed and evangelical doctrine that CCAP Blantyre Synod espouses.

On top of this, there is a section of the church leaders which maintains that the Holy Spirit is adequate empowerment of all believers hence theological training is not only unnecessary but also spiritually retrogressive. As such, such leaders do not show any enthusiasm to participate in theological training.

Church leadership struggles have also erupted in the churches between elders who have gone through theological training and those who have not. At times, participants in theological training are subjectively critical of those who have not participated in the theological training and vice versa. As such, theological training without the leadership of the church minister is bound to create divisions among the leaders.

Financial Support

Respondents indicated that there is need for financial support in order to sustain theological training at the congregation. Some respondents pointed out that the training needs financial subsidy especially in the purchase of training textbooks. The ever-rising purchasing cost of the textbooks is prohibitive for the participation of poor and rural congregants. For example, TEEM CBT set of 15 books rose from US$ 10 in 2013 when it was introduced to US$ 20 in 2019. For the majority of poor participants, the level of fees required for textbooks led to an increase in participants dropping out.

Financial support is also needed for the mobility of the committed facilitators. The evaluation observed that most facilitators are lay leaders of one congregation and run a theological training at a distant congregation. Without deliberate financial support of the host congregation towards the facilitator's mobility, the financial commitment of facilitators is over-stretched and they fail to deliver quality and consistent theological training to enthusiastic participants.

The need for financial support was also argued to be the problem of dependence syndrome. There is a mentality in the church that theological training is supposed to be free. As a result, it becomes hard for the participants themselves to shoulder the financial obligation of supporting the visiting facilitators as well as procuring their own textbooks in spite of poverty among the rural masses.

Value for Theological Training

Understanding the value of theological training cannot be overemphasized both for the church leadership and development of the laity at large. However, the experience of the respondents shows that some lay members of the congregations struggle to appreciate the relevance of theological training especially where the theological training does not add value to their daily lives, family and church.

There is a traditional stereotype with which other members of the laity struggle in order to join theological training. They hold that "theology" is a sacred training specialized for ordained ministers of the Word and Sacrament. As such, the laity mis-conceive that theological training may transform congregants into pastors. Further, theological training may eventually invalidate the role and place of the ordained minister in the grassroots church.

Besides the stereotype, there is a hindering theory that holds that a catechized and baptized member of the congregation does not need any further classes to become a core member of the church. This theory assumes that a catechized member of the church is an individual who has completed a lifelong biblical experience and does not need any other supplementary lessons. The implication is that such lay members no longer feel obligated to participate in theological training.

The understanding of theological training is also complicated with those who have never experienced a spiritual rebirth. Formal and nominal Christians who participate in theological training find a great opportunity to deepen their knowledge of God's Word which either contributes towards their personal encounter with Jesus or hardens their hearts to sinful life. As such, theological training has prevented some formal and nominal members of the church from knowing Jesus better.

Participants in the theological training at the congregation should be adequately recruited through onset awareness. The awareness held at the beginning of the theological training helps potential participants to establish appropriate reasons for undertaking the theological training. Otherwise, participants who do not appreciate the value of theological training do not give priority to theological training classes.

Literacy Levels

Although, the recent fourth Integrated Household Survey (hereafter IHS4) conducted by National Statistics Office (hereafter NSO) reveals that 73% of Malawians are literate,[15] the nature of literacy of lay members has greatly contributed towards the challenges for theological training. Respondents of this chapter found out that many rural congregants dropped out of the theological trainings because of the literacy challenges.

In the experience, theological trainings prefer to use different versions of the Bible. Hence some participants felt that they presented the Word of God in different terms from those to which they were accustomed. As such, facilitators took more time to explain the rationale for the existence of different versions of the Bible. This is common with VERITAS College Course because the modules use *Buku Loyera*, a different translation from *Buku Lopatulika* with which

---

[15] Tinenenji Chakuda, "Literacy Levels now at 73%," *The Nation*, 1 December 2017; retrieved from www.mwnation.com [4.5.2019].

many CCAP Blantyre Synod members are familiar. However, this experience is attributed to the level of literacy of participating members.

In some cases, a theological class may comprise of lay members that possess different literacy and education backgrounds. In such cases, a class of 12 to 15 learners may be made up of individuals who can read and write either Chichewa or English but have different academic qualifications. This set-up creates frustrations for both the highly qualified individuals and those whose education status is very basic. It becomes difficult for the facilitator to balance his presentations so that it suits both groups of individuals in the class. This situation has also put off other individual learners from undergoing theological training.

Time constraint

Time is an important asset in theological training. Many parishioners do not create time for theological training. As such, the registered participants are so low that the unregistered parishioners remain in the active congregations. Besides, both participants and facilitators must observe and keep the consistency of starting and ending times in order to sustain and keep consistency in participants' attendance. In some places, either the facilitator or the participants failed to adhere to the agreed time and this led to likelihood of drop-outs.

Further, theological training must be administered within a prescribed period of time. The experience has been that a prolonged training increases drop-outs and compromises the quality of the training. Due to either limited availability of facilitators or low participants' registration, theological training classes are forced to mix participants of different literacy levels in order to operate a theological class within the minimum requirements. As such, facilitators take time to finish a lesson.

Moreover, ministers in CCAP Blantyre Synod are usually overwhelmed with pastoral duties. Pastoral duties may arise due to the nature of pastoral catchment area covered as well as pastoral responsibilities received within the structure of the CCAP Blantyre Synod. In view of this, ministers fail to find a regular time to operate theological training on a consistent basis.

Therefore, the critical challenges that theological training is facing in CCAP Blantyre Synod is five-fold: leadership support, financial support, value for theological training, literacy levels and time constraints. These bottlenecks stifle the potential success of theological training at the grassroots of the church.

Effects

Regardless of the prevailing problems that theological training is facing, there are negative and positive effects. There are more negative than positive effects experienced. On the negative side, participation in theological training remains very low. The participation ranges from 1% to 10% of the membership of the congregation yet completion is spread between 16% and 90% at most due to low turnout and increased drop-out.

Period

In addition, the period of theological training is discouraging. Theological training is taking longer than anticipated because of a number of factors. First, there is an increase in absenteeism which necessitates make-up classes. This prolongs theological training. Second, the literacy differences among participants in the same class mean that participants' understanding waves are at different paces which forces the facilitator to customize extra classes for slow learners. As such, theological training takes longer time than expected.

Perspective

Further, theological training generates a negative perspective. Non-participative church leaders and members create a perspective against theological training that immunizes them from considering and joining theological training. The negative attitude emerges from either belief that theological training is a liability or not necessary for spiritual development. The negative perspective has created and promoted a general resistance towards participation in theological training by the majority of the membership. As such, theological training is facing not only teething problems but also uphill battles for it to advance at pace.

Pedagogy

On top of this, theological training faces pedagogical challenges. Currently, there are few labourers available to facilitate theological training. The few certified and trained facilitators are facing leadership and financial support which severely discourages their active participation in the development of the church as well as frustrating their further development. With the need for make-up and extra classes due to the nature of literacy differences in theological training classes, the task of facilitation remains hard and demands patience, determination and utmost commitment to serve the Lord.

Calling

However, the positive effects of theological training have been significant. It cannot be overemphasized that the few completed participants have proved their divine calling in the church. This means that participants have found a well guided time to reflect on the gifts, skills and potential that God gave them for appropriate ministries in the church. Out of theological training class, unknown members of the grassroots church have brought out new potential leaders from communicants and at the same time revealed more dimensions of ministry from old leaders.

Capacity Building

As if this is not enough, theological training provides capacity building in various ministries of the church. Both church leaders and members undergoing theological training have gained skills in preaching, teaching, Bible Study, counselling and generally leading others to the Lord Jesus Christ. Theological training gives out a new charge and energy to make personal commitment and contribution to the building of the kingdom of God.

Convenience

Both theologically trained church leaders and lay members of the grassroots church realize their usefulness in the kingdom of God. With this realization, they find it convenient to serve the Lord of the Harvest in the promotion of the Great Commission out of their own willingness and commitment. As a result of theological training, both leaders and members of the church demonstrate increased commitment towards church building and kingdom advancement.

Therefore, theological training has both negative and positive effects on the participants and the church at large. The four negative effects are issues around participation, period, perspective and pedagogy while three positive effects are surrounding calling, capacity building and convenience to serve the Lord. Both of the effects contribute towards the progress of theological training in CCAP Blantyre Synod.

The Role of a Pastor and Lay Leadership

Earlier on, the chapter underlined the critical role of church leadership in general in advancing theological training at the grassroots of the church structure. In particular, the role of a Pastor and lay leadership in their specific jurisdiction is not only crucial but also central to the initiation and promotion of theological training at a congregation.

Modelling

The respondents highlighted four main roles. Pastors and lay leaders must be role models. Parishioners are motivated to participate in theological training when they see that their own pastor is actively taking a critical role. They believe not only that this theological training in acceptable but also they are able to see the direct impact of the training in the life of their own pastor. The increased participation of key and influential elders and deacons in the congregation consolidates the motivation that communicants have cultivated in their pastor.

It is estimated that CCAP Blantyre Synod has over 1,000 prayer houses and over 600 congregations that are served by slightly over 200 pastors. As such, the increased number of congregations and prayer houses against the insufficient number of ordained church ministers means that lay evangelists play a critical role in leading and teaching the church. Their participation in theological training is more transmittable than that of influential elders because they identify with the people in the church more than pastors.

Maintaining

Pastors and lay leaders must maintain theological training. By establishing the best ways of sustaining the work in terms of finance, administration and participation, leaders are able to sustain theological training at a congregation. One way of supporting the theological training is to establish a system that ensures that the leaders are directly overseeing its development. As such, theological training must be included in the annual budget of the congregation as part of the system of the church. The church must appoint the appropriate set-up in the system that is accountable to the Church Session.

Marketing

Theological training needs vibrant marketing. Besides Synod MET processing a successful resolution, the presbyteries and congregations should resolve to promote and implement theological training. Through creative ways, the church leadership should be able to encourage each member to go through theological training. Innovative promotional activities may include but not be limited to holding attractive graduations as a team building event, but also creating space for the graduating members to showcase their newly acquired skills.

On top of this, regular meetings between facilitators, church minister and overseeing structure enables the development of best practices for advancing theological training in every congregation. It is important that congregations, presbyteries and synods adopt theological training as a tool of discipleship. In this way, theological training will be highly promoted in all congregations over time.

Mentoring

Theological training is well received when the church minister and influential elders are involved in mentoring participants. Their roles as mentors not only help to build relationships with subordinates but also facilitate spiritual authority over their members. Through mentoring, members develop stronger trust in their leaders while leaders demonstrate and develop their capacity to lead them well and intimately.

Benefits

Theological training brings forth benefits on three levels namely: individual, family and congregation.

Individual

The benefit of theological training to the individual is immense. Each participant acquires knowledge and skills for leadership development, sermon preparation, people management and pulpit ministry. In general, each participant gains new skills for serving members of the congregation. In addition, the deepened Bible knowledge found in the theological training feeds into the development of one's spiritual life and faith. As such, members of the congregation increasingly serve one another in righteousness.

Family

Respondents established that theological training adds value to the development of the family. For instance, participants are equipped to develop Bible centred and Christ centred family management skills. Such skills enable men and women in the families to deal with marital conflicts and parenting issues which have escalated in recent years. The biblical understanding of family provides stable grounds for participants to lead their families in truth and stability. As a result, the family members are enthused to join theological training. As such theological training leads families to experience a healthy life.

Congregation

The congregation experiences growth due to theological training. Participants sharpen their knowledge of God. Hence, increased knowledge of God provides ground for the growth of one's spiritual life and faith. As knowledge of God increases, their concern and passion for ministry and missions also increases. Therefore, each participant identifies their own passions and gifts and participates in church ministries. As church ministries increase in the congregation, the knowledge of God ensures that quality church decisions are made. Theological training develops interest for further theological pursuits too.

Problems

Individual

The problems of theological training have varied between individual, household and church spheres. Theological training participants are usually under microscopic criticism from peers, family members and non-theological training members of the church. They are either ridiculed for poor performance or their faults are magnified more than their actual magnitude. The peers hold high expectations which generate discouragement and negative attitude when theological training participants fail.

Besides, theological training done by a participant who has never experienced spiritual rebirth leads to the hardening of the heart. As such, participants fail to distinguish between the work of science and that of the Holy Spirit. This failure tends to produce theological hypocrites who rehearse theological rhetoric only without any practice to show for it. In other words, they proclaim right orthodoxy but fail to match with right praxis.

In addition, participants join theological training with wrong motives. They expect to receive financial incentives after completing the training. Failure to live up to the expectation has led them to frustrations and contagious discouragement.

Household

At household level, theological trained members are subjected to harsh ridicule because of their failure to manage household problems better than those who did not receive the theological training. More space is given to those who have theological training in order to serve the church. At times, families have held wrong expectations that theological training is the avenue to pastoral responsibilities.

Church

At the church stage, theologically trained participants are usually overloaded with responsibilities. The overload, at times, can limit their effective service to the church. At most, a section of the church considers the alumni of theological training as people who compete with their own pastors.

Dealing with Problems

Individual level

Theological training participants can deal with their problems in the three dimensions. As individuals, participants must understand each one's vision so that they focus and develop their respective calling and mission. Based on this perspective, they will be able to appreciate different levels of peer expectation not as a source of pressure but motivation to excel.

Participants must also realize the emphatic need to pray and meditate on the Word of God as individuals so that it becomes part of their personal discipline of life. Such disciplines help participants appreciate and understand their own ministry and gift. As part of their ministry, sacrificial giving will be necessary to ensure effective impact on others and the church at large.

Family level

As a family, the participants must accept that their training gives them an edge to expose the members to their leaders as they teach the word of God with confidence and skill. As challenges arise, they must rise to the occasion and apply their theological training with competence for the development of the family.

Church Level

At the church, participants of theological training cannot be competitors of the resident pastor if they realize their nature of calling and ministry under the spiritual authority of the church pastor. In submission and cooperation with the vision of the Pastor, they must strategize to support and promote the church development.

Conclusion

Theological training is an important tool for discipling the CCAP Blantyre Synod and the church at large. The role of church leadership is critical to the promotion and growth of theological training at the grassroots. Church leaders should not only facilitate but also actively participate. Theological training is long overdue in the church of Malawi. Only a theologically trained community can experience transformation that remains Bible centred and Christ centred.

Bibliography

Church of Central Africa, Presbyterian, Blantyre Synod Constitution, Blantyre: Blantyre Synod, 2013.

Church of Central Africa, Presbyterian, Blantyre Synod Strategic Plan 2016-2021, Blantyre: Blantyre Synod Management Team, 2015.

Malongosoledwe a Mapemphero: *Church of Central Africa, Presbyterian Synod of Blantyre,* Blantyre Synod, undated.

Chakuda, Tinenenji, "Literacy Levels now at 73%," *The Nation,* 1.12.2017; www.mwnation.com, [4.5.2019].

Chapter 13

Ministry for All God's People: Laity, Gender and Theological Education in a Rapidly Changing Malawi

Isabel Apawo Phiri

Introduction

The church functions with two categories of people: the laity and the clergy. Throughout the history of Christianity, being clergy comes with a lot of power and privilege while laity means the opposite, especially for lay African women. Renewal in the church and society has also come with redefinition of the role of laity who have a lot to contribute to the church and in the world where they mostly work. This chapter is about affirmation of lay ministry in the church and society, especially for the majority African women who have made the church to be their anchor but have experienced systematic discrimination and oppression due to clericalism.

As a Presbyterian lay woman from Malawi, who has spent one's professional life lecturing in departments of Religious Studies and Theology, faculties and schools of Theology in local and international institutions of higher learning since the 1980s and then transitioned to work for the World Council of Churches, my location is at the intersection of Protestant laity, gender and theological education. My location has influenced the content and my interpretation of what it means to serve God in the church and in the society in a rapidly changing world. Intersectionality is the analytical tool of choice used to help me understand multiple forms of oppression for it encourages examination of how different systems of oppression intersect and affect groups of women in different ways."[1] When the spotlight is put on laity: the people of God, sources of oppression for women becomes a combination of clericalism and patriarchy.

I reflect on the themes of laity, gender justice and theological education from the perspective of my life and work in Malawi, Namibia, South Africa and through the global eye afforded to me as I work for the World Council of Churches. In the first section I will briefly discuss the relationship of clergy and laity. Second, I examine my own journey as a lay woman in the Church of Central Africa Presbyterian (CCAP), Nkhoma Synod and Blantyre Synod; Uniting Presbyterian Church in Southern Africa and in the Church of Scotland in Geneva. Third, I will examine the intersection of female lay theologians and theological institutions (church-owned and state-owned). Fourth, I will draw lessons from how the ministry of the laity has evolved in the ecumenical movement and especially in the area of Public Witness and Diakonia in the World Council of Churches, where I am currently located. Lastly, I will conclude by arguing that, in Malawi we need to prepare the people of God for ministry where every Christian will develop the consciousness that they have to contribute to peace and justice as a response to God's mission.

Clergy and Laity: a Complex Relationship

While the central message of the Gospel that leads to Salvation, which is contained in the Bible has remained the same, how to understand the Scripture and ways of organizing the ministry of the Church has gone through transformation since Christianity was established in the first century. Understanding the concepts of clergy and laity is one example of these changes. According to Richard R. Gaillardetz,

> Although there have been differentiated roles in the church since NT times, for the first 150 years Christianity did not always make a clear

---

1   https://en.wikipedia.org/wiki/Intersectionality.

distinction between laity and clergy. However, a distinction between Christian people as a whole and church leadership had emerged by the 2nd Century. This distinction became hard and fast by the fifth century, as the laity were gradually reduced to passive recipients of clerical ministration.[2]

Elisabeth Adler and Jonah Katoneene add that:

> laypeople are defined by the lack of ordination, the lack of training and competence, and thus are seen as being secondary to the ordained members of the church. The misconception of their place and role in the church has often led to negative connotation regarding the ministry of the laity. Indeed, throughout church history the clergy has seen the laity as objects of its preaching, teaching, pastoral care and theologians have not developed a positive description of function of the laity.[3]

The differentiation on the basis of clergy with power and privilege and laity as follower, is strong in the Catholic Church. The clergy have a lot of power to control the church and in some cases even the social political environment where the church is strong. The Reformation movement of the 16th century was a rejection of such power and privilege, which were often abused at the expense of the followers. The Reformation introduced substantial changes in the understanding of clergy and laity. Martin Luther is well known for using 1 Peter 2:9-10[4] to argue strongly that it is not only ordained priests who have direct access to God. Through Christ all baptized Christians have been given direct access to God. Other relevant

---

2   Richard R. Gaillardertz, "Theology of Laity" in Daniel Patte (ed), *The Cambridge Dictionary of Christianity*, New York: Cambridge University Press, 2010, p. 702.

3   Elisabeth Adler and Jonah Katoneene, "Laity," in Nicholas Lossky, José Miguez Bonino, John Pobee, Tom F. Stransky, Geoffrey Wainwright and Pauline Webb (eds), *Dictionary of the Ecumenical Movement*, 2nd ed, Geneva: WCC, 2003, pp. 658-659.

4   1 Peter 2:9-10 New Revised Standard Version (NRSV): "But you are a chosen race, a royal priesthood, a holy nation, God's own people, in order that you may proclaim the mighty acts of him who called you out of darkness into his marvellous light. Once you were not a people, but now you are God's people; once you had not received mercy, but now you have received mercy."

biblical verses that have been used to support the belief that all Christians are priests are Exodus 19:5–6, First Peter 2:4–8, Book of Revelation 1:4–6, 5:6–10, 20:6 and the Epistle to the Hebrews.[5] Therefore, every Christian has equal potential to minister for God. Out of this teaching came the doctrine of the priesthood of all believers, which is taken seriously by all Protestant Churches. This does not mean that the Protestants do not have a minister who provides leadership. The power of the ordained minister is shared with other lay leaders in the church. For the example, in the case of Reformed churches, the minister is the first Elder among elders responsible for preaching the Word and the Sacraments.[6]

However, although the Protestant churches which came to Malawi believed in the priesthood of believers, for a long time the relationship between the missionaries who were mainly ordained and the laity who had no formal education, was as described by Elisabeth Adler and Jonah Katoneene in the quotation above. Unfortunately, this description of the relationship between clergy and laity has continued even when the churches are now fully in the hands of the indigenous leadership. The congregations located in the city centres of Blantyre, Zomba, Lilongwe and Mzuzu have female and male laity with high professional training as medical doctors, lawyers, judges, theologians, economists, political scientists, educators etc. working for the government or private sector. Any preaching and distribution of church ministries in these cities that does not take this reality into account impoverishes the witness of the Christian faith in the church and in the rapidly changing world. In addition, any use of power and privilege by male clergy that denies the God given gifts of women

---

5   en.wikipedia.org/wiki/universal_priesthood.

6   The Presbyterian Church is ruled by two types of elders: The teaching elder who is called the "Reverend" and the ruling elders who are ordained laymen and women and who also help in preaching the Good news and see to the smooth running of the congregation. The Presbyterians are also classified based on other confessions in addition to the Westminster confession of faith. See "Know your Church" on www.angelfire.com/ex/pcnuyoparish/index1.htm.

fails to help the people of God to experience the abundant life that God promised for all.

My Experience as a Lay Woman in the Presbyterian Church

The Presbyterian church has nurtured me spiritually to know what it means to be a lay woman of faith who desires to live life in the fullness of Christ. As part of my background, I have a variety of traditions from the Presbyterian Church who also hold a variety of teachings on laity and gender roles in the church and society.

First, I inherited from my grandparents a connection with the Dutch Reformed Church Mission, which came from South Africa. My maternal grandfather was a Kerk Session Clerk for a long time at Lobi congregation of CCAP, Nkhoma Synod in Dedza. He is the one who taught me to pray and read my Bible daily. He also taught me the difference between knowing about Jesus and knowing Jesus. He was a very active lay person who in the absence of a minister, lived in the manse. My paternal grandfather was a minister of the Word and Sacrament in the Nkhoma Synod of the CCAP. Since he also lived in the manse at Chilanga congregation in Kasungu, we grew up assuming that both grandfathers were ministers of the Nkhoma Synod of the CCAP, one who wears clerical clothes and the other who does not. It was much later in my life that I realized that one of my grandparents represented the laity and the other the ordained ministries of the Reformed church. Exposure to theological education has also made me realize that the reason why my maternal grandfather was living in a manse is because that congregation did not have an ordained minister due to severe shortage of church leadership.[7] This severe shortage of ministers makes a strong case for the education of laity in theology.

In the context where the gravity of Christianity has shifted from the global North to the global South, the churches in the global south urgently requires an extensive theological programme to equip their lay leadership to contribute to the deepening the faith of their members.

From observing my grandparents and my own experiences in the church, I learnt that women mainly contribute their God given gifts to the church through *Chigwirizano* - Church Women's guild, teaching children through Sunday school and youth Bible studies. This became a topic of interest for me as I pursued my PhD studies at the University of Cape Town, South Africa and majored in African Theology, Mission history and Feminist theology. The title of my thesis was "African Women in Religion and Culture: Chewa women in the Nkhoma Synod of the Church of Central Africa Presbyterian: A Critical Study from Women's Perspective." In my thesis, I argue that *Chigwirizano* provide space for lay women to practise their God given leadership skills.[8] I also highlighted how clericalism and patriarchy has denied women the opportunity to fulfil their calling into leadership positions as teaching and ruling elders and as deacons. The fact that the decision to accept women as elders made in 2011 was rescinded by 2013 is a clear example of patriarchy and clericalism controlling the extent to which women's participation in the church is controlled.

My second Presbyterian church home is the Blantyre Synod of the Church of Central Africa Presbyterian, which traces its roots to the Church of Scotland Mission. This is the church of my parents as they

---

7   See Isabel Apawo Phiri and Dietrich Werner, "Editorial: Handbook of Theological Education in Africa," in Isabel Apawo Phiri and Dietrich Werner (eds), *Handbook of Theological Education in Africa*, Oxford: Regnum, 2013, p. xxviii.

8   Isabel Apawo Phiri, *Women Presbyterianism and Patriarchy: Religious Experiences of Chewa Women in Central Malawi*, Blantyre: CLAIM-Kachere, 1997, p. 80.

worked in Southern Malawi and where I joined the priesthood of all believers through the sacrament of baptism. It is here where I learnt in 1995 that serving God as a lay person through *Mvano* - Women's Guild in Blantyre Synod includes leaving your brains outside as critical thinking about the scriptures or what we were being taught was not allowed. After completing my classes and passing my exams, I was refused membership of the *Mvano* because I was raising gender justice issues in the church and society.[9]

However, a change came in 2000 when the Synod approved the ordination of women into ministry of the word and sacrament. Fortunately, by then there was already a significant number of women with theological education who qualified to take leadership in the church structures as ordained women. Women continue to contribute significantly through other lay ministries of the Blantyre Synod.

My third Presbyterian home has been the Uniting Presbyterian Church of Southern Africa (UPCSA) through the Scottsville congregation in Pietermaritzburg in South Africa since 2000. This church too traces its roots to Church of Scotland Mission work. The UPCSA has accepted the ministry of women both as ordained and as lay people. This is where I began to serve God as a "ruling elder."[10] This is where I saw the senior professional lay members of the congregation being included into the church leadership of the church

---

[9]   See Isabel Apawo Phiri, "Marching, Suspended and Stoned: Christian Women in Malawi 1995," in Kenneth R. Ross (ed), *God, People and Power in Malawi: Democratisation in Theological Perspective*, Blantyre: CLAIM-Kachere, 1996, pp. 63-105.

[10]   The elders are persons chosen from among the congregation and ordained for this service ... However, in many churches, ruling elders retain their ordination for life, even though they serve fixed terms. Even after the end of their terms, they may be active in presbyteries or other bodies, and may serve communion (en.wikipedia.org/wiki/Presbyterian_polity#Elder).

as envisioned by John Knox, the founder of the Church of Scotland, who was a student of John Calvin in Geneva in the 16th century.[11]

My fourth Presbyterian home has been the Church of Scotland in Geneva since 2012, where I have continued to serve God in my lay capacity as a ruling elder.

In summary, although the Presbyterian church comes from the Reformed tradition with its emphasis on priesthood of all believers, how that is applied from one tradition of Presbyterian church to the other differs. In Malawi the gifts of women in the church are mostly exercised through the women's guild - which are powerful in evangelism, *diakonia* work and discipleship of children and youth at church and in their homes. The prophetic *diakonia* where you question why there is injustice and lack of peace in the church and society is not welcomed still, especially when it comes from women. Women, who are in majority in the churches continue to dominate in lay ministries of the church. Substantial renewal is needed value the ministry of lay women in the church in the same way that ordained ministry is accepted.

Lay Professionals in Theological Institutions

As I have stated elsewhere,

> I am an African woman: whose theological education has only been through state universities; who benefited from the World Council of Churches Programme on Theological Education scholarship fund for women without seeking permission from my Presbyterian church in Malawi; who has taught theology in an Ecumenical environment for more than thirty years, within five state universities in three countries in Southern Africa (Malawi, Namibia and South Africa); has been a member of the Circle of Concerned African Women Theologians since

---

[11] Andrew I.M. Kimmitt, "What is an Elder?" in David Plews (ed), *Eldership,* Edinburgh: The Church of Scotland, 2015.

its inception in 1989; and Coordinated the Pan African Circle from 2002 to 2007.[12]

I represent a significant number of African lay women who are lectures in state and church-owned theological institutions where ministers are trained. This is a contested issue in church-owned theological institutions where the majority of the staff are male and ordained. Where you find women lecturers, they are mainly teaching non-theological subjects like English, Sociology or Psychology of Religion. Limitation of lay or ordained female staff in church-owned theological institutions has theological roots. The churches that do not believe in the ordination of women do not allow women to teach biblical and theological subjects. Since Christianity came to Africa at a time when most churches in Europe and North America did not believe in the ordination of women, when the missionaries established bible schools, they excluded women as teachers and as students.

Unfortunately, even after the indigenous people took ownership of the churches, the theological institutions have continued to limit access to their theological institutions to male students and male lectures. The Zomba Theological College has responded to the rapidly changing world by initially accepting lay women to study theology even before the Blantyre Synod of the CCAP accepted the ordination of women. Still even then access to theological education by lay women was limited to those women who were going to work for women's desks of their churches. One needed approval from one's congregation in order to study theology. If a woman wanted to go for Theological Education without the approval of the church, one risked one's education not being recognized by the church. By the time the Blantyre Synod, opened their doors to the participation of women in the leadership of the church as lay or ordained, the

---

12 Isabel Apawo Phiri, "Major Challenges for African Women Theologians in Theological Education (1989-2008)," *Studia Historiae Ecclesiasticae*, December 2008, vol. 34, no. 2, p. 63.

church had a good number of women with church recognized theological education. The ordination of women in the Blantyre Synod also opened the door for ordained women with appropriate theological education to offer biblical and theological courses to students waiting for ordination at Zomba Theological College.

What I have not seen yet is lay women teaching theological subjects to ordained students at church-owned theological institutions. I see that happening in departments of theology in state universities, especially at post graduate level. I have many ordained male students whom I have supervised at masters and PhD level in systematic theology topics with no objections from their churches who may not accept women ordination of women as staff in their church-owned theological seminaries.

Many church-owned theological institutions have special courses for lay women married to ministers so that they can give leadership to the women's guild in their churches. Unfortunately, the quality of this theological education is very basic and it does not match with the complex experiences that spouses of ministers experience when they go back to work in the congregations.

The Circle of the Concerned African women theologians, which consists of both lay and ordained women theologians, have published books to promote a better biblical and theological understanding of the lay and ordained as well as women and men ministries in the church and society for fullness of life for all.

Theological Education by Extension has been key in the equipping the people of God for ministry in the churches and in the world.[13] In my experience, it has been key in the provision of theological education especially to women in African initiated churches who have

13 See Kangwa Mabuluki, "Theological Education for all God's People: Theological Education by Extension (TEE) in Africa," in Isabel Apawo Phiri and Dietrich Werner (eds), *Handbook of Theological Education in Africa*, Oxford: Regnum, 2013, pp. 832-840.

founded their own churches, they still have a secular job and may not have money, or entry qualification for seminaries. As part of my community engagement work while lecturing at the University of KwaZulu Natal I also ran the Centre for Constructive Theology in Durban, South Africa, which had an activity that provided theological education by extension to men and women church leaders of African Initiated Churches in KwaZulu Natal. The majority of our students were women.

Christ in the World: Ministry of the Whole People of God

The World Council of Churches offers a good model of recognition of ministry the ministry of the laity (who are better known as the whole people of God). Historically, it was at the second World Council of Churches assembly in Evanston, Illinois, in the United States of America in 1954 where it became clear that conversation on the ministry of the whole people of God was important to the WCC. Their focus was not to compare the ministry of the ordained, the theologians, the professional church workers but by appreciation of the church in the world. I find this emphasis very important especially in the following description from WCC Evanston assembly in 1954:

> The real battles of the faith today are being fought in the factories and shops, offices and farms, in the political parties, government agencies and countless homes; in the press, radio, television, and in the relationships between nations. It is often said that the church should go into these spheres, but the church is in fact already there. Laypeople are "those members of the church, both men and women, who earn their livelihood in a secular job and who, therefore, spend most of their working hours in a 'worldly' occupation."... The phrase 'the ministry of the laity' expresses the privilege of the whole church to share in Christ' ministry to the world.[14]

---

[14]   Elisabeth Adler and Jonah Katoneene, "Laity," p. 659.

This quotation was meant to boost the self-understanding of the whole people of God that: a) When Christians are doing their normal duties in their various jobs, they are ambassadors of Christ. They are a letter from Christ to the world. This was also echoed at the New Delhi WCC Assembly in 1961. If this message was ingrained in every Christian working in the world today, we would see a massive transformation in every field. In particular, there is widespread corruption in the world, even in predominantly Christian countries like Malawi. The corrupt politicians, economists, judges, lawyers, hospital personnel, educators are Christians who do not take seriously their responsibility to be ambassadors of Christ in their jobs. b) There is also a need to remind the people of God through sermons, Bible studies and morning devotions that they have the responsibility to be ambassadors of Christ at their work place and in their home. In other words, personal renewal of the people of God overflows to their homes and the places where they work.

The second renewal of the ministry of the people of God in the WCC happened at the Uppsala Assembly in 1969 when there was a shift from self-understanding to content of the ministry of the people of God. At this assembly, they focused on the hopes and dilemmas of the world, on development, justice and peace.[15] This was translated into the people of God getting involved in grassroots movements for political, economic and social change which also included sustainable communities and the environment.

The creation of the Programme to Combat Racism, especially in South Africa was a fruit of the action orientated ministry of the whole people of God. This proved to be very controversial and some churches e.g. The Dutch Reformed Church in South Africa cancelled their membership in the World Council of Churches.[16] Those

---

[15] www.oikoumene.org/en/resources/documents/wcc-programmes/public-witness/peacebuilding-and-reconciliation-consultation.

[16] The World Council of Churches had already suspended the Dutch Reformed Church in South Africa in 1961 for heresy by supporting racism theologically.

churches felt that the WCC was too political and was supporting those whom they labelled terrorists e.g. the African National Congress party of Nelson Mandela and Bishop Desmond Tutu in South Africa. When Nelson Mandela came out of prison in 1990 after 27 years of imprisonment and became the first president of a democratic South Africa in 1994, he came to the WCC offices in Geneva, Switzerland to express his personal appreciation to the WCC for its ministry for God's people. It is also important to mention that the Dutch Reformed Church in South Africa renounced racism as sin against God who created all people in God's own image. In 2016 The Dutch Reformed Church in South Africa was restored back into the fellowship of the World Council of Churches. The Programme to Combat Racism is still often cited by the United Nations as the most effective programme of the World Council of Churches.

The emphasis on justice and peace as the ministry for the people of God has continued in the WCC. The WCC 10th Assembly, meeting in Busan, South Korea, under the theme "God of life, lead us to justice and peace," continued the call for peace with justice. The Assembly also reiterated the key role of WCC as convener and facilitator for global ecumenical peace and advocacy work, and the WCC member churches further committed themselves to mobilize the gifts within the fellowship to raise their collective voice for peace across many countries.

The WCC 10th assembly issued an invitation to a pilgrimage of justice and peace.[17] It was an invitation to the worldwide fellowship of Christian churches to deepen their relationship with God and each other by joining together in prayer, witness and service for justice and peace. The invitation was also extended to people of other faiths and people of good will to work and walk together on issues of common concern. In this pilgrimage the assembly identified the following "priority countries" for special attention: the Korean Peninsula, Syria,

---

[17] www.oikoumene.org/en/resources/documents/central-committee/geneva-2014/an-invitation-to-the-pilgrimage-of-justice-and-peace

Israel/Palestine, Nigeria, South Sudan and the Democratic Republic of Congo. Since 2013, the list of countries has expanded to include Iraq, Colombia, Burundi and Ukraine. Besides peacebuilding, invitation also included pilgrimages in addressing issues of Climate Change, Economic Justice and Human Dignity (gender justice, health and healing, racism, migration, xenophobia, statelessness, children, nuclear disarmament). Through engagement with the people of God in Israel and Palestine (2016) Nigeria, Burundi, South Sudan and Democratic Republic of Congo (2017) Colombia (2018) Bangladesh, India, Myanmar, Pakistan, Thailand, (2019) Fiji (2020) WCC has come to understand that on this pilgrimage of justice and people (2016-2020), the major concerns of people are: truth and trauma; land and displacement; gender justice and racial justice.

The approach adopted on the pilgrimage, reflects that all the people of God are on God's mission. Being on a Pilgrimage of Justice and Peace is: participating in God's mission towards life; moving to issues and places relevant for life and survival of people and earth; deepening the fellowship of churches on the way with a strong spiritual dimension of common prayer and theological reflection. It is a journey of hope, looking for and celebrating signs of God's reign of justice and peace already here and now and discovering opportunities for common witness and transformative action that make a difference in today's world with an open invitation to all people of good will.

God is found where people are celebrating their God given gifts, where there is brokenness and people are hurting and we seek to work together to transform the injustices. This requires promotion of justice and peace through advocacy at international, regional and national levels on behalf of and with our member churches. The fellowship is mobilized to accompany people who are in conflict and post conflict countries and consultations are organized to promote theological reflections on the current issues for advocacy and accompaniment. Advocacy and accompaniment must always be informed by theological reflection, which is also informed by advocacy and accompaniment.

Each country is also invited to reflect for itself on what it means for Christians, people of other faiths and of goodwill to be on a pilgrimage of justice and peace.

As I give oversight to the work of the pilgrimage of justice and peace, I have come to appreciate my position as an African lay woman with theological education, bringing the experiences of Africa to the global stage and taking with me back to Africa what I have learnt from the global church. The colleagues whom I work with are professionals in their fields: doctors, lawyers, economists, political analysts, theologians and educators. We are mostly lay people who have a lot to contribute to the work of the church in the world.

Conclusion

I grew up in Malawi in the 1970s to early 1990s when theological education was separated from what people were experiencing in politics and economy. South African liberation theology and feminist theology helped to engage my faith with the signs of our times. I wish this kind of learning were available to all the people of God in Malawi. This can only happen with continuing education of the people of God to show them that they are not just receivers of messages from the clergy but they are to reflect for themselves on what are the signs of our times and what is God calling them to do. In Malawi, we need to prepare the people of God for ministry where every Christian will develop the consciousness that they have to contribute to peace and justice in response to God's mission.

Bibliography

Adler, Elisabeth and Jonah Katoneene, "Laity," in Nicholas Lossky, José Miguez Bonino, John Pobee, Tom F. Stransky, Geoffrey Wainwright and Pauline Webb (eds), *Dictionary of the Ecumenical Movement*, 2nd ed., Geneva: WCC, 2003, pp. 658–664.

Gaillardertz, Richard R., "Theology of Laity," in Daniel Patte (ed), *The Cambridge Dictionary of Christianity*, New York: Cambridge University Press, 2010, pp. 702-703.

Mabuluki, Kangwa, "Theological Education for all God's People: Theological Education by Extension (TEE) in Africa" in Isabel Apawo Phiri and Dietrich Werner (eds), *Handbook of Theological Education in Africa*, Oxford: Regnum, 2013, pp. 832-840.

Phiri, Isabel Apawo and Dietrich Werner, "Editorial: Handbook of Theological Education in Africa," in Isabel Apawo Phiri and Dietrich Werner (eds), *Handbook of Theological Education in Africa*, Oxford: Regnum Books International, 2013, pp. xxvii-xxxiii.

Phiri, Isabel Apawo, *Women Presbyterianism and Patriarchy: Religious Experiences of Chewa Women in Central Malawi*, Blantyre: CLAIM-Kachere, 1997.

Phiri, Isabel Apawo, "Marching, Suspended and Stoned: Christian Women in Malawi 1995," in Kenneth R. Ross (ed), *God, People and Power in Malawi: Democratisation in Theological Perspective*, Blantyre: CLAIM-Kachere, 1996, pp. 63-105.

Phiri, Isabel Apawo, "Major Challenges for African Women Theologians in Theological Education (1989-2008)," *Studia Historiae Ecclesiasticae*, December, 2008, vol. 34, no. 2, pp. 63-81.

Raiser, Elisabeth, "Inclusive Community," in John Briggs, Mercy Amba Oduyoye and Georges Tsetsis (eds), *A History of the Ecumenical Movement. Volume 3 1968-2000*, Geneva: WCC, 2004, pp. 244-277.

Chapter 14

(Financial) Viability of Grassroots Theological Education

Volker Glissmann

Introduction

Theological Education is at the heart of the life of the church.[1] Theological education prepares those serving in numerous roles within the church community and it exists to serve God through equipping God's servants for life, for ministry, for witnessing. Unfortunately, theological education is sometimes reduced to focus exclusively on leadership development to serve the church's own internal organizational needs. Yet, comprehensive grassroots theological education is and remains an important internal development need of the church.[2] Overall, theological education exists on a continuum that addresses a whole range of different educational needs: grassroots, ministerial and academic or higher theological education.[3] Overall, the church has a commitment and a

---

[1] Education is not always the highest priority in all parts of Malawi, especially rural Malawi. That effects the mission of the church too. The Malawi school education system with its huge classes, minimal personal attention by the teachers and limited (to non-existent) learning materials and a resulting teacher-centred learning are contextual challenges especially to grassroots theological education. However, the benefits of learning are usually embraced by the grassroots when the opportunity arises. For a discussion of attempted learner based education see: Wezzie Chiziwa, *Curriculum Reform. Initial Primary School Teachers' Experiences with Outcome Based Education in Malawi*, Mzuzu: Livingstonia Press, 2020.

[2] Grassroots theological education explicitly includes Christian education and the Christian education department within the church.

[3] Christian education is part of theological education though I prefer the term grassroots theological education, for a detailed discussion see Volker Glissmann,

calling to provide (ongoing) theological education to the clergy as well as to the laity or the grassroots. This is generally accepted on all sides.

Institutions for ministerial and academic theological education have developed wide-ranging systems, approaches and methods to ensure comprehensive training can be offered to the highest theological, and educational standards. Yet, these two forms of theological education also continuously evolve, develop and change in order to offer even better theological education. The same is true for institutions (both church-internal and ecumenical institutions) that offer grassroots theological education. One of the key questions is how best to equip the grassroots for life, faith and service? This conversation has to happen within our church context, where some city congregations have thousands of members and where pastors look after multiple congregations. For CCAP Blantyre Synod a congregation has a minimum of 200 members and pastors look after multiple congregations and prayer houses. The Malawian context is on one where the leadership need of the church is much greater than which could be met by a relatively small number of full-timer clergy. Additionally, a literate and highly competent grassroots has many gifts and skills that can be released for service in the church and outreach of the church through appropriate theological education. A related question is how can ministers be supported to comprehensively train their leaders and members of the congergation? Traditionally, ministers are expected to provide (member) education that goes beyond their preaching ministry. Preaching and teaching are not the same, teaching is distinctly different form of

<hr>

"Grassroots Theological Education," p. 54-55. See also Dietrich Werner who lists under theological education a broad range of different activities including "theological lay education, ministerial formation, theological education by extension, continued education for pastors and church-workers, distance learning theological education," see Dietrich Werner, "Ecumenical Learning in Theological Education," p. 1.

ministry from preaching.[4] In the traditional four-fold ministry division of ministers - teaching is one of the key pastoral roles.[5] One assumption in ministerial theological education is that pastoral knowledge "trickles down" through preaching and teaching to the grassroots. Ross Kinsler evaluated the assumptions that theological knowledge will eventually "trickle down" to the grassroots and especially churches in the rural areas. He concluded that it does not happen in any meaningful way.[6] The other issue is that "trickle down" does not lead to actually ministry preparation of the grassroots. Kinsler proposes to release the energy of the believers and their local leaders for primary ministry. He continues, "Fulltime "ministers" should no longer be allowed to pre-empt the ministries of their congregations; they must play an essential but *auxiliary* role – to enable and support local leaders who should carry the *primary* responsibility for ministry."[7]

The teaching role or office of ordained ministers is a historical precedent that arose at a time when church ministry was significantly differently understood and when the church's teaching was limited to theological and biblical knowledge mainly delivered through sermons to an audience of comparatively less-educated individuals than the pastors. In the Malawian context where a few full-time clergy are responsible for the education of so many individuals, the question of the fitness for purpose of education simply trickling down is questioned.

---

4   Thomas Oden helpfully summarizes this when he says, "teaching is done generally through proclamation [preaching], worship, Eucharist, and pastoral care, but more particular through catechesis, confirmation, and deliberate efforts at Christian education" (Oden, *Pastoral Theology: Essentials of Ministry*, p. 141).

5   Traditionally, there were four main areas identified for pastoral formation: preaching, pastoral care, (member's) education (also called "teaching" which includes catechesis, confirmation, baptism preparation, Bible studies) and leadership.

6   See Kinsler, 'Ministry by the People,' p. 4.

7   Kinsler, 'Ministry by the People,' p. 9, emphasis original.

The need, scope and content of grassroots theological education has significantly grown in the last half century. Church life in the 21st century has moved and changed dramatically beyond the exclusive theological-biblical teaching requirements of previous generations of ministers. Grassroots ministry empowerment requires additional inputs by pastors to deliver highly specialized and often additional material beyond the classic theological-biblical content that defines the church's ministry and the content of their own theological ministerial education. This includes (but is not limited to): teaching methodologies for Youth and Sunday School Teachers, Bible study skills and small group dynamics, theories of human development for the Youth and Sunday School Teachers, financial and budget management of the church session, conflict management and resolutions, pastoral care skills (as well as marriage counselling) for lay leaders which is informed by theological-biblical reflections on culture as well as insights from sociological and psychological contemporary research on human development, knowledge of the (ever changing) government regulations and laws so that the church supports the government's efforts toward human wellbeing in society for example through child protection and labour laws. That is even before we spoke of the many partnerships to improve the life and wellbeing of Malawians that the church and congregations are involved in, through farming and food security projects, water and well drilling, houses for the vulnerable, work with street children and mentally handicapped individuals, entrepreneurship and income generation projects, tree planting and environmental protection and of course the other two key pillars of the Malawian church: its health and education work. Here in Malawi, we know that the majority of the diverse church ministry is actually done by the lay Christians. The bottom line is that the teaching ministry that is expected to be delivered by the teaching elder/pastor for grassroots empowerment has grown so much and has become so diverse that realistically speaking, no minister can fulfil this ministry solemnly by developing teaching materials by themselves or even to exclusively rely only on their theological education which might not always prepare ministers

259

to equip grassroots leaders to run both theological-biblically informed as well as contemporarily relevant ministries of the church.[8]

This is the context in which the reflections about the viability of grassroots theological education takes place. It is good to reflect about biblical revelation and theological insights in order to empower the grassroots church as theologians and church leaders have done in this volume. However, without addressing the elephant in the room, namely the viability as well as the funding of grassroots theological education, not much is gained. Traditionally, the words "viability" and "financial" go together. However, the idea of reducing viability to only one aspect of viability, namely financial viability, should raise some serious theological questions within the church community about the very nature of theological education and reflection. Therefore, this chapter will approach the question of the viability of grassroots theological education by firstly, looking at viability as covenant faithfulness, secondly, by looking at covenant faithfulness as requiring broad or comprehensive theological education and thirdly, (comprehensive) theological education requires church-based.

Viability as Covenant Faithfulness

The question of viability is asking whether something can work successfully? Or in other words, whether something can achieve its intended purpose? Is it fit for purpose? The idea of sustainability on the other hand asks the question if something can be maintained at its current level. In that regard, the "viability" question is not exclusively about finances but more importantly about whether an organization, namely the church, is currently able to successfully

---

[8]   Theological education traditionally focusses on leadership development for future church ministers and might or might not be best placed to equally empower them with the specialized knowledge required to run specialized ministries in the church. That is why theological institutions increasingly offer courses for Youth and Children Ministry or Music Ministry and even Urban or Rural Ministries.

achieve its overall goals. It is important to ask the viability question not with an exclusive focus on the individual institutions that the church set up to achieve its goals. Rather the question explicitly needs to include the church because it is the church that initiated institutions to aid the church's own objectives. Viable theological educational allows the church, in all its many manifestations, to work successfully and fully participate in the mission of God in the world. A key question here is, is it actually viable for the church *not* to comprehensively train the grassroots and instead focus predominantly on ministerial theological education?

Within the church, too often viability is treated predominantly in terms of financial viability.

> All too often people think of viability in terms of the financial sustainability of the institutions. But financial viability is not the fundamental issue. The fundamental issue is how an educational process can *renew*, give life (*la vie*), transform people, churches and other institutions and the world. In other words, the funding question should never be dissociated from the vision question.[9]

Then the question becomes, can we afford it? Is it not too expensive? Yeow Choo Lak reflecting on decades of leadership in church and theological education responds poignantly to the exclusive financial question, "*If you think education is expensive, try ignorance.*' The same sentiment can be extended to theological education: '*If you think theological education is expensive, try heresy.*'"[10] Theological Education is expensive and wholistic quality theological education is very expensive. To look at viability only through a set of financial questions is not an adequate theological response. There are three related questions that require theological answers first of all: Do we want theological education? Secondly, how comprehensive do we

---

[9] John Pobee, 'The Viability of Tertiary and Theological Institutions: Problems and Promises,' p. 38, emphasis original.

[10] Yeow Choo Lak, 'The Financial Viability of Ecumenical Theological Formation,' p. 97, emphasis original.

want our theological education to be? Thirdly, is it viable not to invest significantly in grassroots theological education? Educated clergy is vital for the spiritual wellbeing and ministry of the church, an educated grassroots is also vital for the spiritual wellbeing and ministry of the church. In the words of the great African theologian, John S. Pobee:

> I must address a thing about our African situation. In Ghana, my home, people often associate, if not equate reading theology with training for ministry and priesthood. In that way they signal that theology is for those to be set apart for the priesthood of the church and not something for all and sundry. Here is a fundamental error that needs correcting so as to release energies for viability. In our churches, especially since the Reformation and in the ecumenical movement, we have affirmed what is theologically stated as the priesthood of all believers. In other words, by virtue of our baptisms we are each and all consecrated and constituted into a people of God with a mission to the ends of the world.[11]

Theological education for all the people of God (both clergy and grassroots) will release the right energies for the witness of the church: well-trained clergy and well-trained grassroots. This then allows for the full participation of all the people of God in the mission of God. The church can only succeed in its witness if everyone is equipped, if everyone is informed and if everyone can fully participate in God's mission to be a witness of his goodness to the world.

Not surprisingly, this is also apparent in the reflection of Hosea the prophet. During the Assyrian crisis, Hosea the prophet gave a profound and disturbing reflection on the state of covenant faithfulness within the Kingdom of Israel. Hosea's reflections are crucial because he spoke just before the end of the Kingdom of Israel at the hand of the Assyrians. Hosea concluded his assessment of the nation by highlighting that God's people "are destroyed for lack of

---

[11] John Pobee, "The Viability of Tertiary and Theological Institutions: Problems and Promises," p. 39.

knowledge" (Hosea 4:6). Neither the vertical relationship with God was right nor the horizontal relationship among the people of God was right. This lack of knowledge manifested itself profoundly,

> there is no faithfulness or steadfast love, and no knowledge of God in the land; there is swearing, lying, murder, stealing, and committing adultery; they break all bounds, and bloodshed follows bloodshed. Therefore the land mourns, and all who dwell in it languish, and all the beasts of the field and the birds in the heavens, and even the fish of the sea are taken away. (Hosea 4:1-3)

Ultimately, the complaint of the prophet is that the whole covenant community is not an honour-bringing witness to the life and witness of God's people in their entirety (as co-regent with God) to the greatness and life-sustaining guidance of the God of Israel. Israel, the people and the nation, were not blessed because God's guidance for successfully living (as the covenant community) in the Torah was not followed.[12] The people died because of a lack of knowledge of their covenant God (Hosea 4:6). The remedy to avoid calamity falling upon the covenant community is emphasizing the need for knowledge about God and His ways among all the people of God. This is the essential spiritual reason why grassroots theological education is so vital. The church cannot exist without knowledgeable clergy and knowledgeable members and this makes ministerial and grassroots theological education paramount to the life of the church.

A Deuteronomistic reading of the Old Testament emphasizes the fault of the kings of Israel in the downfall of the Kingdom of Israel (Northern Kingdom). This can be seen in the final and summarizing report of the Fall of Samaria to the Assyrians in 2 Kings 17:1-23, which blamed the sins of the people on the sins of King Jeroboam of Israel. The sins of King Jeroboam are of course central to the

---

[12] Torah generally means guidance. A more poignant translation of the "law of Moses" would be the "guidance/Torah of Moses."

downfall of the Kingdom of Israel.[13] But it was not the sin of one individual but rather the example set by the nation's leadership that deprived the people of guidance about their ancestral covenant relationship. Ultimately, it was the sin of the people in their entirety that caused God's rejection of the people. The background to the rejection of the Kingdom of Israel is of course the covenant idea that all Israel is called to be priests and a holy nation (Exodus 19:6 cf Isaiah 61:6). The prophet Hosea on the other hand, adds insights to the Deuteronomistic emphasis that only the political leadership was to blame for the downfall and for the ignorance of the people. Hosea continues to expand his insights into the lack of covenant faithfulness in Israel by highlighting the failure of the priests (as well the prophets), when he says, "Yet let no one contend, and let none accuse, for with you is my contention, O priest" (Hosea 4:4, ESV). The priests and the prophets were supposed to guide the nations in their covenant relationship, but they failed (Hosea 4:5). Hosea emphasizes this as the result of the rejection of the priesthood, "My people are destroyed for lack of knowledge; because you have rejected knowledge, I reject you from being priests to me. And since you have forgotten the law of your God, I will also forget your children" (Hosea 4:6, ESV). The Jewish priesthood learned from its failure that led not only to the Assyrian captivity but also to the Babylonian exile. The lesson that the Jewish priests learned was that the teaching and instruction of all of God's people developed especially as a result of the Babylonian exile. Grassroots theological education is one of the key developments of Israel's reflection about the reasons why the nations lost its ancestral covenantal homeland. "The priests, whose primary duty was to teach the law of God to the

---

[13] There are 23 references throughout the books of 1 and 2 Kings to the sin of Jeroboam which caused Israel to sin -- see 1 Kings 14:16. Later kings of Israel continued the sins of Jeroboam: see 1 Kings 15:30, 15:34, 16:2, 16:7, 16:19, 16:26, 16:31, 21:22, 22:52, 2 Kings 3:3, 10:29, 10:31, 13:2, 13:6, 13:11, 14:24, 15:9, 15:18, 15:24, 15:28, 17:21, 17:22, 23:15.

people, had failed to do so."[14] Therefore, the priests emphasised after the exile their role to teach the people the law of God. One important corrective to the failed reliance on the exclusive priestly guardianship of knowledge developed during the Babylonian exile, in the move from Temple worship to synagogue worship, from liturgy towards Torah reading, from individual and priestly intermediation to community and communal piety. The Babylonian exile formulated a diversification of knowledge into the community away from the custodianship of the priest/teacher towards grassroots education as a viable solution. We see this among those that returned from Babylonian exile, Nehemiah 8 retells the story of the returnees from exile and their desire to build the new community upon the ancestral covenant – the Torah of Moses. Nehemiah 8:1 highlights the essential theological reformulation and democratization of building the life of the community around God's guidance. The initiative goes out from "all the people" who had gathered, "they" told Ezra to bring "the book of the Law of Moses." Then Ezra read to them. The story is an important reminder that spiritual initiatives also originate from the grassroots when they have been theologically empowered.

It is of spiritual and theological essence for the covenant community – the church – that "all the people" are theologically informed, spiritually vibrant and engaged in God's mission. Dietrich Werner, the former Ecumenical Theological Education Programme Coordinator at the World Council of Churches (WCC), neatly summaries the key reflections that were prompted by the Edinburgh 2010 centenary conference which started a renewed global engagement on the role of theological education.[15] Here are some of the key summaries from that process,

---

[14] Douglas Carew, "Hosea," in *Africa Bible Commentary*, Grand Rapids: Zondervan, 2006, 1013–26. p. 1017.

[15] The Programme on Ecumenical Theological Education (ETE) of the World Council of Churches developed out of its predecessor the Theological Education Fund (TEF) which was formed during the Ghana Assembly of the International

Theological education is the most essential key and strategic factor for the renewal of the church's life and mission. Without proper and relevant theological education the very future of the Christian church, its dialogue with society and its participation in the daily struggles and longings of ordinary people is endangered; the less churches and their leaders are investing in theological education, the more the future of Christianity will be left to those who promote a distorted image of the Christian identity and endanger dialogue and co-existence with other churches as well as other religious traditions. Theological education is thus vital for the transmission of Christian tradition from one generation to the next and essential for the renewal and continuity of the church and its leadership. Theological education is a matter of survival for an authentic and contextual mission of the church in contemporary contexts. ... With all legitimate attention and emphasis on ministerial formation, an inclusive approach emphasizing theological education as a process of renewal and formation for all God's people always needs to be kept in mind.[16]

The theological (as well as spiritual) viability of the church depends on utilizing quality theological education in order to empower the church and all its members.

Churches cannot function properly with an ignorant laity. How much more would the church benefit from empowered and informed laity? The pastoral vision for the congregation cannot function without the laity. How much more would the pastor benefit from empowered and informed grassroots? In reality, many churches and many potential candidates for the ministry, as well as many ministry jobs are poorly resourced. This is not going to change anytime soon nor is it a uniquely Malawian issue. Full-time theological education is financially viable only for the few and bi-vocational church ministers

---

Missionary Council in Accra 1958. Edinburgh 2010 refers to a major mission conference that looked at mission in the 21st century. It was held on the centenary of the World Missionary Conference held in Edinburgh 1910. Major publications arose from the conference, see www.edinburgh2010.org, [12.2.2020].

[16] Werner, "Ecumenical Learning in Theological Education," pp. 6–7.

which might be increasingly necessary (here in Malawi as well as in the West). Against this background, grassroots empowerment is vital. Ultimately, there are spiritual and theological reasons, besides financial and practical considerations, that demand grassroots empowerment because it is at the heart of the covenant relationship between all the people and their God.

Within the Malawian context with its challenges of few full-time ministers in relation to the vast grassroots the need for a training the grassroots through the pastoral the teaching role seems like an overwhelming task. However, the alternative of not training the grassroots seems even more overwhelmingly negative especially in light of Hosea's reflection and the two subsequent exiles that are attributed to a lack of knowledge that destroyed the people of God. Grassroots Theological Education is important because without it covenant faithfulness will decline. The measure for viable grassroots theological education is a systematic theological education system that provides knowledge for the people to be faithful to the covenant and empowers them to participate. A viable theological education system requires to focus on knowledge for all.

Covenant Faithfulness Requires Broad or Comprehensive Theological Education

Any training is better than no training, but broad or comprehensive training is better than any training. And covenant faithfulness requires a broad or comprehensive approach to grassroots theological education which allows for full participation in life through the blessings of God, full ownership of individual's faith and preparation for allowing gifts and skills to be used in the service and ministry of God.

The closest societal equivalent to the question of viability for theological and especially grassroots theological education is "secular" education. Education is the attempt of our societies to empower every generation for full participation in the economic and political life of our societies. It is something that we might take for granted today, however, these are rights that previous generations have fought for (and current generations in many places still fight for today). Education is a right for the country's citizen. Education is the dream of a society for equal opportunity, for equal participation and fundamentally for allowing those that are gifted intellectually to rise to the top to contribute to the welfare of society (for example through engineering innovations or medical research). Most societies have free Primary and Secondary School education and this is understood as an investment in the next generation of tax payers. The aim is to achieve, for most members of society, full participation in the life of society. Literacy (both reading and writing) are cornerstones of society which will enable individuals to read their medical prescription, to understand the laws of the land and to be self-empowered in forming political views and to be informed and participate in the elimination of evils identified by society (e.g. HIV and AIDS). Some societies also have free tertiary level education. For these societies the reason is the same as for Primary and Secondary School Education.

What is true for General Education is also true for theological education and especially church-based grassroots theological education. Theological education is essential for the life of the church as it empowers individual members to fully participate in the life of the church. A well trained and informed grassroots will feed into the growth and development of the church through expertise, theological reflection on areas of personal expertise, by full (aka informed) participation in the mission of God and the church.[17] An additional

---

[17]   Cf. Engel who observed, "the charismata of Christians are so manifold and the challenges which the churches face in each continent deserve new activities and emphases in funding ... missionary innovation and a new spirit can be found among people, who would like to be more actively involved in the life of the churches who seek education for the purpose: as an ordained minister, as a lay person or as members of independent Christian groups," see Engel, "Funding of Theological Education," p. 139.

benefit of developing qualified grassroots leaders will then create a pool from which experienced and proven ministerial candidates can be drawn.[18]

The full participation of all of God's people in the mission of God and full participation in the life of the church is a mark of viable theological education. Important in that regard is the consistent theological argument and application to the idea of the full participation of all of God's people which is centrally expressed in the idea of the priesthood of all believers within the context of the *missio Dei* (the mission of God in and through the life of the church). Full participation of the grassroots means that grassroots theological education in general should be emphasised but it also means that ministerial grassroots theological education and training needs to be offered to those members of the grassroots who are involved in any kind of church-based ministry.[19] Generally speaking, the grassroots in its entirety needs to be educated as they fully participate in the *missio Dei*. Additionally, some members of the grassroots will be elected or appointed to leadership positions in ministries of the church. For these, additional ministerial grassroots theological education is also paramount. For church-based theological education and trainings' reason for the theological and educational empowerment of grassroots leaders, be they Elders, Deacons, Evangelists, Sunday School Teachers, Children and Youth Leaders or Worship Team Leaders, is fulfilling the essential request of the church to train the next generation. Theological education is concerned with empowering all the people of God to live in harmony

---

[18] Traditional hierarchical societies have a traditional leadership style based on seniority which can cause friction when young and often inexperienced young theological graduates are installed as leaders. For further discussion, see Yeow Choo Lak, "The Financial Viability of Ecumenical Theological Formation," in *Towards Viable Theological Education: Ecumenical Imperative, Catalyst of Renewal*, Geneva: WCC, 1997, pp. 94–102 [97–98].

[19] The importance of theological education does not undermine the plurality of important issues that churches are engaged in.

with God and in harmony with each other and in harmony with God's creation as God's appointed co-regents (or representatives) here on earth.

Grassroots theological education requires a broad and comprehensive approach to grassroots theological education (in the same way that ministerial theological education is board and comprehensive). The aim of grassroots theological education is to prepare the grassroots for life faith and ministry. One of the failures of pre-exilic Israel and Judah was that the people didn't know and thereby didn't live by God's covenant even though they were called by his name. Some members of the grassroots will not only require theological knowledge but also appropriate ministry training so that they can fulfil their grassroots ministerial call, as elders, deacons, Sunday school teachers, children and youth leaders as well as in response to the many gifts and skills that that the grassroots has been given to support the ministry of the local church. This is why grassroots theological education should be broad and comprehensive, rather than piecemeal and sporadic. Grassroots theological education in order to aid the viability of the church needs to be systematic, comprehensive, need-based, ongoing and responding to the local contexts. Only a broad and comprehensive approach to grassroots theological education can be called viable grassroots theological education, it has to prepare for life, for faith and for ministry. One of the lessons of the exile was not to limit theological knowledge and religious participation among the people but this required that a broad and comprehensive knowledge needed to be made available to the ordinary people, so that they once empowered through knowledge were empowered to live faithful to the covenant. This broad foundation of knowledge was important for the Jewish communities who lived far away and couldn't participate in the temple worship, yet these communities where able to use the Sabbath family meal as an essential element of maintaining their faith as it was anchored not in the priests but in the actual family meal within the family. The broad knowledge was also important when the apostles went to Jewish communities in the diaspora to proclaim Christ, because these communities comprehensively knew their Old Testament so it was easy to prove that Jesus was the promised Old Testament Messiah because of the people's broad knowledge which saved them.

Broad or Comprehensive Theological Education requires Church-based Funding

Financial viability is important but it is only one element of the sustainability or viability of theological education both for ministerial and for grassroots theological education. It is nearly impossible for ministers to do all the needed and required grassroots theological education without the help from outside. This is partly because of time and will remain a key problem until churches have significantly more clergy to look after the grassroots church. The other reason is that it is nearly impossible in the 21st century for ministers to develop their own contextual, systematic, comprehensive and pedagogically designed training programme that will empower the grassroots they look after. On the other hand, why would minsters not try to rely on the expertise of theological training institutions that actually can offer the kind of contextual, systematic, comprehensive and pedagogically designed grassroots education programmes that are needed? Ministers have access to denominational as well as ecumenical (and church-owned and approved) residential and distance learning institutions that have the needed expertise (or should have the expertise).

The foundational funding idea for theological education is that "financial responsibility lies primarily upon the local church or churches."[20] Yet a balanced and practical approach has emerged out of the practicalities of church life, namely that it is "a combination of

---

[20] See Herbert M. Zorn, *Viability in Context: The Theological Seminary in the Third World - Seedbed or Sheltered Garden?* Bromley: Theological Education Fund, 1975, p. 27.

sources of revenue from local contributions, fees and endowment which provides the greatest financial viability."[21] Here "local contributions" refers to the aforementioned responsibility of the church. A key area of sustainability for theological education is the relation between the church and theological institutions. In theory the theological institutions train for the church, but it is the church that needs to ascribe relevance to theological colleges and their graduates. This is more of a problem for interdenominational institutions than for denominational institutions. Yet, there is also too often a widening gap between the needs of the church and the services and programmes offered by institutions. The sustainability model for denominational institutions can fail if theological institutions are not fully participating in the life and training of the church. Too often, theological institutions are self-identifying and self-labelling as "leadership training" which usually refers to ministerial theological education and increasingly to ministerial higher theological education. The relevance of the theological training's institution for the life of the church will ultimately determine its own financial viability in the long run. One of the missiological founding ideas of the church, especially in Sub-Saharan Africa, is: self-sustaining, self-propagating, self-governing and increasingly the emphasis is also on self-theologizing.[22] Underlying all of the above is the assumption that church communities pay for those that serve them.[23] The same assumption is applied to the funding of theological education in general and grassroots theological education

---

[21] See Herbert M. Zorn, *Viability in Context*, p. 29.

[22] See McGinnis, "From Self-Reliant Churches to Self-Governing Communities." Also Shenk, "The Contribution of Henry Venn to Mission Thought." The fourth "self" of self-theologising was highlighted by David Bosch who follows Paul G. Hiebert, see Bosch, *Transforming Mission: Paradigm Shifts in Theology of Mission.*

[23] Similarly, John Pobee appealed to the churches to accept full responsibility for theological education and ministerial formation within their context, see "Pobee, "Financial Viability of Ecumenical Theological Education." Similarly, "The church must accept responsibility for theological education and ministerial formation" (Engel, "A Response by Lothar Engel [to Yeow Choo Lak]," p. 106.

in particular: the students should pay for their own training. Yet, at the same time, most ministerial theological education (including upkeep) is paid for by the church (often through international funding) in Malawi. Yet as Luzy Wanza highlights so poignantly about the aspirational gap within the developing world church, "most Churches desire to have adequately trained personnel but are unable to generate enough local resources to undertake training for those who are called to ministry. Moreover, as part of its mission of evangelization, some Churches desire to build more churches, clinics and resource centres as well as equip lay people for their role in ministry."[24] The goal for local churches remains self-reliance or self-sustainability. The goal is not disputed as an overall aspiration. Yet, at the same time the universal church is one body, interconnected to local witnessing communities who might have or might not have all the gifts necessary (including financial) to do its work. Rather, we need to work towards inter-dependence where we are all contributing to the overall witness of the church. What is true for the global-local church relationship is also true for the relation local church-local theological educational institutions who might not have all the resources necessary to do its work.

However, the question that needs answering is it possible for all church ministry including the medical work through health centres/hospitals, variety of mercy ministries (to help the poor) and of course theological education to be self-sustainable? Some services offered by the church are free, while other services attract a minimal contribution. A few years ago, a friend who worked for a Christian NGO, challenged me to explain why it is theologically correct (and not just a budgetary matter) to insist that theological education needs to achieve financial viability. He pointed out that up until recently (and in some countries still today), all secular education is free. His sentiment is partially incorrect as education is never free. The

---

[24] Wanza, "Self-Reliance: A Management Strategy for Socio-Economic Sustainability of the Church in Africa," p. 61.

question is just who pays for it? "Free" education is paid for through the contributions of the citizens or the community through taxes and contributions. It is the whole community that invests in education on the assumption that the whole community will benefit long term through its educated members. Most secular societies do not expect or require education to be viable or sustainable – it is an essential service to the citizens.[25] Could it be that in theological education and especially grassroots theological education financial viability might actually not be desirable? The question is, should the whole community share the cost of the education or should individuals pay by themselves as they are the ones to benefit? In support of the latter the argument is that because an individual's prospects are enhanced by the education they should pay. While in support of the former, the whole community benefits from the education of some of its members and these members become more effective in their roles.

A major study on viability in the Developing World was conducted in 1975 by The Theological Education Fund (TEF) under the guidance of Herbert Zorn.[26] The study is still valuable today because

---

[25] Here the nation state collects taxes from its citizens so that it can collectively and on behalf of the citizens, provide for essential human community services that support and keep its citizens safe, like education, health, defence, policing, food safety standards, etc.

[26] It is not surprising that the work of the TEF (Theological Education Fund) and its successors of PTE (Programme on Theological Education), and the ETE (Ecumenical Theological Education) feature prominently here as, as Kaunda rightly observed something that is not only true for PTE but also for TEF and ETE, "the PTE believed that theological education cannot be an end in itself or simply an academic endeavour; it is not even bound to any one institution, but is an instrument of the mission of God. This understanding also necessitated the PTE to search for alternative models, such as the Theological Education by Extension (TEE) in order to give the whole people of God full access to and "recapture for theological education the missionary passion and missionary vision it never should have lost" (Castro 1983:xi). See Kaunda, "Imagining a Just and Equitable African Christian Community," 79. The Castro citation is from Castro, "Foreword." See

the funding models did not fundamentally change since then. Unfortunately, since the 1980s the issue of theological reflection on viability of theological institution did not produce major continent-wide or even nationwide reflection. In the study, Zorn looked at the financial viability of theological education and he examined in detail a number of financing options. The aim of the study was not to identify one universal funding model but rather to highlight the strengths and weaknesses of certain models. It is important to remember that the 1970s-1980s was the period of increasing indigenization of mission-funded and mission-run theological education. It was a period of change and also a period of reduction in international funding. It was also a period increasing the universification of theological education whereby the higher education paradigm increasingly became the norm. Zorn discusses the pros and the cons of eight suppositions related to variations in viability.[27] The eight models can be reduced to two main approaches

---

also Kinsler, "Relevance and Importance of TEF/PTE/ETE: Vignettes from the Past and Possibilities for the Future."

[27] The eight suppositions are: (1) Viability requires basic and major financial support from the churches which are served by theological education; (2) In a viable system of theological education, students should support themselves and pay significant tuition fees, even if they must get the money from their churches; (3) Endowment is a viable form of reducing dependence of theological education upon foreign subsidy; (4) A combination of sources of revenue from local contributions, fees and endowment provides the greatest financial viability; (5) University related theological education is the most viable approach to adequate theological education; (6) Foreign subsidy in finance and personnel is ipso unviable, at best a necessary and temporary evil; (7) Overseas assistance in capital projects, especially building, encourages viability by freeing the local churches to meet running expenses; (8) Theological education by extension is a major breakthrough toward viability.

Theological education by extension (TEE) is discussed in Zorn's study as was then the first major non-residential form of theological education due to its emphasis on on-the-job training combined with teaching seminaries. However, Zorn might have been too hopeful to label TEE a major breakthrough in viability, for a (plus a third, which is a hybrid approach that combines elements of the first two):

a) the church/denomination pays for the ministries that it has (grant-funded approach);[28]

b) the ministry has to be self-funded through collecting tuition fees or programme contributions (tuition-funded model);

c) a combination of sources of revenue from church contribution and fees (plus endowments).[29]

Viability in Context was published in 1975 and the general conclusions and observations still generally stand. However, Zorn's study needs to be upgraded to include contemporary issues surrounding theological education. The key challenge for churches remained unchanged and mostly unaddressed since the publication of *Viability*

---

discussion on TEE and funding, see Mabuluki, "The Relevance of TEE in African Training for Mission."

[28] This funding model includes overseas contributions, though within the church context it is generally recognized that the overseas funding temporarily does not come from the local church but the universal church.

[29] These models were already included by Zorn (see Zorn, *Viability in Context*, 27–35.) Another model that exists nowadays is the Christian University model, though it does not fundamentally change the funding models. A similar model was discussed by Zorn under the heading "university related theological education." The model of the 1970/80s basically outsources theological education to a state university, similar to where graduates of theological seminaries join the TRS Department of Chancellor College of the University of Malawi after graduation to further their theological education. The fees are either covered by a grant (through the church or Student Loan Providers) or the students themselves pay the fees. A variation is that the profits of the Christian university subsidize the costs of the theology department. This is a variation of the grant model whereby the profits of the university are turned into a grant to pay the fees of the students in the theological faculty. Early indicators show that generally tertiary level education is so costly to run that it does not generate sufficient income to fully support the theological faculty. Again, a helpful discussion on the purpose of the Christian university can be found in Bellon, "Theological Education in Africa: Business or Mission?"

in Context. It is actually, the major viability issue for all churches which have a rural presence. The ministry viability in rural areas of the "professionally-paid" ministry model.[30] The same is true for ministry viability in mission and church-planting contexts where churches are still small and unable to contribute meaningfully to the costs. Rural churches (here in Malawi but similar in the Western Developed World) cannot raise enough funds to support a professionally-paid minister (with or without a tertiary level education). Ironically, especially here in Malawi, the greatest need for effective, relevant and quality theological education lies with the rural churches where the Christian witness is the weakest. The other issue that Zorn's study did not address is the question underlying this article: the viability of grassroots theological education. Grassroots theological education does not greatly differ from other forms of theological education, with the exception that the tuition-funded model most clearly does not apply.

First of all, we will look at the grant-funded model of theological education; secondly, the tuition-funded model, thirdly, the issue why the tuition-funded model cannot apply for grassroots theological education and finally we will conclude with some recommendations for the strengthening of grassroots theological education here in Malawi.

Grant-funded Models of Theological Education

A widespread funding model for denominational education in general is budget allocation to the education departments (or the Theological Colleges) from the denominational central budget including the salaries for administrative, support and teaching staff. In this regard, different educational programmes or departments (like children ministry, youth ministry, women and men's ministries and Christian education departments) are supported through funding allocations

---

[30] Yeow Choo Lak, "Financial Viability in Theological Education in Our Region," p. 315.

from the central denominational budget. This model has worked reasonably well as – through the support of the wider church – specialized expertise can be employed, tailored programmes developed to a) generally supported individual churches and church members in providing quality access to assist non-educators with educational expertise; b) to develop programmes that address current issues facing the church as well as empower existing groups to gain a better understanding of their faith.

The main funding is provided through budget allocation based on denominational priorities. These departments usually ask for a small minimal fee to attend their training. The fee is not used to cover the actual staff costs (salaries) as well as the costs for running and developing educational programmes for the denomination.

Increasingly, theological ministerial education however, often seems to fall outside of the denominational funding model and moves to a tuition-funding model. Specialized support ministries and institutions, are not denominational but interdenominational (though still owned by denominations). Often these are not included in the theological grant-funding model and rely on membership contributions and more often than not unfortunately, have to rely on selling their products. Here in Malawi this would include the Bible Society, CLAIM and TEEM, just to name a few.

Tuition-fee funded Models of Theological Education

Tuition-funding education views the institution as a service provider to students who will pay for the service through tuition fees. In this model the responsibility for covering the cost of the education is solemnly placed on the students to pay for his/her theological education.[31] However, few students have the financial support

---

[31] The last two or so decades have seen a significant change within both the Malawian as well as the British Higher Education financing. Theological educators who benefited from much lower tuition fees at the time of their studies should seriously reflect on how they themselves would manage to study today.

(through family or churches via theological study grants) that will pay for their theological studies. This then means that students will either rely on government loan schemes or not study because they cannot afford it. This funding model also assumes the presence of deposable income from families to support their children's higher education. With the current costs of higher education courses easily in the millions of Kwacha the real question has to be: who can afford this? The concern is that this model "will lead to elitism of students from financially able families or larger congregations. The able student from a small, struggling congregation at the cutting edge of the church is eliminated."[32] A lot of our current church leaders and theological educators have benefited previously from generous church grants to allow them to fulfil their ministerial calling. This is one of the reasons why church grants should continue into the next generation. In the same way it also needs to be acknowledged that – not surprisingly – there is the desire within the church (both in pastoral ministry as well as in educational and specialized ministry) and for further studies from Diploma to Bachelor, from Bachelor to Master, from Master to PhD as well as the need for specialization within the vast field of theological education (like Master in Theological Education, Online and Distance Education, Curriculum Design) to remain relevant in an ever changing and ever developing professional context of ministry. The one underpinning hope of self-funding in higher education is the belief that the huge investments in theological and theological-professional qualifications will lead to an increase in salaries which then can be used to pay back the student loan investment.[33] This is mostly a myth that educational loans can

---

[32] Herbert M. Zorn, *Viability in Context*, pp. 28–29.

[33] Tuition-funded ministerial education needs to recognize that the church has a huge need for theologically and professionally trained individuals, however, assuming that individuals will continuously invest (out of their own pocket) into their theological and/or professional development does not take into account the financial pressure on living and on family life in general. In that regard the church

be repaid easily through increases in church salaries. Only in very few cases within the context of the church and its ministry and mission does an additional theological and/or theological-professional qualification increases one's salary.[34] This is an essential observation that is especially shared by the current generation. The question of viability in theological education in the 21st century needs to be discussed within the challenges of exorbitant student debt in the Western world as well as income inequality which excludes not only those that are academically not qualified but more importantly disqualifies those that are called and spiritually qualified but who do not have access to finances. It is always ironic to study these two factors (financial and academic requirements) that prevent those that are called to minister in the light of Jesus picking a bunch of backwater Galilean fishermen to proclaim his gospel.

Non-applicability of Exclusive Tuition-funded Education to Grassroots Theological Education

Programmes of higher education have at least the theoretical opportunity to charge fees to cover the majority of their running costs through tuition fees, based on the assumption that students will be able to see the tuition fee as an investment which will generate

---

is different from other careers, where furthering one's education generally leads to new opportunities and higher salaries.

[34] I recently finished a Master in Theological Education programme (which was funded by my church). It has helped me professionally and it has led to additional professional opportunities within the area of theological education, but these did not add anything to my bank account, with the exception, that I was asked to assist as an adjunct lecturer in the Master in Theological Education programme. This is a part-time course and only takes place every other semester. Out of the 30 graduates thus far, only one is involved in the programme. That was because I had a higher qualification and I had just finished the Master's when one of the lecturers needed replacement. The point of the story is that the majority of graduates will not be absorbed as lecturers in theological education. A few years ago, I applied for a vacancy in my alma mater, a small Bible College, and yet over 100 applicants applied for the academic vacancy.

higher personal income in the years to come. On a global scale, this model increasingly shows its conceptual shortcomings by increasing personal debt but, too often, failing to deliver a return for the tuition investment. This trend is even more pronounced within the church context which is generally marked by lower salaries and the calling paradigm to explain why stipends and not salaries are paid.

Grassroots theological education (both in independent as well as denominational settings) cannot charge its grassroots audience a price that will cover any substantial part of its actual operating cost. This is because the courses are mostly non-accredited and do not lead to higher professional qualifications. The majority of grassroots courses are for knowledge. The actual operational costs for grassroots theological education in Malawi are made up as follows: a) staffing cost which includes salaries of office staff both admin and teachers/facilitators; b) training costs (travel, promotions, graduations, advertising and also printing of training material); c) governance costs (financial audits, Board and Trustees meetings); d) development cost for new material (cost for engaging subject and educational experts if the work cannot be done in-house. Rarely do grassroots educational institutions have the depth of expertise on their staff to cover the development of new materials in relevant subjects or even the expertise to regularly revise existing material in order to keep the material relevant). This is why a tuition-based funding model will always be non-applicable to grassroots theological education.

Evaluation and Conclusion

The advantage of the grant-funded model is that it recognizes that overall responsibility for the funding of theological education lies with the church community. It also recognizes that interconnectedness of the church, its members and the funding for both ministerial and grassroots theological education. Most importantly, it allows for gifted (and called) individuals, independent of their financial background, to be trained for the wellbeing of the church (otherwise, these gifted members would not be available for the ministry of the church). It allows for the specialization of much needed ministry expertise which otherwise would not be available to the church if it solemnly would depend on its members paying themselves for additional professional qualifications. It has been widely used as a model within the Malawian church both for clerical training and further education.

The other funding model that is available is the tuition fee model for grassroots theological education. The main issue that disqualified it is that grassroots theological education (because of its informal nature) can never share for a non-accredited grassroots course anything that can contribute to cover its operational cost. Yet, grassroots theological education is essential for the viability of the church. Tuition fee-based models will - by their very nature of being self-funded -- will not have the welfare and the need of the church/ institutions at heart but will be undertaken in support of the assumed professional trajectory of the learner. It is likely that in the foreseeable future the false promise of self-funded higher education, which is based on the myth of an increase in salary, will see enrolment dropping significantly and highlight the unsustainability of the tuition-fee model for theological higher educational.

The only funding model with a long-term sustainability for grassroots theological education is the grant-funded model. Especially if it is understood to be part of the viability of theological education that is concerned about achieving covenant faithfulness through broad or comprehensive grassroots theological education in order to support the full participation of all its members in the ministry of the church as an investment in the wellbeing, maturity and growth of the church.

Acknowledgements

I would like to thank Blair Bertrand and Kenneth Ross for their useful comments on an earlier version of this chapter.

Bibliography

Bellon, Emmanuel. "Theological Education in Africa: Business or Mission?" *InSights Journal for Global Theological Education* 2, no. 2 (2017), 21–33.

Bosch, David J., *Transforming Mission: Paradigm Shifts in Theology of Mission*, New York: Orbis, 1997.

Carew, Douglas, "Hosea," in *Africa Bible Commentary*, Grand Rapids: Zondervan, 2006, 1013–1026.

Castro, Emilio, "Foreword," in *Ministry by the People: Theological Education by Extension*, ed Ross F. Kinsler, Geneva: WCC, 1983, ix–xii.

Engel, Lothar, "A Response by Lothar Engel [to Yeow Choo Lak]," in *Towards Viable Theological Education: Ecumenical Imperative, Catalyst of Renewal*, Geneva: WCC, 1997, 103–8.

Engel, Lothar, "Funding of Theological Education," in *Theological Education in Africa: Quo Vadimus?*, edited by John Pobee and J. N. Kudadjie, Accra: Asempa, 1990.

Glissmann, Volker, "Grassroots Theological Education," *InSights Journal for Global Theological Education* 5, no. 1 (2019), pp. 53–67.

Kaunda, Chammah J. "Imagining a Just and Equitable African Christian Community: A Critical Analysis of the Contribution of Theological Education Fund/Ecumenical Theological Education (1910-2012)," PhD, University of Kwazulu-Natal, 2013.

Kinsler, Ross F., "Ministry by the People," *Ministerial Formation* 5 (1979), pp. 3–11.

Kinsler, Ross F., "Relevance and Importance of TEF/PTE/ETE: Vignettes from the Past and Possibilities for the Future," *Ministerial Formation*, 110 (2008), pp. 10–17.

Lak, Yeow Choo, "Financial Viability in Theological Education in Our Region," *Asia Journal of Theology* 23, no. 2 (2009), pp. 310–322.

Lak, Yeow Choo, "The Financial Viability of Ecumenical Theological Formation," in *Towards Viable Theological Education: Ecumenical Imperative, Catalyst of Renewal*, Geneva: WCC, 1997, 94–102.

Mabuluki, Kangwa, "The Relevance of TEE in African Training for Mission." In *Reflecting on and Equipping for Christian Mission*, edited by Stephen Bevans, Teresa Chai, Nelson Jennings, Knud Jorgensen, and Dietrich Werner, Oxford: Regnum, 2015, pp. 79–89.

McGinnis, Michael D., "From Self-Reliant Churches to Self-Governing Communities: Comparing the Indigenization of Christianity and Democracy in Sub-Saharan Africa," *Cambridge Review of International Affairs* 20, no. 3 (September 2007), pp. 401–416.

Oden, Thomas C., *Pastoral Theology: Essentials of Ministry*, New York: HarperCollins, 1983.

Pobee, John, "Financial Viability of Ecumenical Theological Education." *Ministerial Formation* 65 (1995), pp. 51–55.

Pobee, John, "The Viability of Tertiary and Theological Institutions: Problems and Promises," *Ministerial Formation* 84 (1999), pp. 37–42.

Shenk, Wilbert R., "The Contribution of Henry Venn to Mission Thought," *Anvil* 1, no. 1 (1985), pp. 25–42.

Wanza, Luzy, "Self-Reliance: A Management Strategy for Socio-Economic Sustainability of the Church in Africa," *AFER* 57, no. 1–2 (2015), pp. 60–84.

Werner, Dietrich, "Ecumenical Learning in Theological Education: The World Council of Churches Perspective," *The Expository Times* 123, no. 1 (October 2011), pp. 1–11.

Zorn, Herbert M., *Viability in Context: The Theological Seminary in the Third World - Seedbed or Sheltered Garden?* Bromley: Theological Education Fund, 1975.